Remake Television

Remake Television

Reboot, Re-use, Recycle

Edited by Carlen Lavigne

LEXINGTON BOOKS
Lanham • Boulder • New York • Toronto • Plymouth, UK

Published by Lexington Books
A wholly owned subsidiary of Rowman & Littlefield
4501 Forbes Boulevard, Suite 200, Lanham, Maryland 20706
www.rowman.com

10 Thornbury Road, Plymouth PL6 7PP, United Kingdom

Copyright © 2014 by Lexington Books

British Library Cataloguing in Publication Information Available

Library of Congress Cataloging-in-Publication Data

Remake television : reboot, re-use, recycle / edited by Carlen Lavigne.
pages cm
Includes index.
ISBN 978-0-7391-8333-5 (cloth : alk. paper) — ISBN 978-0-7391-8334-2 (ebook)
1. Television remakes—United States—History and criticism. 2. Television adaptations—United States—History and criticism. 3. Television programs—Social aspects—United States. I. Lavigne, Carlen, 1976–
PN1992.3.U5R47 2014
791.45'75—dc23
2013048980

∞™ The paper used in this publication meets the minimum requirements of American National Standard for Information Sciences Permanence of Paper for Printed Library Materials, ANSI/NISO Z39.48-1992.

Printed in the United States of America

Contents

Acknowledgments

This collection would not have been possible without the intelligent, industrious, and good-natured authors who wrote it—thanks, everyone. You are a pleasure and a privilege to work with.

I am grateful for funding from the Red Deer College professional development committee, and for the support of Torben Andersen and Jane MacNeil. As usual, Heather Marcovitch heads my list of academic co-conspirators. I also get by on a daily basis with the help of RDC colleagues and friends including Nancy Batty, Tera Dahl-Lang, Elaine Spencer, and Larry Steinbrenner.

Thanks to the gracious editors at Lexington, a great team which has included Lenore Lautigar and Lindsey Porambo.

Thanks always (infinity plus two) to James and Elizabeth Lavigne, and Erica Pereira.

And, yes, still thanks to coffee. Of course.

Introduction

Carlen Lavigne

On October 11, 2012, the US network Adult Swim premiered its recurring special *The Greatest Event in Television History* (2012–present). The faux-format "mockumentary" detailed the preparation for a supposedly troubled multi-million-dollar film shoot. It was presented with tongue-in-cheek gravitas by *Survivor* (2000–present) host Jeff Probst:

> In just a few hours, in this historic Hollywood movie theater, Hollywood's most important Hollywood types will have arrived to watch what will surely be one of the most important events to ever be televised from this historic Hollywood theater here in Hollywood: a shot-for-shot recreation of the opening title sequence of the 1980s television show *Simon & Simon* with *Mad Men*'s Jon Hamm and *Parks and Recreation*'s Adam Scott.

The series—created by Adam and Naomi Scott—pokes fun at both Hollywood hype and the remake phenomenon; its second installment, aired on June 6, 2013, stars Adam Scott, Amy Poehler, and Horatio Sanz in a (remarkably accurate) reshoot of the opening sequence to *Hart to Hart* (1979–84).

It is oddly appropriate that each episode of the series will continue to position itself as "the greatest event in television history" as it retools classic televisual images over and over, further repeating its own format and each time claiming (facetiously) to be even more spectacular than before. The "making of" mockumentary may be a comedy, but its basic premise—that an old series might be re-shot with contemporary actors, and that such a series might be both expensive and highly publicized—seems a rueful acknowledgment of our current fascination with reworking and revisiting past media.

Remakes are pervasive in today's popular culture, whether they take the form of reboots, "re-imaginings," or overly familiar sequels. Television remakes like *Hawaii Five-0* (2010–present) and *Nikita* (2010–13) have proven popular with producers and networks interested in building on the nostalgic capital of past hits (or giving a second chance to underused properties). Some TV remakes have been critical and commercial successes, while others haven't made it past the pilot stage; all have provided valuable material ripe for academic analysis. *Remake Television* examines

1

the changing contexts and challenges provided by generational, cross-cultural, and transmedia format shifts. In this anthology, authors from a variety of backgrounds offer multinational, multidisciplinary perspectives on remake themes in popular television series from cult classics to current ratings giants.

The precise array of chapters collected rested on a vital question of definition: what is a remake? In terms of television, is it a reboot program like *Battlestar Galactica* (2004–09) that re-envisions a narrative from the beginning but shares its name and copyright with an older property? Is it a program retooled across international borders, like the US version of the UK's *The Office* (UK 2001–03; US 2005–13)? Do we consider adaptations (e.g., film to television, or book to television) like *Parenthood* (2010–present) or *Game of Thrones* (2011–present)? What about series that serve as sequels, as in *Star Trek: The Next Generation* (1987–94), or prequels, like *The Carrie Diaries* (2013–present)? What if a television series like *Terminator: The Sarah Connor Chronicles* (2008–09) picks up where a film left off? All of these texts are potential candidates for the category of "remake" — each incorporates tropes, characters, names, or narrative canons from earlier works. Which do we consider?

This anthology welcomed as many different interpretations as possible — as a result, it covers a variety of reboots, adaptations, continuations, and cross-cultural television works. The collection includes wide-ranging analysis from scholars seeking to explore new approaches to television remakes.

We open with William Proctor's overview of remake and adaptation debates, and follow with chapters from Steven Gil, Ryan Lizardi, Heather Marcovitch, and James W. Martens, all of whom challenge or expand accepted definitions of "remakes." This first section highlights our cultural fascination with recycled media. Proctor pieces together the many scattered parts of the complex "zombie matrix" that influences and informs *The Walking Dead* (2010–present). Gil offers *The X-Files* (1993–2002) as a study of a remake that may borrow (and lend) specific aesthetic and narrative tropes without directly sharing a name with any of its predecessors or descendants. Lizardi examines themes of nostalgia in contemporary television series, advertisements, and programming, concerned that a cultural preoccupation with our glossy personal media pasts could threaten our ability to engage more critically with these same texts. Finally, Marcovitch and Martens posit *Fringe* (2008–13) and *The Avengers* (1961–69), respectively, as programs that remake *themselves* mid-run — either through the multiple universes and timelines of *Fringe,* or the frequent recasting and retooling that marked *The Avengers* as part of England's rapidly changing Swinging 60s.

The next section of the volume concentrates specifically on the cultural contexts of twenty-first-century US television remakes. I examine *Beauty and the Beast* (2012–present) as a post-9/11 fairy tale centered on military/crime themes indigenous to early twenty-first-century America. Matthew Paproth discusses the unlikely positioning of *Friday Night Lights* (2004; 2006–11) as 2012 US election fodder, and analyzes the implicit political leanings of both the film and the television series. Cristina Lucia Stasia suggests *Charlie's Angels* (2011) as a postfeminist series that retroactively highlights the more feminist positioning of its 1976–81 predecessor.

Finally, we open to a wide range of remake discussion. Karen Hellekson asks about intercultural notions of morality and ethics in the Danish *Forbrydelsen* (2007–12) and its American remake *The Killing* (2011–present), while Kimberley McMahon-Coleman discusses onscreen metaphors for disability in both film and television iterations of *Teen Wolf* (1985; 1987; 2011–present). Lorna Piatti-Farnell and Lynnette Porter separately analyze the consistent popularity—and frequent reconfiguration—of two prominent fictional figures: the vampire and Sherlock Holmes. Piatti-Farnell examines the continued cultural flexibility of the Gothic in *Dark Shadows* (1966–71; 1991) and Porter compares the successes of two very different contemporary Holmes remakes: *Sherlock* (2010–present) and *Elementary* (2012–present). Helen Thornham and Elke Weissmann examine *Jamie's School Dinners* (2005) and its US remake *Jamie Oliver's Food Revolution* (2010–11) in discussing the implications of adapting public service programming to a for-profit network. Paul Booth and Jef Burnham ask how progressive versions of an ongoing series like *Doctor Who* (1963–89; 1996; 2005–present) may engage fan audiences differently, and how contemporary media may enforce specific, less-flexible readings of a program. Finally, Peter Clandfield explores *The Prisoner* (1967–68; 2009) in questioning whether the popularity or cult status of a primary series may hamper meaningful engagement with a remake.

As remakes, reboots, and adaptations flood our televisions, they provide a vibrant source of material for academic analysis. What does this wave of nostalgia mean? What are the implications of our fascination with cultural recycling? What might differences between old and new texts tell us about changing social and political contexts? The authors in this anthology collectively ask what constitutes a remake, why remakes are so popular, and what remakes might tell us about television—or about ourselves.

FILMS AND TV SHOWS

The Avengers. BBC, 1961–69.
Battlestar Galactica. The SciFi Network. 2004–09.
Beauty and the Beast. CBS, 1987–90.
Beauty and the Beast. The CW, 2012–.
The Carrie Diaries. The CW, 2013–.
Charlie's Angels. ABC, 1976–81.

Charlie's Angels. ABC, 2011.
Dark Shadows. ABC, 1966–71.
Dark Shadows: The Revival Series. ABC, 1991.
Doctor Who. BBC, 1963–89.
Doctor Who. BBC, 2005–.
Doctor Who. Directed by Geoffrey Sax. 1996. Fox Network.
Elementary. CBS, 2012–.
Friday Night Lights. Directed by Peter Berg. 2004. Universal Pictures.
Friday Night Lights. NBC, 2006–11.
Fringe. Fox Network, 2008–13.
Game of Thrones. HBO, 2011–.
The Greatest Event in Television History. Adult Swim, 2012–.
Hawaii Five-0. CBS, 2010–.
Nikita. The CW, 2010–13.
The Office. BBC, 2001–03.
The Office. NBC, 2005–13.
Parenthood. NBC, 2010–.
The Prisoner. AMC, 2009.
The Prisoner. ITV, 1967–68.
Sherlock. BBC, 2010–.
Star Trek: The Next Generation. Paramount Pictures, 1987–94.
Teen Wolf. Directed by Rod Daniel. 1985. Atlantic.
Teen Wolf. MTV, 2011–.
Teen Wolf Too. Directed by Christopher Leitch. 1987. Atlantic.
Terminator: The Sarah Connor Chronicles. Fox Network, 2008–09.
The Walking Dead. AMC, 2010–.
The X-Files. Fox Network, 1993–2002.

ONE

Interrogating *The Walking Dead*

Adaptation, Transmediality, and the Zombie Matrix

William Proctor

There are precious few stories that have not been 'lovingly ripped off' from others. In the workings of the human imagination, adaptation is the norm, not the exception. —Linda Hutcheon[1]

Thomas Leitch puts forth the proposition that "only movies are remade": plays are "reinterpreted," comic books are "occasionally revived by new artists," ballet is "recreated or rechoreographed," and short stories or novels are "often adapted for stage or screen." But only films can be described as remakes.[2] How, then, do we begin to discuss remaking practices that are becoming a significant feature of the television landscape if "only movies are remade"? Surely it is less than helpful to semantically erect impermeable boundaries around remaking practices to isolate each from the other, whether it be an adaptation, a so-called "reimagining," a cover version of a popular song, or—to throw contemporary vernacular into the stewing pot—a franchise "reboot,"[3] or even a sequel or prequel. It behooves us to take a step backwards and view these practices as a "freewheeling cultural process, flagrantly transgressing cultural and media hierarchies, willfully cross-cultural, and more web-like than straightforwardly linear in its creative dynamic."[4]

Henry Jenkins discusses the notion of transmediality[5] that pulls a profusion of texts within a centrifugal whirlpool of cross-media pollination that encompasses multiple media formats including comic books, film, television, internet, merchandising, and so on. This orchestration of cross-platform activity is, according to Murray, "clearly . . . adaptation operating under a different name."[6] In short, following recent work in the field of adaptation studies and a turn from fidelity criticism towards poststructural paradigms of dialogism and intertextuality, remakes *are* adaptations, and vice versa (as are cover versions, reimaginings, reboots, recreations, and so forth).

What I am interested in here is the notion that an adaptation—in this instance, AMC's *The Walking Dead* (2010–present)—not only operates as a remake, but that the "source" or "original" text—the Image comic book series written by Robert Kirkman—can be seen as *already a remake* of existing discourses, tropes, quotations, and allusions alongside narrative components and generic features rather than a simplistic, dyadic relationship between "original" and "copy." By way of interrogation, this chapter looks at *The Walking Dead* phenomenon as tethered to a process of transmediation and intertextuality that expands the analytical playing field in interesting ways; this process is infinitely more complex and "messy" than traditional models of adaptation and remaking illustrate. Rather than focusing on adaptation as a translation between media forms or, as Verevis states, "the movement between *different semiotic registers*,"[7] a text such as *The Walking Dead* "might be better understood through a comparative rather than medium-specific lens, one that rejects cultural hierarchies and embraces intertextuality."[8] It is not only films that are remade—from this perspective, all texts "repeat recognisable narrative units,"[9] to some extent, and, as Brooker claims, texts "cannot fail to brush up against thousands of living dialogic threads."[10] From this position, then, an adaptation is a remake that "is caught up in the ongoing whirl of intertextual reference and transformation, of texts generating other texts in an endless process of recycling, transformation, and transmutation, with no clear point of origin." As Barthes points out in his seminal, oft-quoted, "The Death of the Author," a text is "a multi-dimensional space in which a variety of writings, none of them original, blend and clash. The text is a tissue of quotations drawn from the innumerable centres of culture."[11]

This chapter is split into two sections. The first deals with *The Walking Dead* as belonging to a matrix of zombie fiction without any discernible root, a rhizomatic network that spreads and sprawls without origin, end, or hierarchical organization.[12] The second section returns to the question of fidelity and asks whether this remains integral to an understanding of adaptation/remakes. Christine Geraghty states that "perhaps it is time to move on"[13] from criticisms of fidelity yet also argues that "faithfulness matters if it matters to the audience."[14] As Dudley Andrew insists, fidelity simply cannot be thrown into the dustbin. It is

> the umbilical cord that nourishes the judgement of ordinary viewers as they comment on what are effectively aesthetic and moral values after they emerge from *Romeo + Juliet* (Luhrmann, 1996), *The Color Purple*

(Spielberg, 1985), or even *Passion of the Christ* (Gibson, 2004). If we tuned in on these discussions, we might find ourselves listening to a vernacular version of comparative media semiotics.[15]

While poststructural paradigms of intertextuality and deconstruction can help illuminate the yellow brick road of textual interconnectivity, this may operate in abstraction rather than practice and it is important to give the reader a voice here to illuminate the praxis of interpretation. As John Storey points out, "only a reader can bring a temporary stability to a text."[16]

A. THE WALKING DEAD: A (BRIEF) HISTORY

Issue 1 of *The Walking Dead* comic book series was published by Image Comics in 2003 and, at the time of writing, has reached issue 110 with no indication of cessation on the horizon. Outside of the "big two" of comic publications—that is, DC and Marvel—this is a monumental achievement for a continuing graphic serial. Its circulation averages between 60,000 and 70,000 per calendar month. 2012's milestone issue 100 topped the Diamond Distributor's comic book chart and sold 383,000 copies, "making it the biggest selling indie comic since issue 11 of *The Darkness* in 1997,"[17] and also making it the number one comic for the year by a significant margin. In 2010, *The Walking Dead* received an Eisner award—the comic equivalent of the Oscar—for best continuing series.[18]

Written by Robert Kirkman and featuring art by Charlie Adlard and Tony Moore, the narrative of *The Walking Dead* (both comic book series and TV show) follows protagonist Sheriff Rick Grimes who, in the opening scene, is hospitalized following a violent shoot-out. Upon waking from a coma, he finds the hospital deserted, at least by the living: mutilated corpses line the hallways and zombies (reanimated corpses hungry for human flesh) populate the hospital canteen. He flees in terror and witnesses the stark truth of it all: the world is populated by these "undead" creatures and humanity has become a victim of an extinction-level event which, at the moment, remains shrouded in mystery. Thus begins Rick's quest to find his family and fight for survival in a post-apocalyptic scenario where the foundations of civilization have collapsed.

Since "its humble beginnings as a small indie comic, the harrowing tale of survival in a zombie-infested world has grown to become a worldwide multimedia phenomenon."[19] Merchandising consists of a clothing range: t-shirts, hoodies, and fancy dress costumes for men and women;[20] two different series of action figures, one based on the comic and one on the TV series;[21] drinking mugs, sew-on patches, posters, and so forth. There are two board games—again, a TV variation and a comic book version—a monthly magazine and a "talk show," humorously titled *The Talking Dead*, which follows AMC's broadcast of new TV episodes. Additionally, two tie-in novels of a planned trilogy have been released, written by creator/writer Robert Kirkman and Jay Bonansinga—*Rise of the Governor* and *The Road to Woodbury*, respectively—which chart the origin story of Phillip Blake, or to use his *nom de guerre*, the "Governor," a nefarious character who torments Rick and his band of survivors in gruesome ways in what has been considered *the* seminal arc of the comic book diegesis hitherto. The novels act as parallel narratives—or "sidequels"[22]—to the comic book series and, by extension, the AMC adaptation, which extend and enhance the story world of *The Walking Dead* through transmedia operations.

In 2012, another "sidequel" emerged, this time as a videogame which won multiple game of the year awards.[23] Telltale Games' series of "point-and-click" narratives adhere to comic book continuity but, as designer and co-project leader, Jake Rodin implies,

> [i]t's from the comic book world but it's similar to the TV show. . . . The comic is sort of the hub and the TV series is a spoke off of that and we're another spoke. But *The Walking Dead* is *The Walking Dead*—so for someone who's seen the TV show, when you go and play the game you won't be "fuck, what is this?" We want it to be available to everyone.[24]

This statement is rather telling and brings into play the thorny issues of continuity and fidelity. For many comic book fans, continuity is a sacrosanct issue and breaching it can incur the wrath of many a hardened reader. For Reynolds, serial continuity in comic books is the "same kind of continuity preserved in . . . TV soap operas" which operate according to an Aristotelian cause-and-effect logic with a back story, or history, which comprises "all the episodes previously screened, with their explicit or implied content [which] needs to remain consistent with the current storyline."[25] That said, the TV show has veered away, sometimes radically, from the trajectory of the comic book, bringing issues of fidelity and faithfulness into the analytical equation. The idea of the textual universe of *The Walking Dead* as "spokes on a wheel" with the comic book as "center" or, as the above statement posits, "hub," with other media artifacts connected via alternate spokes that may or not function in tandem—sometimes shifting events or excluding them completely with new characters and arcs introduced—is a central feature of intertextuality. In short, not all texts within the "wheel" act as examples of "transmedia storytelling" *per se* as multiple plot points and continuations spread across media platforms whilst still adhering to a cause-and-effect logic. *The Walking Dead's* transmediality is both continuous and, at times, discontinuous. It is important to point out at this juncture that recent works in adaptation studies decry fidelity criticisms which invariably position film or, in this case, television, as inherently inferior to literature. But television may be more culturally valued and valorized than the graphic medium of comic books, at least in some circles. While I do not want to imply that audience figures can be used to measure cultural worth, it is interesting that, as discussed above, *The Walking Dead* comic series regularly sells between 60,000 and 70,000 issues per month (which does not take into account online downloads and readers who purchase collected editions that are released every six months) while the season three finale of the TV show attracted 12.4 million viewers, a new record for cable.[26] The difference between the comic book audience and those who tune into AMC to watch the TV adaptation is important, especially when it comes to issues of fidelity. Fidelity for whom?

As we can see, *The Walking Dead* comprises a number of texts beneath its diegetic umbrella which function as extensions and/or contradictions—counterfactual narratives—to the established story world. However, rather than "spokes on a wheel" with a central "hub," it is more accurate to draw upon Brooker's concept of a "matrix." The metaphor of the wheel is thus inadequate to contain the multiplicity of texts spiraling within and without *The Walking Dead*—both centripetally and centrifugally. This poses interesting questions: where is *The Walking Dead*? When did it begin? With issue one of the comic book series? Is the TV show an adaptation in the traditional sense, acting as a facsimile of the "original" and thereby setting itself up in the status of "copy," inferior and parasitical? Drawing upon Derrida, it becomes fruitful to ask, "[w]hat are the borderlines of a text? How do they come about? What is its upper edge?"[27] Do we begin with its title—in this case, *The Walking Dead*?

> If we are to approach [aborder] a text, for example, it must have a *bord* [edge, brink, verge, border, boundary, limit, shore]. . . . But when do you start reading it? What if you started reading after the first sentence (another upper edge), which functions as its first reading head but which itself in turn folds its outer edges back over onto inner edges whose mobility—multilayered, quotational, displaced from meaning to meaning—prohibits you from making out a shoreline? There is a regular *submerging* of the shore.
>
> When a text quotes and requotes, with or without quotation marks, when it is written on the brink, you start, or indeed have already started, to lose your footing. You lose sight of any line of demarcation between a text and what is outside it.[28]

"Beginnings" are rather difficult to track and map with any accuracy. All analysis is interpretative and depends on the position of the reader. Each reader possesses an intertextual encyclopedia that varies according to many factors which will, in turn, lend themselves to the interpretation of a text and how it is manifested at the point of consumption. As Hutcheon describes it, "differently knowing audiences bring different information to their interpretation of adaptations."[29] Thus, "beginnings" may not always begin in the same place. The "bord" or "first reading head" of *The Walking Dead* could very well be located at the point of origin: issue 1 of the comic book released in 2003. But the very notion of "point of origin" is saturated with instability, an attempt to fix a center upon a text that incorporates "thousands of living dialogic threads."[30] Edward W. Said argues that "a beginning immediately establishes relationships of either continuity or antagonism or some mixture of both. . . . Is the beginning of a given work its real beginning, or is there some other secret point that starts the work off?"[31] In order to address this issue, and search for the beginning of *The Walking Dead*, we must push further at the so-called boundaries of the text in order to collapse the structure and unearth the foundations that have its roots deeply entwined in history and what I — drawing from Brooker — describe as the "zombie matrix."

B. ENTER THE MATRIX

Will Brooker describes the Christopher Nolan Batman films — *Batman Begins* (2005), *The Dark Knight* (2008), and *The Dark Knight Rises* (2012) — as part and parcel of a vast intertextual matrix that comprises the many facets of the Batman mythos: comic books, video games, animations, films, and so forth. Rather than operating as a sole author dispensing a singular "vision," Brooker sees Nolan as a Barthesian "scriptor," one "who filters, selects and rearranges aspects of the already-said . . . a kind of editor, negotiating the encyclopaedic existing versions of Batman continuity and selecting certain aspects for his compilation."[32]

> [E]very new Batman story is always already an adaptation of existing elements and earlier stories, combined in a new order with a twist and a handful of innovations. Authorial expression, and the pleasure of these texts for the reader, lies neither in the reassuring repetition of entirely familiar patterns and motifs or in the surprise of entirely new inventions, but the dynamic between the two.[33]

Similarly, *The Walking Dead* comic book and its transmedia extensions are not forged from a firmament of "pure" originality, *creatio ex nihilo*: it draws on a wealth of narrative tissues which populate the intertextual database, or what Allen describes as the *déjà*: "the already written or read."[34] As Umberto Eco puts it, "It is not true that works are created by their authors. Works are created by works, texts are created by texts, all together they speak to each other independently of the intentions of their authors."[35]

Lorna Jowett and Stacey Abbott point towards *The Walking Dead* as an amalgamation of pre-existing tropes and "familiar conventions" drawn from zombie texts or, more pointedly, zombie *films*:

> [A] man wakes up in hospital to find it and the surrounding town abandoned while bodies decay in the street (*à la 28 Days Later*); a seemingly innocuous man stumbling around in the background of the image is revealed to be the walking dead (*Night of the Living Dead*); a group trapped in a department store surrounded by the living dead

(*Dawn of the Dead*); racial tension erupts between the human survivors (*Night of the Living Dead*); a character conceals that he has been bitten and slowly becomes infected (*Land of the Dead*); two survivors smother themselves in blood in order to walk among the undead unnoticed (*Shaun of the Dead*); a scientist trapped alone in his facility tries to find a cure to the infection (*I am Legend*).[36]

Many commentators cite George A. Romero's "midnight movie phenomenon,"[37] *Night of the Living Dead* (1968), as the "first reading head" of the zombie genre, at least in its most ubiquitous form: that of the shambling, soulless, flesh-eating "undead." Gerry Canavan argues that Robert Kirkman's objective is to extend the work of Romero, "to employ the hyperbolic temporal continuity native to the comic form to create the feel of a Romero film that never ends."[38] But Romero as "origin point" is rather problematic and warrants further investigation. Although Romero introduced a "new breed" of zombie, one not tethered to the Haitian voodoo tradition, but repopulated into the American experience, this does not provide a demarcation point, cleanly severed without connective limb or tissue—in fact, it explicitly *relies* on the antecedent rather than disavowing it, as subversion or reinterpretation invariably involves connectivity. Furthermore, Romero's *Night of the Living Dead* took as its inspiration Richard Matheson's 1954 novel, *I am Legend,* and also the film based upon the book, *The Last Man on Earth* (1964). Deborah Christie writes that Romero's indebtedness is "generally acknowledged" but the connection has not been sufficiently probed, a critical neglect she seeks to address in the article, "A Dead New World: Richard Matheson and the Modern Zombie."[39]

Before Matheson and Romero, the zombie figure's genealogical roots can be traced historically to Haitian voodoo traditions and, as Dan Hassler-Forest informs us, "the United States' military occupation of the former slave state from 1915 to 1934."[40] Kyle William Bishop also links the zombie form to the Haitian voodoo tradition and its cultural export to the military occupation of Haiti by the United States. Moreover, he explicitly links the rise of the *American* zombie to the publication of William B. Seabrook's "sensational travelogue," *The Magic Island* (1929), which brought "the zombie out of the misunderstood superstitions of Haiti and into the light of mainstream America."[41] Seabrook describes "the zombie" as

a soulless, human corpse, still dead, but taken from the grave and endowed by sorcery with a mechanical semblance of life—it is a dead body which is made to walk and act and move as if it were alive.[42]

Seabrook's description is remarkably akin to the zombie figure in the contemporary period, although one may point towards the phrase "endowed by sorcery" as the point for departure for Romero as he severed the dark magic of voodoo from the equation and re-situated the zombie epidemiologically.[43] Interestingly, however, Romero's *Night of the Living Dead* was not the first to do this: Boluk and Lenz point towards *Zombies of Mora Tau* (1957) as the first film to treat the zombie in such a fashion. Additionally, the turn to epidemiological explanations for the walking dead also features in science fiction texts of the same decade, most effectively in *Invasion of the Body Snatchers* (1956) which explicitly positions the zombie sub-genre within a larger field of horror, sci-fi, and fantasy. Romero is writing onto a palimpsest where the trace of history stains the parchment and seeps through.

Many cite Victor Halperin's 1932 film, *White Zombie*, which is often regarded as the "first reading head" in narrative fiction, but this can also be challenged as an unstable reference point due to Seabrook's book and a 1932 play titled simply *Zombie* which Halperin arguably based his film on.[44] David Flint states that the term "zombie" had entered the *Oxford English Dictionary* as early as 1819, over a hundred years before Seabrook and Halperin.[45] Given the wealth of texts, practices, and historical examples spiraling across the intertexual matrix, is it even possible to search and, indeed, excavate the "first reading head" of *The Walking Dead*? The examples marshalled above are simply illustrative and in no way point towards an exhaustive study. Furthermore, this "mapping" of the zombie phenomenon is subjective and may differ slightly, or largely, depending upon the position of other readers. Connections have been made between the zombie as "figure of contagion" and Daniel Defoe's 1722 work, *A Journal of the Plague Year*,[46] whilst Hogle sees genealogical roots in the neo-Gothic tradition "that began in literature with Horace Walpole's 1764 novella *The Castle of Oranto: A Gothic Story*."[47] It would seem that trying to seek the "source," "the first reading head," is a fruitless task, one that shifts according to readership and interpretative fields, amongst other variables. Suffice to say, we have not even begun to scratch the surface of the zombie matrix. I have not discussed Romero beyond the cursory, and the spread of the zombie contagion across popular culture in the latter half of the twentieth century was so wide that it emigrated from the American experience and into international locations. The Italian zombie film cycle, for example, is an important episode in the history of the genre as practiced by influential directors such as Lucio Fulci and Bruno Mattei. Mark McKenna[48] examines the multiplicity of Italian zombie films that unofficially "sequelize" Romero's works—films such as *Zombi 2* (aka *Zombie Flesh Eaters,* 1979), Fulci's follow-up to *Zombi* (the Italian title for Romero's seminal *Dawn of the Dead,* 1978). The Italian tradition of "filoni"—simply "in the tradition of" ("when you bring a script to a producer the first question he asks is not 'what is your film like' but 'what film is your film like'"[49])—signals the repetitive strategies rather more explicitly. One could ask a similar question of *The Walking Dead*, also: what is *The Walking Dead* like? The answer, as I have hopefully demonstrated, lies within the ebb and flow of the zombie matrix, an infinitely complex and intricate ocean of intertextuality.

C. THE 21ST-CENTURY ZOMBIE RENAISSANCE

The Walking Dead is but one instance of zombie fiction in the new millennium. Many critics and commentators cite the events of 9/11 as symptom for the resurgence in the genre as the zombie is often discussed as a harbinger of socio-cultural crises—Saussure and Lacan's "floating signifiers," if you will. Through the zombie, as Hogle argues, "we look at ourselves, albeit in a kind of distortion mirror."'[50] Tony Magistrale argues that all literature, both in print and on screen, addresses society's most pressing fears and is "nothing less than a barometer for measuring an era's cultural anxieties."[51] While these are important considerations, this chapter's purview cannot attempt even a brief overview of the factors at work here. For a more detailed study on these and other issues, there are a growing number of academic works in the area of zombie narratives.[52]

The reason I bring the twenty-first-century renaissance into the discussion is to highlight the plethora of zombie texts that are spiraling across the matrix in multiple media forms: in literature (Max Brooke's *World War Z*, 2006; Seth Graham Smith's *Pride and Prejudice and Zombies*, 2009); "Young Adult" books (Carrie Ryan's *The Forest of Hand and Teeth*, 2009; Charlie Higson's *The Enemy*, 2008, and its sequels); video games (the *Resident Evil* series, 1996–present; *Little Red Riding Hood's Zombie BBQ*, 2008; *Dead Space*, 2008); comic books (Garth Ennis's *Stitched*, 2011–present; *Marvel Zombies*,[53] 2005–06; and *Key of Z*, 2011); film (*28 Days Later*, 2002; Romero's *Land of the Dead*, 2005, *Diary of the Dead*, 2007, and *Survival of the Dead*, 2009; *The Revenant*, 2009; *Shaun of the Dead*, 2004); and, of course, television. Although *The Walking Dead* is often described as television's first foray into zombie fiction, the 2007 pilot *Babylon Fields* failed to be picked up by US networks and was subsequently discarded. In the UK, Charlie Brooker's 2008 zombie five-part serial, *Dead Set*, situates a group of *Big Brother* (2000–present) contestants amidst a post-apocalyptic uprising of the walking dead whilst shows such as *Dark Shadows* (1966–71) and *Buffy the Vampire Slayer* (1997–2003), alongside anthology programs, also have episodes featuring flesh-eating zombies.

And this is the tip of the proverbial iceberg. At the moment, zombies are everywhere, plaguing multimedia platforms and infecting the cultural landscape. *The Walking Dead* is a minuscule limb within a veritable mass of seething "undead" hordes. The next and final section of this chapter returns to the question of fidelity and poses the question: does it matter? Remember that the texts discussed above operate in an abstract sense and the zombie matrix is not an exhaustively delineated transmedia map, but shifts and mutates, waxes and wanes, depending upon receivership.

D. ADAPTATION STUDIES IN THE NEW MILLENNIUM OR WHAT ABOUT FIDELITY?

Brooker describes intertextuality as "a process whereby the meaning of a text is not found within the text itself, but in constant communication with and relation to other meanings within a network, like stations on a multidimensional subway map."[54] But how does this work in practice? Is meaning only contained through dialogic relations? Could one argue that the poststructural project that repudiates the "locking down of meaning" actually "locks down meaning"? In its disavowal of meta-narratives, what if poststructuralism (and, indeed, intertextuality) becomes a meta-narrative itself? As Allen argues,

> [t]o recognise that the text's meaning does not spring from an author combining a signifier (writing) with a signified (concept), but springs in fact from the intertextual, does not mean we can simply move to the intertextual level to unite signifier and signified. To say that a text is constructed from a mosaic of quotations does not mean that we can find the text's intertexts and then view them as the signified of the text's signifiers.[55]

In the twenty-first century, the study of adaptation—and, indeed, remaking/rebooting practices—has entered a so-called "new wave" governed by a turn to poststructuralist paradigms of dialogic relations and intertextual matrices. Stam argues that the field of adaptation studies was beset by comparative analyses between source and translation that invariably reinscribes "the axiomatic superiority of literature to film"—and, by extension, television and "other visual media."[56] Stam cites McLuhan's concept of "rear-view logic," which creates a hierarchy between art-forms based on cultural longevity: "[t]he venerable art of literature, within this logic, is seen as inherently superior to the younger art of cinema, which is itself superior to the even younger art of television."[57]

> The conventional language of adaptation criticism has often been profoundly moralistic, rich in terms that imply that the cinema has somehow done a disservice to literature. Terms like "infidelity," "betrayal," "deformation," "violation," "bastardization," "vulgarization," and "desecration" proliferate in adaptation discourse, each word carrying its specific charge of opprobrium.[58]

This shift to poststructuralism within adaptation studies, then, serves to deconstruct the prejudicial bifurcation between "the cotton candy of entertainment and the gourmet delights of literature,"[59] thus opening up the analytic playing field. The binary logic between "original" and "copy," with the source text valorized and the adaptation vilified, is destabilized due to what Bakhtin describes as "heteroglossia"; that is, a compilation of many competing voices operating in a palimpsestuous manner. Simone Murray pulls no punches about the discipline prior to the poststructural shift:

> It did not help that adaptation studies scholars in the second half of the twentieth century were often their own worst enemies, producing a seemingly endless stream of repetitious and theoretically timid comparative book/film case studies that served largely to confirm both disciplines' direst views of the field as an academic backwater . . . adaptation studies turned in on itself, becoming in the process increasingly intellectually parochial, methodologically hidebound and institutionally risible.[60]

But, still, for some critics, adaptation studies is "haunted by fidelity." As Leitch decries, "[o]f all the ways to classify adaptations, surely the decision to classify them as more or less faithful to their putative sources . . . is one of the most fruitless."[61] I would argue, however, that the "undead spirit" of fidelity haunts the field precisely because it *does* matter. I reiterate Geraghty's statement that "faithfulness matters if it matters to the audience."

My own readership of *The Walking Dead* began with the comic book series and then the AMC TV show. On a weekly basis I would visit my friend and academic colleague, Rob Jewitt, in his office at the University of Sunderland and we would debate the decisions made by Kirkman and AMC that, quite simply, "keep getting *The Walking Dead* wrong!" The TV show introduces new characters—brothers Merle and Daryl Dixon, for example—and "re-version" narrative arcs, such as the deaths of Shane and Lori. It also introduces new scenes and remakes whole swathes of narrative that, for some reason, would annoy and confuse in equal measure. For both me and Jewitt, fidelity matters, but not simply because of re-translation and revision. The TV show, for us, and as we shall see, other readers, is simply not "as good" as the comic book series due to miscasting—especially The Governor—and a general narrative malaise. Of course, we are dealing with value judgments and subjectivities here, but this is an important factor to consider when dealing with the issue of fidelity. Remember, "faithfulness matters if it matters to the audience." Rather than sweep issues of fidelity away, research needs to be conducted with the audience in order to analyze how readers interpret texts in practice as well as debating theoretical perspectives.

To illustrate: on internet forums, readers often negotiate and argue their individual interpretative positions. On thewalkingdeadforums.com, in a thread debating the differences between the comic book and its televisual counterpart, SVTRay, Zombie Hunter, from Texas states that "the TV showisn't [sic] even on the same level . . . [the] added material slows down the pace of the show and frustrates most people . . . I think they should stick to the original material."[62] Shanefan946, in response, disagrees: "well thats [sic] your opinion. Most people I know like the tv show better . . . I find the comics characters pretty shallow."[63] Phantomzombielord appreciates both mediums and likes "the necessary shock value that comes from the 'I can't believe they did that when they were supposed to do this' familiarity you think you have reading the comic."[64] These examples illustrate three positions: SVTRay views the comics as "the original material" which the TV show should "stick to," a perspective that highlights the importance of faithfulness; Shanefan946 disavows the comic book characters as "pretty shallow" and prefers the TV show—as do "[m]ost people I know"; whereas Phantomzombielord straddles the fulcrum between mediums and likes the shock value that comes with *un*faithfulness. Although these are selected examples, hopefully it demonstrates that fidelity and faithfulness matter to *some* people and should not be repudiated from the analytical table completely.

E. CONCLUSION

Clearly, there are different ways to analyze remakes and adaptations. Leitch attributes the poststructuralist turn to Stam and Raengo who "sought to reorient adaptation studies decisively from the fidelity discourse universally attacked by theorists . . . to a focus on Bakhtinian intertextuality . . . and this attempt was largely successful."[65] But, Leitch continues, this did not redraw the field exclusively but "stirred the pot," which provoked "a welcome outburst of diverse work on adaptation."[66] Similarly, work on remaking practices, such as Constantine Verevis' path-breaking study, *Film Remakes* and his edited anthologies, *Second Takes: Critical Approaches to the Film Sequel* (co-edited with Carolyn Jess-Cooke), and, more recently, *Film Remakes, Adaptations and Fan Productions* (co-edited with Kathleen Loock), have engaged with multiple methods of analysis that expand the field rather than shoehorn everything into processes of dialogism and intertextuality.

Texts such as *The Walking Dead* are "afloat upon a sea of countless earlier texts from which it [can] not help borrowing."[67] I am not seeking to recant intertextuality; in fact, to borrow a phrase from Derrida, "I am convinced of it." But this is not the only method of analysis available to us as scholars. More, not less, work is required in the area of fidelity—and, indeed, the multiplicity of approaches will help bolster the arena rather than collapse it entirely as privileging one approach as the only valid approach. There are many approaches available; I, for one, look forward to the next wave of study in the area of adaptation, remaking and rebooting in the twenty-first century.

FILMS AND TV SHOWS

28 Days Later. Directed by Danny Boyle. 2002. 20th Century Fox.

Batman Begins. Directed by Christopher Nolan. 2005. Warner Bros.

Big Brother. Channel 5, 2000–.

Buffy the Vampire Slayer. The WB, 1997–2001. UPN, 2001–03.

The Color Purple. Directed by Steven Spielberg. 1985. Warner Bros.

The Dark Knight. Directed by Christopher Nolan. 2008. Warner Bros.

The Dark Knight Rises. Directed by Christopher Nolan. 2012. Warner Bros.

Dark Shadows. ABC, 1966–71.

Dawn of the Dead. Directed by George A. Romero. 1978. United Film.

Dead Set. E4, 2008.

Diary of the Dead. Directed by George A. Romero. 2007. The Weinstein Company.

I Am Legend. Directed by Francis Lawrence. 2007. Warner Bros.

Invasion of the Body Snatchers. Directed by Don Siegel. 1956. Allied Artists.

Land of the Dead. Directed by George A. Romero. 2005. Universal Pictures.

Night of the Living Dead. Directed by George A. Romero. 1968. The Walter Reade Organization.

The Passion of the Christ. Directed by Mel Gibson. 2004. Newmarket Films.

The Revenant. Directed by Kerry Prior. 2009. Lightning Entertainment.

Romeo + Juliet. Directed by Baz Luhrman. 1996. 20th Century Fox.

Shaun of the Dead. Directed by Edgar Wright. 2004. Universal Pictures.

Survival of the Dead. Directed by George A. Romero. 2009. Magnet Releasing.

The Talking Dead. AMC, 2011–.

The Walking Dead. AMC, 2010–.

White Zombie. Directed by Victor Halperin. 1932. United Artists.

Zombi 2. Directed by Lucio Fulci. 1979. The Jerry Gross Organization.

Zombies of Mora Tau. Directed by Edward L. Cahn. 1957. Columbia Pictures.

NOTES

1. Linda Hutcheon, *A Theory of Adaptation* (New York: Routledge, 2006), 177.

2. Thomas Leitch, "Twice-Told Tales: Disavowal and Rhetoric of the Remake," in *Dead Ringers: The Remake in Theory and Practice*, ed. J. Forrest and L.R Koos (Albany: State University of New York Press, 2002), 37.

3. See William Proctor, "Regeneration and Rebirth: Anatomy of the Franchise Reboot," *Scope: An Online Journal of Film and Television Studies* 22 (2012): http://www.scope.nottingham.ac.uk/February_2012/proctor.pdf

4. Simone Murray, *The Adaptation Industry: The Cultural Economy of Contemporary Literary Adaptation* (London: Routledge, 2012), 2.

5. Henry Jenkins, *Convergence Culture: Where Old and New Media Collide* (Albany: New York University Publishing Press, 2006).

6. Murray, *Adaptation Industry*, 2.

7. Constantine Verevis, *Film Remakes* (Edinburgh: Edinburgh University Press, 2005), 82.

8. Henry Jenkins, "Should We Discipline the Reading of Comics," in *Critical Approaches to Comics: Theories and Methods*, ed. M.J Smith and M.J Duncan (London: Routledge, 2012), 7.

9. Verevis, *Film Remakes*, 1.

10. Will Brooker, *Hunting the Dark Knight: Twenty-First Century Batman* (London: IB Taurus, 2012), 37.

11. Roland Barthes, "The Death of the Author," in *Image/ Music/ Text*, R. Barthes (London: Fontana, 1977), 146.

12. Adolphe Haberer, "Intertextuality in Theory and Practice," *Literatura* 49 (2007): http://www.leidykla.eu/fileadmin/Literatura/49–5/str6.pdf

13. Christine Geraghty, *Now a Major Motion Picture: Film Adaptations of Literature and Drama* (Plymouth: Rowman and Littlefield, 2008), 1.

14. Ibid., 3.

15. Dudley Andrew, "The Economies of Adaptation," in *True to the Spirit: Film Adaptation and the Question of Fidelity*, ed. Colin MacCabe, Kathleen Murray, and Rick Warner (New York: Oxford University Press, 2011), 28.

16. John Storey, *Cultural Theory and Popular Culture: An Introduction—Sixth Edition* (Sussex: Pearson, 2012), 128.

17. Ian Berriman, "The Long Walk Ahead," *The SFX Book of The Walking Dead* 1 (2013): 9.

18. Rob Jewitt, "Adapting The Walking Dead for Television: 'It's Not About the Zombies'" (Conference Paper, University of Sunderland, *Adventures in Textuality: Adaptation Studies in the 21st Century*, 2013).

19. Berriman, "The Long Walk Ahead," 8–15.

20. See here for range of clothing items: http://www.amazon.co.uk/s/ref=nb_sb_noss?url=search-alias%3Dclothing&field-keywords=walking%20dead

21. Jewitt, "Adapting The Walking Dead for Television."

22. A "sidequel" is a parallel storyline that may or may not converge with the mainline narrative.

23. Jewitt, "Adapting The Walking Dead for Television."

24. Steve Jarratt, "Playing Dead: The Walking Dead Videogame," *The SFX Book of The Walking Dead* 1 (2013): 102–103.

25. Richard Reynolds, *Superheroes: A Modern Mythology* (University Press of Mississippi, 1994), 8.

26. Jewitt, "Adapting The Walking Dead for Television."

27. Jacques Derrida, "Living On," in *Deconstruction and Criticism*, ed. H. Bloom, Paul de Man, Jacques Derrida, Geofreey Hartman, and J. Hills Miller (London: Continuum, 1979), 70.

28. Ibid., 67.

29. Hutcheon, *A Theory of Adaptation*, 8.

30. Brooker, *Hunting the Dark Knight*, 37.

31. Edward W. Said, *Beginnings: Intention and Method* (London: John Hopkins University Press, 1975), 3.

32. Brooker, *Hunting the Dark Knight*, 39.

33. Ibid., 66.

34. Graham Allen, *Intertextuality* (London: Routledge, 2000), 73.

35. Umberto Eco quoted in Haberer, "Intertextuality in Theory and Practice," 57.

36. Lorna Jowett and Stacey Abbott, *TV Horror: Investigating the Dark Side of the Small Screen* (London: IB Tauris), 31. Thanks to Rob Jewitt for recommending this book and quote.

37. Dan Hassler-Forest, "Cowboys and Zombies: Destabilizing Patriarchal Discourse in *The Walking Dead*," *Studies in Comics* 2 (2011): 341.

38. Gerry Canavan, "'We *Are* the Walking Dead': Race, Time, and Survival in Zombie Narrative," *Extrapolation* 51, no. 3 (2010): 435.

39. Deborah Christie, "A Dead New World: Richard Matheson and the Modern Zombie," in *Better Off Dead: The Evolution of the Zombie as Post-Human*, ed. D. Christie and S.J. Lauro (New York: Fordham University Press, 2011), 67.

40. Ibid., 67–81. Although Boluk and Lenz argue its origins can be located in African myth; see Stephanie Boluk and Wylie Lenz, "Generation Z, the Age of Apocalypse," in *Generation Zombie: Essays on the Living Dead in Popular Culture*, ed. S. Boluk and W. Lenz (London: McFarland, 2011), 5.

41. Kyle William Bishop, *American Zombie Gothic: The Rise and Fall (and Rise) of The Walking Dead in Popular Culture* (London: McFarland, 2010), 13.

42. Chera Kee, "'They are not men…they are dead bodies': From Cannibal to Zombie and Back Again," in *Better Off Dead: The Evolution of the Zombie as Post-Human*, ed. D. Christie and S.J. Lauro (New York: Fordham University Press, 2011), 67–81.

43. Boluk and Lenz, "Generation Z," 4.

44. Ibid. See also Gyllian Phillips, "White Zombie and the Creole: William Seabrook's The Magic Island and American Imperialism in Haiti," in *Generation Zombie: Essays on the Living Dead in Popular Culture*, ed. S. Boluk and W. Lenz (London: McFarland, 2011), 27–40.

45. David Flint, *Zombie Holocaust: How the Living Dead Devoured Popular Culture* (London: Plexus, 2009), 11.

46. Boluk and Lenz, "Generation Z," 3.

47. Jerrold E. Hogle, "Foreword," in *American Zombie Gothic: The Rise and Fall (and Rise) of The Walking Dead in Popular Culture*, ed. Kyle William Bishop (London: McFarland, 2010), 2.

48. Mark McKenna, "'What Film is Your Film Like?' Retitling as Adaptation and Paratext" (Conference Paper, University of Sunderland, *Adventures in Textuality: Adaptation Studies in the 21st Century*, 2013).

49. Luigi Cozzi quoted in McKenna, "'What Film is Your Film Like?'"

50. Hogle, "Foreword," 3.

51. Quoted in Bishop, *American Zombie Gothic*, 9.

52. For example, see Kyle William Bishop, *American Zombie Gothic: The Rise and Fall (and Rise) of The Walking Dead in Popular Culture* (Jefferson: McFarland, 2010); Stephanie Boluk and Wylie Lenz, eds., *Generation Zombie: Essays on the Living Dead in Popular Culture* (Jefferson: McFarland, 2011); Stephanie Boluk and Wylie Lenz, "Generation Z, the Age of Apocalypse," in *Generation Zombie: Essays on the Living Dead in Popular Culture*, ed. Stephanie Boluk and Wylie Lenz (Jefferson: McFarland, 2011), 1–17.

53. The first issue of which Kirkman penned and also crossed over with the *Evil Dead* saga in *Marvel Zombies vs The Army of Darkness,* thereby adding more interconnections.

54. Brooker, *Hunting the Dark Knight*, 48.

55. Allen, *Intertextuality*, 73.

56. Robert Stam and Alessandra Raengo, *Literature and Film: A Guide to the Theory and Practice of Film Adaptation* (Oxford: Blackwell, 2005), 4–5.

57. Ibid., 4.

58. Ibid., 3.

59. Robert Stam and Alessandra Raengo, *Literature and Film: A Guide to the Theory and Practice of Film Adaptation* (Oxford: Blackwell, 2005), 7.

60. Murray, *Adaptation Industry*, 2.

61. Thomas Leitch, "Adaptation Studies at a Crossroads," *Adaptation: The Journal of Literature on Screen Studies* 1, no. 1 (2008): 63.

62. SVTRay, http://www.walkingdeadforums.com/forum/f102/watching-tv-show-reading-comics-2530.html

63. ShaneFan946, http://www.walkingdeadforums.com/forum/f102/watching-tv-show-reading-comics-2530.html

64. Phantomzombielord, http://www.walkingdeadforums.com/forum/f102/watching-tv-show-reading-comics-2530.html

65. Leitch, "Adaptation Studies at a Crossroads," 64.

66. Ibid.

67. Ibid.

TWO

A Remake by Any Other Name

Use of a Premise Under a New Title

Steven Gil

Discourse surrounding remake television largely focuses on the outright remaking of a series or the adaptation of a property from another medium. In such discourse, a series which is not identified as a remake or adaptation is usually labeled an original. Taking terms such as "original" and "remake" at face value suggests an unbalanced distribution of creative agency and overlooks the similarity of intertextual influences in both cases. An entire show need not be subject to remaking. Several originals utilize basic narrative elements from earlier texts, thus remaking only aspects of their predecessors. This chapter analyzes the concept of remaking a premise to illustrate the complexity of the remake phenomenon. It does this through the examination of a succession of originals centered on *The X-Files* (1993–2002). Created by Chris Carter and featuring initially, and most famously, the efforts of FBI agents Fox Mulder (David Duchovny) and Dana Scully (Gillian Anderson) to investigate mysterious events in a search for the truth, the series provided new variations on old themes and also iconographic tropes of its own. Due to this combination of being influenced and influential, *The X-Files* provides a salient case study for the remaking of narrative elements that occur in television fiction. Much of what follows focuses on the genre of science fiction (SF), as this is the series' main generic location, and also the source of many of the particular narratives upon which it draws. To provide theoretical grounding for the analysis, the first section examines definitions of "remake" alongside other terms such as adaptation, sequel, reboot, and par-

ody. In doing so, it shows the interrelatedness of this body of classificatory labels and establishes how each denotes a particular intertextual relationship. Following sections examine *The X-Files* as first a remake and
then a source for remakes.

A. WHAT MAKES A REMAKE

Before examining *The X-Files,* it is necessary to briefly evaluate critical
theory on remakes and related classifications in order to establish the
intertextual nature of remaking. Often when remakes are mentioned,
they are thought of as new productions bearing the same names as previous intellectual properties. Examples include *The Twilight Zone* (1959–64)
remakes of 1985 and 2002, and the *Knight Rider* (1982) remake of 2008
where the first season DVD box set bore the sub-title, "An Icon Reborn."
Poignantly, Arnzen comments, "A remake's marketing strategy reduces
text to title, packing a narrative body into a reified 'brand name' which
can be mass-produced and recycled over time."[1] Criticism of the remade
Battlestar Galactica (2004–09)[2] as "Galactica in Name Only,"[3] however,
raises questions of what besides a name is maintained or need be maintained in order for a series to constitute a remake (as opposed to an
independent property that overtly copies only selective elements, or uses
the older property largely for its nostalgia value). Carroll argues, "the
status of the remake or adaptation as remake or adaptation is not inherent in the text itself, but is a product of the discourses which surround
it."[4] Some prominent remakes such as *All in the Family* (1971–79), based
on *Till Death Us Do Part* (1965–75), drop the name and remake the premise, giving credence to views that a television show's status as a remake
extends beyond the title and rests, in part, on how that show is framed.

   For this chapter, the texts form the focus. In addition to titles, each of
the earlier examples shares more than a name with older properties, taking on stylistic as well as narrative traits. In *BSG* II, the central narrative is
kept—a group of human survivors attempts escape from a maliciously
genocidal artificial life form—but many of the particulars of this narrative
are changed. We see this as the same property, due both to title and
content, despite the sometimes major alterations. So while industrial and
marketing discourse, as well as scholarship and paratextual commentar-
ies, can position shows as remakes, there are nevertheless textual features
which substantiate that positioning.

   The common criticism of remakes as unoriginal stems from their reliance on existing properties. Verevis notes the association of creative lazi-
ness with the phenomenon of remaking films, where remakes are seen as
acts of commercial opportunity to turn a quick and reliable profit on past
successes, established material, and audience nostalgia.[5] By Carroll's esti-
mation, "where originality and creative autonomy prevail as criteria of

evaluation, the remake and the adaptation tend, by definition, to be found wanting."[6] But it is flawed reasoning to suspect only remakes of being creatively indebted to earlier texts or lacking in originality. In challenge to popular conceptions, Forrest and Koos rightly observe:

> While many remakes are indeed uninspired copies of their originals— probably in proportion to the uninspired "original" films produced annually—the existence of many critically acclaimed remakes hinders us from adopting as a general rule the widely accepted notion that all remakes are parasitical and not worth any critical consideration outside a political and economic evaluation of Hollywood's commercial filmmaking practices.[7]

Remakes are not all so indebted to their originals that their creativity is compromised. In fact, the creativity of an original—any text that is not called a remake, adaptation, or similar term—may be equally compromised. By looking at *BSG* we can see how the term "original" is not a guarantee of originality. Even though the earlier series was not a remake, it still noticeably drew on Mormonism as well as *Star Wars* (1977), in the latter case so much so that a lawsuit was involved. The former influence was due to creator Glen A. Larson's Mormon upbringing and the latter due to the massive influence of the first *Star Wars* film. Creativity in a remake can be evaluated in the same way as creativity in an original as each may utilize established tropes and narrative conventions to varying degrees of similarity to the wealth of cultural texts that precede them. Either is capable of being highly derivative or highly innovative and so it should be remembered that "original" denotes a particular intertextual association rather than attesting to a text's creativity, novelty, or even originality.

Turning to "adaptation" as a related term that overlaps with "remake" and suffers from similar complaints about creative status, one can further demonstrate the creativity involved in new articulations of a property. Comparing the two classifications provides useful insight on the ways that the narratives of remakes are formed. Offering a contrast of the terms, Verevis writes:

> A remake is generally *a remake of another film,* whereas one of the principal arguments of adaptation theory is concerned with the movement between *different semiotic registers,* most often between literature and film . . . adaptation does not simply involve a retelling (*rereading*) of a story[.][8]

Applying this logic to television, remakes occur when one television show is made again, and adaptations when a film or work of literature is turned into a television show. It could be that when moving a property from one medium to another, the expectation is that distinct changes need to occur to make the text suitable for its new situation. In the case of a novel's adaptation to film, significant redaction may be required, or in

the reverse circumstances scenes that previously relied on visual establishing shots would have to be articulated through the written word.
Contrastingly, the expectation is that remaining in the same medium
would not engender these issues. However, no medium is homogenous
enough for this simple outline to work in practice. Production context
may be fundamentally different between remakes and their respective
originals for a number of reasons, as Carroll argues: "[D]ifferences in the
context of production can be as crucial to the remake as the adaptation,
whether those differences concern historical context, national provenance, authorship or indeed medium (such as film 'remakes' of television
series)."[9]

US remakes of British shows are produced in markedly dissimilar
industrial conditions. Even looking at a single national locus, one has to
accept that production context changes over time, meaning a television
series being remade in recent years will be subject to considerations that
did not necessarily impact older programming. *BSG* II illustrates this
point as it was made for its contemporary television environment. Although both series of *BSG* were produced for television, the most recent
featured the kind of complex serialized narrative that has become a
prominent feature of narrative fiction in the medium whereas the original
was highly episodic, thus keeping to the expectations of its own time.
BSG II matches what Leitch calls the *"true remake,* which combines a focus
on the . . . original with an accommodating stance which seeks to make
the original relevant by updating it."[10] That updating reshapes the tone,
topicality, and narrative structure of the series. One could view this as the
adaptation of an older text to a new cultural environment. It is also worth
noting that adaptation does not operate solely between print and audiovisual media as a film may be adapted to television or television to film.

Adaptation from film to television can also involve changes in accor-
dance with new actors playing established characters. For instance, the
character of Jack O'Neill in *Stargate SG-1* (1997–2007), sometimes explicitly labeled an adaptation of the film *Stargate* (1994), is altered to better fit
with Richard Dean Anderson's desire to perform a version of the character with a sense of humor, contrasting Kurt Russell's performance in the
film. A similar impact occurs in the case of television remakes, once more
illustrated by *BSG*: Edward James Olmos and Lorne Green have different
acting styles and histories with each shaping their performances as Ada-
ma, and Lloyd Bridges is a much different Commander Cain to Michelle
Forbes' Admiral Helena Cain. Remakes certainly involve some of the
same creative practices as adaptation, including the alteration of content
for a new format, context, and audience. It is unclear what really distinguishes the remake from the adaptation and whether these should even
be seen as mutually or contrasting exclusive categories.

Consideration of "sequel" provides further evidence that some remakes are able to be classified under multiple (overlapping) critical cate-

gories as well engaging in creative utilization of source material without simply repeating a given narrative. *Knight Rider* II is not actually a recreation but continues the original series' story, set twenty-five years after its events and featuring the son of the original series' Michael Knight (David Hasselhoff) as its lead. In that respect, one can view it as a sequel telling the story of the next generation of man and machine, despite the title giving no indication of that fact. Further illustrating the co-presence and complications of remake and sequel as terms of classification, Leitch argues:

> [S]ome sequels, like *Friday the 13th*, Parts 4–6, gravitate towards remakes, and occasional remakes like *Invasion of the Body Snatchers* (1978), contain elements of sequels. . . . The audience for sequels wants to find out more, to spend more time with characters they are interested in. . . . The audience for remakes does not expect to find out anything new in this sense: they want the same story again, though not exactly the same[.][11]

A sequel is seen as having to carry on a narrative that has been established by a preceding text. The word "text" is used in this instance to stand in for a variety of media-specific terms. Each of Leitch's examples is a film as the sequel of another film, but it is equally possible for a television series to act as the sequel to a film. Examples include *Stargate SG-1* and *Terminator: The Sarah Conner Chronicles* (2008–09), which directly extend film narratives. Despite various changes, *SG-1* never seeks to retread or completely disregard the major events of *Stargate*, instead using these as the foundation of an ongoing narrative. Print media may also present sequels, as in the case of the *Star Wars* Expanded Universe, which spreads across comics, novels, and short stories, extending almost every facet of the film franchise.[12] Additionally, the episodes of a television series, especially those which present a serialized narrative, could likewise be viewed as a set of sequels. A closely related term is "prequel," which denotes many of the same aspects as the sequel but refers to a continuation of the narrative that precedes what has already been seen instead of following on from the extant narrative. A sequel or prequel uses the original as source material for a developing narrative, incorporating the original narrative as diegetic history; the remake also uses the original as source material but is typically seen to overwrite the original's narrative instead of building on it. Whether audiences want to see the same story or not, a remake requires less of a prior investment in a given diegesis, as it proceeds from a new beginning. Both draw on an original but the remake might be regarded as more independent than the sequel.

"Sequel" and "adaptation" are far from the only terms that could be said to overlap with "remake." Another term of significance is "reboot." Urbanski examines *BSG* II and *Star Trek* (2009) as reboots.[13] What may be said to immediately identify a reboot is the fact that it initiates a series of texts. In the case of a television show, this is rather inevitable, with the pilot leading to the first season and potentially others. The contrast is perhaps greater in regards to films where no sequels may be intended. For example, *The A-Team* (2010) film is a remake of the television series and also an adaptation due to the change of medium. But at present, it is a self-contained narrative with no additional film or television sequel. In contrast, J.J. Abrams' *Star Trek* film is a remake, an adaptation, and also a reboot, as it was meant to revive the franchise's film presence and has already resulted in one sequel (*Star Trek Into Darkness*, 2013). "Parody" also has some overlap with remake. In this case one may say a parody is a remake directed at explicitly humorous ends. The *Laugh it Up, Fuzzball* trilogy from *Family Guy* (1999–present)—"Blue Harvest" (2007), "Something, Something, Something, Dark Side" (2009), and "It's a Trap!" (2010)—is a parody of the original *Star Wars* trilogy. However, it may also be regarded as an adaptation of that narrative both to television and to the stylistic and comedic focuses of *Family Guy*. Adding further terms, Verevis writes:

> Tim Burton's *Planet of the Apes* is not a remake but a "re-imagining" of Schaffner's film (and Pierre Boulle's novel); George A. Romero's zombie movie *Dawn of the Dead* (1979) is "re-envisaged" by Zach Snyder (2004); and *Solaris*, a 1972 film by Andrei Tarkovsky (from the novel by Stanislaw Lem) is "revisited" by Steven Soderbergh (2002).[14]

What we have in each case is a description of the intertextual relationship between television shows and other cultural texts. As Stam and Raengo observe, "virtually all films, not only adaptations, remakes, and sequels are mediated through intertextuality and writing."[15] Speaking to the creative interaction of texts, Sanders argues, "Any exploration of intertextuality, and its specific manifestation in the forms of adaptation and appropriation, is inevitably interested in how art creates art, or how literature is made by literature."[16] In other words, we are dealing with the mutual influences that texts can have on each other, specifically the impact of the older on the newer. To paraphrase Sanders, one can see this chapter as an examination of how television, the content not the medium, creates television. Clearly such terms as adaptation, sequel, and remake are not mutually exclusive;[17] however, each nevertheless conveys specific connotations that describe the relationship between one text and another. The above examination of terms offers an intertextual mapping of specific relationships and provides the grounding for analyzing the remaking of narrative elements instead of entire shows.

B. *THE X-FILES* AS REMAKE

The X-Files does not suit classification as a remake in the typical sense of being a new production of an older property—there is no *original* for *The X-Files* in the same way that there is for *Knight Rider* II or *BSG* II. As such, some aspects of the creativity of a remake do not apply, including the performance of roles by new actors/actresses. However, the series does draw on precursory texts in a way not far removed from such explicit remakes. In that regard, *The X-Files* exemplifies the intertextual connections discussed above and the ways in which an original can be regarded as remaking narrative premises. Several specific and generic precursors to *The X-Files* have been noted. Backstein lists horror films, "1950s B sci-fi," *Kolchak: The Night Stalker* (1974–75) ("Carter's stated inspiration"), conspiracy thrillers, and early 1990s blockbusters including *The Silence of the Lambs* (1991).[18] *Quatermass* (1979) and alien invasion films from the 1950s are also cited by Booker.[19] One could also add *Twin Peaks* (1990–91) to the list for its FBI protagonist, serial narrative, and strange occurrences. Positioning *The X-Files* within the history of SF, Vest further explains:

> *The X-Files* . . . developed a fresh narrative approach to many SF conventions during its nine broadcast seasons. . . . Just as *The X-Files* has affected later SF programs, it has also been influenced by previous literary, cinematic, and television SF texts. Many journalists, reviewers, and scholars have noted the debt that *The X-Files* owes to *Kolchak: The Night Stalker*, *The Twilight Zone*, and *Invasion of the Body Snatchers*. Less acknowledged, however, is how the science fiction of Mary Shelley, Abraham Merritt, and H.G. Wells provided narrative contexts. . . . As so often happens, the elements introduced by earlier SF authors become part of a generic lexicon that later writers freely employ without realizing their specific origins. . . . The truth of the genre is that its most powerful concepts often outlast their individual creators, coming into public consciousness stripped of their sources.[20]

The number of precursory texts that can be said to form the lineage of *The X-Files* demonstrates the breadth of intertextual connections present. Such examples have had varying degrees of influence, with remaking occurring in multiple ways from the rationale and structure of the series to individual episodes. These are the particular levels at which a connection between the series and the remake phenomenon can be examined. One could surmise from Vest's assessment that these intertextual influences are at least partially unacknowledged. The concept of the "unacknowledged remake" has been presented by Greenberg.[21] For this chapter, it is the cited and open examples of intertextuality that form the focus of analysis. Such direct connections solidify the inclusion of the series in considerations of remake television.

Insofar as *The X-Files* can be said to be remaking a specific show, that television series is possibly the most acknowledged of its precursors—

Kolchak: The Night Stalker. The eponymous Carl Kolchak (Darren McGavin) is a newspaper reporter in Chicago who has confrontations with witches, ghosts, and other paranormal or science fictional entities as a result of his investigating strange cases. Only lasting for one season (with some episodes not even produced), the series was an extension of two made-for-television movies. However, the character of Kolchak was first conceived in a novel written by Jeff Rice. The series offers a dual case of adaptation—once from print to screen then from movie format to ongoing series. Rice's then unpublished novel, *The Kolchak Papers*, was adapted into a screenplay by *I Am Legend* (1954) author and *Twilight Zone* alumnus Richard Matheson. *The Night Stalker* (1972) saw Kolchak tracking down a serial killer who turns out to be a vampire in Las Vegas. A follow-up TV movie, *The Night Strangler* (1973), also written by Matheson, features Kolchak hunting another serial killer, this time in Seattle. While conducting research for Kolchak, Titus Barry (Wally Cox) discovers earlier sets of murders, occurring at twenty-one-year intervals and matching those that Kolchak is investigating. Together, the pair deduce and discover the killer to be a 144-year-old surgeon/alchemist who uses the blood of his strangled victims to create an "elixir" that temporarily prolongs his life and renews his vitality for twenty-one years at a time. Initially skeptical authorities are finally convinced but nevertheless cover up the story. The first film's narrative is mentioned several times within the second, making *Night Strangler* a direct sequel.

Those familiar with *The X-Files* will see immediate parallels with episodes from the series where a serial killer is discovered to possess paranormal abilities. One particularly resonant example is "Squeeze" (1.03) where the killings occur at thirty-year intervals to preserve the life of the killer. Replace Kolchak with a pair of FBI agents and one has *The X-Files*. That replacement is central to the adjusted premise which Carter used in the formation of his series. As recounted by Lowry:

> Though it provided his inspiration, Carter didn't remember many specifics. . . . When he revisited the show he realized that it had a confining premise: Carl Kolchak, an unlucky newspaper reporter, kept stumbling upon vampires, werewolves, and zombies. . . . Carter began to refine his premise, trying to figure out "how not to fall into the big pit that [*Kolchak:*] *The Night Stalker* had fallen into." . . . He knew he needed a concept that would provide a more hospitable series framework, something sustainable week after week without stretching the parameters of credibility. . . . With some further modification and research, Carter had his foundation—namely, that there must be someone at the FBI investigating unexplained cases. . . . Reporter Carl Kolchak kept bumping into monsters by happenstance, calling for a huge suspension of disbelief. In *The X-Files*, agents Mulder and Scully would look for the paranormal after someone else encountered it, with the Bureau as a logical divining rod.[22]

When Carter wanted to update *Kolchak: The Night Stalker*, he did not try to overtly remake the series. Noticing the flaws in that series' execution, he was able to adopt the premise and adapt its set-up to provide a more coherent framing. The notion of Kolchak chasing cases, then encountering the paranormal and extraordinary, was well suited to self-contained movie narratives but far less convincing as a recurrent plot device that had to be re-enacted each week. Whereas anthology shows such as *The Twilight Zone* are able to present individual encounters, the series format necessitates the same protagonists appearing in each subsequent episode. By providing a stronger rationale for Mulder and Scully's regular engagements with the occult, Carter made the premise more suitable for series television.

Further points of difference resulted from the use of the FBI. Setting aside the two films, Kolchak found all these occurrences locally whereas those in *The X-Files* are spread out across a larger geographic area (mainly, but not restricted to, the continental US) again facilitated by the shift to FBI agent protagonists. Additionally, Kolchak had an often antagonistic relationship with law enforcement while Mulder and Scully enjoy the authority that comes from their status as FBI agents, allowing them access to information and crime scenes not as easily or plausibly obtainable by a reporter.

There are also points of similarity worth mentioning. While many earlier narratives lean more towards *encounters* with the occult, both *Kolchak: The Night Stalker* and *The X-Files* feature *investigations*. Mulder and Scully, like Kolchak before them, actively pursue the seemingly impossible. Much like Mulder, Kolchak often shows a strong commitment to his theories before having sufficient evidence to convince anyone else. That conviction is not one of pure belief though, and as with instances from *The X-Files* it rests on a willingness to be led by evidence towards an unlikely conclusion. Questions of factuality are central to the narrative of *The Night Strangler*. When Kolchak encounters opposition to his suggestions that the murderer is an animated corpse with superhuman strength, he cites hard evidence from the victims' bodies and eyewitness testimony as the basis for his conclusion. Although Mulder is the typical source of such claims in *The X-Files*, we also see Scully taking on this role in "Humbug" (2.20). Both series evince a greater willingness to discover and experience, as well as prove the existence, of the as-yet unknown.

Despite the major changes which differentiate *Kolchak: The Night Stalker* from *The X-Files*, there is still a strong intertextual connection between the two, such that the latter can be seen as a remake of the former's premise. As *The X-Files* progressed, it established its own identity but still maintained links back to Kolchak, showing that intertextual indebtedness does not delimit the possibility of a series being creatively independent. When Darren McGavin appears in *The X-Files*, he does not reprise his role as Kolchak but is framed as former special agent Arthur Dales, who established the X-files and was the first to investigate them (5.15, "Travellers"; 6.13, "Agua Mala"). In this way the series integrates its extra-diegetic legacy into the narrative.

The *X-Files* also remakes older texts by incorporating them as episodes. One particularly salient example is "Ice" (1.08). Parallels have been drawn between this episode and John Carpenter's 1982 film, *The Thing*. "Ice" is an adaptation due to the change of medium and context, as well as a remake due to the explicit connection back to Carpenter's film. Glen Morgan, who co-wrote the episode, cited an article from *Science News* as the initial inspiration for a tale about the discovery of an alien life form beneath the ice,[23] but Carter has also explicitly noted J.W. Campbell's "Who Goes There?" (1938) and Carpenter's *The Thing* (itself an adaptation of Campbell's story, and remake of *The Thing from Another World* [1951]) as influences.[24] The episode stages the basic narrative of Campbell's story and Carpenter's film within the diegesis of the series, featuring Mulder and Scully. Nevertheless, the episode features a research team uncovering an alien entity which then proceeds to take over and kill the human members and create a scenario of distrust and paranoia. Shearman observes:

> [H]owever derivative Ice may be, it finds a way of taking its borrowed material and finding within it something which defines The X-Files . . . what Morgan and [James] Wong so skillfully extract from The Thing is its desperate paranoia and its fear of identity loss.[25]

In effect the series is incorporating its own generic lineage (of SF horror) by positioning the narrative as part of a broader set of such encounters with alien or unknown life forms. To maintain the ice-bound setting while also justifying the presence of FBI agents, the location is shifted from Antarctica to Alaska. Instead of a shape-shifting creature, *The X-Files* depicts a small worm able to infest human hosts. Themes of paranoia and loss of selfhood are resonant with *The X-Files*, perhaps explaining why the film and novella are so successfully adapted into the series' canon. An independent narrative is thus integrated into the series through the remaking of its premise as structured around the demands of *The X-Files'* diegesis. This is not a direct utilization of an earlier property but rather demonstrates the creative agency that can be found within specific instances of remaking.

C. *THE X-FILES* REMADE

In many of the same ways as it was drawing on earlier material, *The X-Files* has itself been a source of narrative elements for other television shows. In a discussion of *The X-Files* remakes, these are considered to have a similar relationship to that between the series and *Kolchak: The*

Night Stalker. That is to say, the narrative premise has been remade instead of the totality of the program serving as a direct template.

Before *The X-Files* finished its fourth season, it already had one imitator of sorts: *Dark Skies* (1996–97). Lasting for only one season, the series followed the efforts of congressional aide John Loengard (Eric Close) and his fiancé Kim Sayers (Megan Ward) to stop an alien invasion that was already underway but covered up by mysterious forces within the US government. Official facilitation of alien invaders is reminiscent of the Syndicate from *The X-Files*. In contrast to the contemporary setting of *The X-Files*, *Dark Skies* episodes take place across the 1960s, mixing fictional scenarios with real occurrences as though giving the secret history behind major events. Usually these entail the series' alien antagonists—the Hive—trying to further their invasion plot and being hindered by Loengard and Sayers, sometimes with the help of figures such as Jim Morrison (Brent David Fraser) and Carl Sagan (Joe Urla). This combination of the real and the fictional formed a crucial part of the marketing associated with *Dark Skies*. As reported by series co-creator Bryce Zabel:

> The essence of the pitch was that Brent [V. Friedman] and I had met a man named John Loengard who wanted to get the truth out about UFOs and felt that telling the story as fiction was the only way.[26]

Zabel and Friedman continued to maintain that Loengard was a real person who had provided them with information and presented this paratextual claim of an actual alien presence as a point of difference from *The X-Files*. Although *The X-Files* has been described as "blurring boundaries" in some postmodern sense,[27] *Dark Skies* is not considered in the same discourse despite its being a more solid example of fiction that purports to be fact. Perhaps due to the series' lack of success, or the proximity of its premise to that of *The X-Files*, *Dark Skies* is overlooked in many discussions of SFTV. While clearly derivative, the series remains distinct from *The X-Files* in ways which illustrate how remaking can produce new creative texts, especially in cases where producers have to distinguish their product from legally protected or concurrent properties.

Another series with evident connections to *The X-Files* in its premise and format is *Fringe* (2008–13). Created by J.J. Abrams, Alex Kurtzman, and Roberto Orci while the trio were working on the reboot of *Star Trek*, *Fringe* centers on three characters—scientist Walter Bishop (John Noble), his con artist/genius son Peter (Joshua Jackson), and FBI agent Olivia Dunham (Anna Torv)—working for the "Fringe Division" of the FBI and Department of Homeland Security. Like *The X-Files*, *Fringe* takes on SF concepts that precede either series. However, towards the end of *Fringe*'s run, Abrams stated, "The idea was to do a show that was in the same vein as some early [David] Cronenberg movies or *Altered States* [1980], a little bit of *Twilight Zone* and *X-Files*."[28] Having a fictional group working within the FBI systematically investigate strange occurrences is a premise clearly taken from *The X-Files*. Furthermore, as Clarke Stuart observes:

> *The X-Files'* Agent Scully is a clear precursor to Olivia's character, not only in terms of her occupation as a detective-soldier but in her reserved nature. . . . Like her "fringe science" predecessor, Agent Scully . . . she is rational, practical, and quietly passionate, in contrast to the man who helps her along her hero's path—the quirky, impractical Walter Bishop.[29]

Dynamics between the central protagonists are similar in some respects in each series. Influences are also evident in individual episodes such as "What Lies Below" (2.13), which replicates *The Thing*-inspired events of *The X-Files'* "Ice." There appears to have been some anxiety about the similarity, with Abrams addressing claims about the series and insisting it was not "directly inspired by" *The X-Files*.[30] Certainly there are differences, with the serial narrative focusing on parallel universes instead of alien colonization and government conspiracy. Unlike *The X-Files'* characteristic lack of closure, wherein there are often no definitive explanations, investigations within *Fringe* render more outright conclusions and also place the US government into a more central and less oppositional role. In that regard, the Fringe Division is more like the Stargate Program and NID from *Stargate SG-1*. Several other non-*X-Files* parallels are also evident: the role and visage of *Fringe's* Observers resembling that of the Watchers from Marvel Comics;[31] the use of high-frequency vibration to move through solid walls (1.10, "Safe"), a mainstay of DC Comic's The Flash for decades;[32] and countless other tropes borrowed implicitly from the SF canon. Overall, *Fringe* has connections to texts other than *The X-Files*. However, at the level of the premise and format there is a clear influence, making the intertextual influence foundational rather than total.

Additionally, the format of self-contained episodes and a broader mythology arc is also replicated by *Fringe*. When the series was first going to air in 2008, Orci described this format as something new, stating, "Lately you can either have a procedural or you can have something extremely serialized and very culty. . . . And to us the idea of seeing if you can do both simultaneously is a new kind of storytelling."[33] Mixture of procedural and seriality is not a new kind of storytelling, crucially because, as Short notes, *The X-Files* "pioneered a format that rewarded regular viewing, via a developing mythology, while self-contained episodes encouraged casual viewers."[34] A similar mixture of serial and episodic narrative was used in *Twin Peaks*, and Booker also notes that *Blake's 7* (1978–81) had the same structure as *The X-Files* in "linking individual episodes into a sequential 'myth arc' plot."[35] Regardless of whether *The X-Files* was the first to employ this format, it certainly popularized it within SFTV and related genres. For example, *Stargate SG-1* uses this model, as does *Super-*

natural (2005–present). Indeed, *Supernatural* was influenced by *The X-Files* in many of the same ways as *Fringe*, depicting episodic narratives unfolding through a procedural structure with varying degrees of connection to a larger narrative arc.[36] As Johnson notes, "dual narrative structure" enables a series "to be accessible to the casual viewer, while simultaneously rewarding the loyal viewer with character and story development."[37] In this format, Abrams saw a means of avoiding the issues that had arisen with *Lost* (2004–10), where viewers were alienated if they missed any episodes. It is interesting that the highly intricate serial narratives (exemplified by *Lost*) that Abrams is more readily associated with are eschewed in order to adopt *The X-Files'* structure. Far from an innovation by the time he and his co-creators utilized the format, the combination of episodic and serial elements had already been brought to prominence by *The X-Files* and become a staple of television fiction.

Before leaving the topic of *X-Files* remakes it is worth mentioning two final but fundamentally different examples. Whereas *Dark Skies* and *Fringe* are both fiction, *Miracle Detectives* (2011) can be regarded as a non-fiction remake of *The X-Files*. According to the program description:

> Randall Sullivan, a strong believer and Indre Viskontas, a scientist and supernatural sceptic, travel throughout the United States to uncover answers to mysterious incidents that transcend logic. Performing an in-depth examination of these bizarre cases, Randall and Indre visit the sites of each incident to hear first-hand accounts of these incredible stories[.][38]

As the title implies, each segment follows a procedural format wherein two presenters—a male "believer" and a female skeptic—assess the validity of a given paranormal claim. Similarly to *Miracle Detectives*, the National Geographic series *Ancient X-Files* (2010) also takes a non-fiction approach. In this case the mysteries are not as contemporary, coming instead from myths, conspiracy theories, and pseudohistory. The co-presence of "controversial" claims and critical evaluation attempts again to replicate the tonality of *The X-Files'* own investigations. Each program demonstrates the cross-over of ideas from fiction to reality, and also encapsulates the belief held by some viewers that *The X-Files* was depicting events with some real-world facsimile.

D. CONCLUSION

In this chapter, questions have been raised over the scope of the remake phenomenon. Far from being limited to a set of revived properties, we can now see remaking as a cultural practice that operates at multiple levels. Textual aspects of narrative and premise can be remade, thus showing the intertextuality of television series that is present even in those examples which are labeled as original. Originals can still engage in remaking by adapting basic narrative elements to new ends or altering these such as to avoid perceived flaws in the source material. Through *The X-Files*, a set of examples has been examined showing a form of remaking in even the production of new narratives. It is possible to trace the creative lineage of a television series and assess the ways that an original's own creativity is formed out of the way it remakes earlier concepts and premises.

FILMS AND TV SHOWS

The A-Team. Directed by Joe Carnahan. 2010. 20th Century Fox.
All in the Family. CBS, 1971–79.
Altered States. Directed by Ken Russell. 1980. Warner Bros.
Ancient X-Files. National Geographic Television, 2010.
Battlestar Galactica. ABC, 1978–79.
Battlestar Galactica. The Sci-Fi Network, 2004–09.
Blake's 7. BBC, 1978–81.
Dark Skies. NBC, 1996–97.
Family Guy. Fox Network, 1999–.
Fringe. Fox Network, 2008–13.
Invasion of the Body Snatchers. Directed by Philip Kaufman. 1978. United Artists.
Knight Rider. NBC, 1982–86.
Knight Rider. NBC, 2008.
Kolchak: The Night Stalker. ABC, 1974–75.
Lost. ABC, 2004–10.
Miracle Detectives. The Oprah Winfrey Network, 2011.
The Night Stalker. Directed by John Llewellyn Moxey. 1972. ABC.
The Night Strangler. Directed by Dan Curtis. 1973. ABC.
Quatermass. Thames Television, 1979.
The Silence of the Lambs. Directed by Ridley Scott. 1991. Orion Pictures.
Star Trek. Directed by J.J. Abrams. 2009. Paramount Pictures.
Star Trek Into Darkness. Directed by J.J. Abrams. 2013. Paramount Pictures.
Star Wars. Directed by George Lucas. 1977. 20th Century Fox.
Stargate. Directed by Roland Emmerich. 1994. Metro-Goldwyn-Mayer.
Stargate: SG-1. The Sci-Fi Network, 1997–2007.
Supernatural. The CW, 2005–.
Terminator: The Sarah Connor Chronicles. Fox Network, 2008–09.
Till Death Us Do Part. BBC, 1965–75.
The Thing. Directed by John Carpenter. 1982. Universal Pictures.
The Thing From Another World. Directed by Christian Nyby. 1951. RKO Radio Pictures.
The Twilight Zone. CBS, 1959–64.

The Twilight Zone. CBS, 1985–89.
The Twilight Zone. UPN, 2002–03.
Twin Peaks. ABC, 1990–91.
The X-Files. Fox Network, 1993–2002.

NOTES

1. Michael A. Arnzen, "The Same and the New: "Cape Fear" and the Hollywood Remake as Metanarrative Discourse," *Narrative* 4, no. 2 (1996): 175.
2. For the purposes of clarity, where two series bear the same name, Roman numerals are used to denote the remake—for instance, *Knight Rider* II refers to the 2008 series and *BSG* II to the 2004–2009 series.
3. Lynette Porter, David Lavery, and Hilary Robson, *Finding Battlestar Galactica: An Unauthorized Guide* (Naperville: Sourcebooks, 2008), 3.
4. Rachel Carroll, "Affecting Fidelity: Adaptation, Fidelity and Affect in Todd Hayne's Far From Heaven," in *Adaptation in Contemporary Culture: Textual Infidelities*, ed. Rachel Carroll (London; New York: Continuum, 2009), 38.
5. Constantine Verevis, *Film Remakes* (Edinburgh: Edinburgh University Press, 2006), 4.
6. Carroll, "Affecting Fidelity," 34–35.
7. Jennifer Forrest and Leonard R. Koos, "Reviewing Remakes: An Introduction," in *Dead Ringers: The Remake in Theory and Practice*, ed. Jennifer Forrest and Leonard R. Koos (Albany: State University of New York Press, 2002), 3.
8. Verevis, *Film Remakes*, 82.
9. Carroll, "Affecting Fidelity," 36.
10. Thomas M. Leitch, "Twice-Told Tales: The Rhetoric of the Remake," *Literature/Film Quarterly* 18, no. 3 (1990): 145.
11. Leitch, "Twice-Told Tales," 142.
12. The Expanded Universe of course raises question of canonicity. While *SG-1* is effectively an official sequel due to its being produced by the owners of the original intellectual property, the Expanded Universe could just as easily be discounted if future *Star Wars* films produce a new version of events to follow the narrative of the existing six films.
13. Heather Urbanski, *The Science Fiction Reboot: Canon, Innovation and Fandom in Refashioned Franchises* (Jefferson: McFarland, 2013), 5–7.
14. Verevis, *Film Remakes*, 10.
15. Robert Stam and Alessandra Raengo, *Literature and Film: A Guide to the Theory and Practice of Film Adaptation* (Malden: Blackwell, 2005), 45.
16. Julie Sanders, *Adaptation and Appropriation* (New York; London: Routledge, 2006), 1.
17. A full taxonomy of "remake" or classificatory scheme was not attempted in this section. Instead the intention was to outline terms, sometimes seen as competing, that are here argued to be overlapping. For typologies of remake see: Michael B. Druxman, *Make it Again, Sam: A Survey of Movie Remakes* (A.S. Barnes, 1975); Leitch, "Twice-Told Tales"; and Harvey Roy Greenberg, "Raiders of the Lost Text: Remake as Contested Homage in *Always*," *Journal of Popular Film & Television* 18, no. 4 (1991): 164–171. For an account of scholarship concerning remakes see: Verevis, *Film Remakes*. This scholarship principally concerns Hollywood films.
18. Karen Backstein, "Flexing those Anthropological Muscles: X-Files, Cult TV, and the Representation of Race and Ethnicity," in *Cult Television*, ed. Sara Gwenllian-Jones and Roberta E. Pearson (Minneapolis: University of Minnesota Press, 2004), 117.
19. M. Keith Booker, *Science Fiction Television* (Westport: Praeger, 2004), 6.

20. Jason P. Vest, "The Truth is Back There: The X-Files and Early Science Fiction," in *The X-Files and Literature: Unweaving the Story, Unraveling the Lie to Find the Truth,* ed. S.R. Yang (Cambridge: Cambridge Scholars Press, 2007), 125–126.

21. Greenberg, "Raiders of the Lost Text," 170.

22. Brian Lowry, *The Truth is Out There: The Official Guide to* The X-Files (London: Harper Collins, 1995), 10–11.

23. Lowry, *The Truth is Out There,* 118–119.

24. Jane Goldman, The X-Files *Book of the Unexplained: Volumes I and II* (New York: Harper Entertainment, 2008), 94.

25. Robert Shearman, *Wanting to Believe: A Critical Guide to* The X-Files, Millennium & The Lone Gunmen (Des Moines: Mad Norwegian Press, 2009), 17.

26. Bryce Zabel. "*Dark Skies*: The Write Stuff," February 17, 2006, http://www.brycezabel.com/newsviews/2006/02/dark_skies_was_.html

27. Cf: Douglas Kellner, "*The X-Files* and the Aesthetics and Politics of Postmodern Pop," *The Journal of Aesthetics and Art Criticism* 57, no. 2 (1999): 161–175.

28. Quoted in Natalie Abrams, "Fringe Oral History: Building the World of 'Science Fact'," last modified January 13, 2013, http://www.tvguide.com/News/Fringe-Series-Finale-Oral-History-Abrams-Jackson-Torv-Noble-1059131.aspx

29. Sarah Clarke Stuart, *Into the Looking Glass* (Ontario: ECW Press, 2011), 8 and 14.

30. James Hibberd, "J.J. Abrams: 'Fringe' isn't Directly Inspired by 'X-Files'," last modified July 14, 2008, http://www.hollywoodreporter.com/blogs/live-feed/jj-abrams-fringe-isnt-inspired-50508

31. Clarke Stuart (*Into the Looking Glass,* 142–3) also notes the similarity to the Watchers as well as Isaac Asimov's Eternals, Kurt Vonnegut's Tralfamadorians, and the aliens from *2001: A Space Odyssey* (Stanley Kubrick, 1968) and *The War of the Worlds* (1898). Besides the Eternals, these other examples are far less direct than that with the Watchers, a race who ostensibly watch over parallel and alternate realities as the Observers also do.

32. Barry Allen, the second character to hold the moniker of The Flash and perhaps the most well known, was the first capable of this feat.

33. Quoted in Kathie Huddleston, "J.J. Abrams, Alex Kurtzman and Roberto Orci dig deep to discover 'the pattern' in their new Fox series," last modified September 8, 2008, http://web.archive.org/web/20090319031033/http://www.scifi.com/sfw/interviews/sfw19440.html

34. Sue Short, *Cult Telefantasy: A Critical Analysis of The Prisoner, Twin Peaks, The X-Files, Buffy The Vampire Slayer, Lost, Heroes, Doctor Who and Star Trek* (Jefferson: McFarland, 2013), 63.

35. Booker, *Science Fiction Television,* 83.

36. *Supernatural* is less opaque about the fantastical elements it presents, with investigations often leading to definitive discoveries of the supernatural. Additionally, the conspiracy is one of demons instead of governmental forces. Perhaps due to its greater distinction from *The X-Files,* the series is able to be more playful about potential comparisons, with demon hunting brothers Sam (Jared Padalecki) and Dean Winchester (Jensen Ackles) occasionally masquerading as FBI agents under the aliases "Mulder" and "Scully."

37. Catherine Johnson, "Quality/Cult Television: *The X-Files* and Television History," in *The Contemporary Television Series,* ed. Michael Hammond and Lucy Mazdon (Edinburgh: Edinburgh University Press, 2005), 65.

38. Discovery Press Web, "Miracle Detectives," accessed April 5, 2013, http://press.discovery.com/emea/tlc/programs/miracle-detectives/

THREE

The Nostalgic Revolution Will Be Televised

Ryan Lizardi

Contemporary media trends have increased the tendency to construct nostalgic subjects as subjectively fixed on their own affectively charged media pasts. These viewing subjects are not encouraged to be engaged citizens who can compare the past to the present and gain knowledge from the juxtaposition of continuities and discontinuities. Rather, the consumer of televisual nostalgic media is presented with a flattened distinction between the past and the present. Texts and brands beloved from the past are presented as persistently relevant and activate a yearning for an eternal return of the same. Freud described melancholia as the attempt to eternally recreate the past, demonstrating the "loss of capacity to adopt a new object of love" compared to a healthy mourning of the past that learns and adapts for the future.[1] Similarly, remakes and other nostalgic television programming/advertising mark an individual and solipsistic yearning that is fixated on and focused through a mediated history by constructing our pasts as comprising only the constellations of texts we individually loved as children, which I am calling our personal "playlist pasts." We may all have a different "playlist," but repetitively consuming this type of media encourages a melancholic concentration of libidinal energy on the individual nostalgic text and takes focus away from a comparative view of history.

I will demonstrate a melancholic nostalgia in the televisual medium that discourages the release of beloved childhood texts by consistently encouraging the consumption of their contemporary remake counterparts. Todd Gitlin describes the remake phenomenon as part of a recom-

37

binant media trend, which is not only economically beneficial for media producers because they can "capitalize on and mobilize demonstrable tastes," but also stands as "consumer society's tribute to our hunger for a stable world."[2] This form of nostalgia in television acts as a neutering force that limits the potential for critical gazes into the past by defining the difference between then and now through comparisons of original and remake. The problematic tendencies of televisual nostalgia will be compared to several normative aims of modern enlightenment politics that consider the use of history as a way to make social progress. The remake melancholic nostalgia mode, which has emerged as a cultural dominant, works contrary to these norms. The remake nostalgic ethos aims neither for revolutionary nor progressive change; rather, it serves to recreate, pacify, and distract, thereby reaffirming dominant ideologies and a hegemony of the past that seeks to encourage an engagement with the past that is uncritical and defined by surface-level differences between texts.

Remakes are not the only way television is nostalgic; however, considering their prominence in both programming and commercials, they are the most extensive. This chapter will attempt to contextualize the whole of televisual nostalgia. Not every show and every commercial is nostalgic, or a remake, but there is a growing nostalgic phenomenon that presents itself at every televisual level. From *Elementary* (2012–present) to *How I Met Your Mother* (2005–present) and the accompanying advertisements, television presents itself as a hyper-nostalgic medium. Connections can be drawn here to Jameson's model of postmodernism as a dominant cultural modality, as he stated that though he is "very far from feeling that all cultural production today is 'postmodern,'" it is still helpful to "project some conception of a new systemic cultural norm" to avoid falling into the trap of "random difference."[3]

Johanna Hofer coined nostalgia as "homesickness" and a "pathology that decimated the ranks of the Swiss Army."[4] Hofer was describing a longing for a localized home, much like nostalgia for post-communist cities explored by Svetlana Boym.[5] Over time, nostalgia progressed from pathology to "melancholia or depression."[6] Important for these theorists was how nostalgia became "crucial for those trying to define how much of the past we need to be able to recapture, and when too much of the past captures us."[7] How much and how little should be remembered was socially constructed, and Freud posited that nostalgia and yearning were the basis for all desire.[8] In this chapter, nostalgia similarly refers to a yearning for the past or some past state, which results in a consistent focus on past objects and reassuring, already-held ideological positions. Nostalgia is not universally regressive or problematic, but many critics have argued to be wary of the "dangers of stasis, the failure to change."[9] These theorists counterpose stasis with a preferable comparative focus on the past, which can have inherent adaptive potential if properly utilized.

Two organizing heuristics may be used as avenues to help us grasp this unwieldy topic. The first helpful heuristic for thinking about television's reconstruction of mediated pasts can be found in Fredric Jameson's discussions about the allegorical value of historical knowledge. In his thinking about postmodernity, Jameson laments the "disappearance of the American radical past" or a loss of the ability—caused by the postmodern representation of historical objects without difference—to see the time periods that came before as different than one's own.[10] There is critical potential in a radical past, and losing this can lead to a parallel loss of discussion-provoking discourse. In Jameson's discussion of this past/present conflation, the implication is that the goals and ideologies that we as a culture strive to achieve appear as unchanging and stable. With stability, the past is used as a stagnating force, creating a form of nostalgia that self-perpetuates because the longing for the past is folded onto itself. Television remakes consistently strive for an unchanging and stable past.

The second heuristic is Marcel Proust's description of automatic or involuntary memory, used throughout this chapter to understand how contemporary television works on the memories of its constructed nostalgic viewers.[11] Proust's topic is a visit with his mother, imbued with nostalgia already, where through the consumption of cake and tea the "vicissitudes of life became indifferent to me" and unidentified happy childhood memories come to mind.[12] Emotions drive transportation to a different memory place by activating senses that are "connected with the taste of tea and cake."[13] Proust remarked that emotionally activated memories have "magnetism" towards the identical moment being experienced in the present through emotional repetition.[14] In contemporary nostalgic media, the television commercial or program that repeats and remakes asks its viewers to remember the original emotional moment. Remake viewers are offered memory triggers in the form of beloved childhood texts or eras. These texts are designed to force the identical media-defined memory that had been "embedded at a great depth" to leave its "resting place" and rise to the surface.[15] Michael Wood calls this Proustian "involuntary memory" dynamic a "recovery of reality" for its attempt to both recall and recreate a time that can now only exist in the mind.[16] Once recalled, events that occurred in the past become idealized and exaggerated due to their distanced nature. All forms of the televisual nostalgic modality likewise tend to trigger automatic memories in viewers so they are perpetually enticed to look backwards on their own individualized and media-defined pasts. With theorists like Jonathan Gray, Henry Jenkins, and John Caldwell discussing the fragmentation of what it means to talk about "television," the points of nostalgic contact and remake ethos that trigger Proustian nostalgic involuntary memories exist at multiple places, including programs, advertisements, and ancillary outlets of content access, making the exploration of these issues all the more important.[17]

I seek to unveil the symbolic representations of the past in nostalgic texts and explore the connotations of media that validate an eternal return to an idealized and media-defined history. Encouraging this form of past engagement engenders a subjective hypernostalgic worldview in which viewers' pasts are nothing more than compilations of affectively charged texts for which they yearn. Viewing subjects are led to believe that through the effective use of smart media tailored to their particular tastes, they might return to this idealized and impossible past. Coming to terms with subjects who are the result of this kind of construction means having to understand how the texts themselves work to encourage and promote certain interpretations over others. Understanding how these texts speak to the viewing subjects' desires for the perpetual experiences of their individual playlist pasts becomes paramount. The texts that will be explored in this chapter are exemplary, though inherently not comprehensive. While some are explicitly nostalgic in their historical representations, such as *Elementary*, others, like *How I Met Your Mother*, contain a more implicit version of nostalgia that validates an eternal desire to return to an individualized past.

A. THE TELEVISION REMAKE

In the realm of television content, the most explicitly nostalgic programming is the remake. Film is not the only medium to take the business of remakes quite seriously, as television has recently caught the reboot bug. From new versions of *Hawaii Five-0* (2010–present), *Charlie's Angels* (2011), *V* (2009–11), and *Battlestar Galactica* (2004–09), to US adaptations of the UK's *The Office* (2005–13) and *Life on Mars* (2008–09), the contemporary television landscape looks very familiar. A show like *Nikita* (2010–13) is right at home on network television, as it is a remake of the television show *La Femme Nikita* (1997–2001), itself a remake of the French film *Nikita* (1990), which was remade as *Point of No Return* (1993) in the United States. This rash of remakes works to define history through the re-experience of nostalgic media texts and focuses the viewing subject's attention on an uncritical past. The playlist past nostalgic finds plenty of triggers in the televisual medium—including the explicitly nostalgic remake text, which extends to representations of historical eras and characters as well as channels dedicated to nostalgic programming.

Examples of remakes are plentiful, and all are asking viewers to reach backwards in time on some level, but this analysis is most interested in a specific mode of nostalgic encouragement—namely, texts that simplify and de-radicalize the past by recreating and enhancing classic hegemonic power structures. Even more problematic are remakes that "sanitize" or adjust past texts that may have stood slightly outside the hegemonic norm, bringing them more in line with an "accepted" history. For example, the television remake *Elementary* (2012–present), which steadily gained popularity in the 2012–13 season, draws from the very familiar Sherlock Holmes textual legacy but changes important gender dynamics that may have previously served to complicate hegemonic assumptions. Holmes is already no stranger to television, with shows like the British *Sherlock* (2010–present) running concurrently and pseudo-remakes like *House, M.D.* (2004–12) carrying the arrogant and brilliant detective torch despite being set in a hospital. *Elementary* furthers the idealization goals of contemporary nostalgic television programming by updating characters and elements that may be considered hegemonically problematic. Most significantly, Watson is recast as female in this version, thereby heteronormalizing the relationship between Watson and Holmes that has been the subject of homoerotic speculation in previous iterations.[18] Much fan fiction has been devoted to this subtextually homosexual relationship, and the current films featuring Robert Downey, Jr., and Jude Law seem to take pride in the well-placed innuendo. Though Holmes and Watson are not explicitly involved romantically in *Elementary*, there is consistent speculation from other characters about their relationship, which leads to audiences being encouraged to consider them as linked in this manner.

Holmes's greatest enemy, Moriarty, is also revealed to be a woman. The series' first season hinges on Sherlock's loss of his only true love, a woman named Irene Adler, whose death precipitated his spiral into heroin addiction and predicated the hiring of Watson as his sober companion. Adler is revealed to be alive two episodes before the season finale, and revealed to be Moriarty shortly after. This big twist is accompanied by Moriarty explaining her need for gender secrecy as a "potential client might struggle with my gender, as if men have a monopoly on murder." This might point towards a progressive feminist ideology; however, refracted through the lens of the remake, this dynamic is a still an important shift in gender politics. Moriarty and Holmes do not share nearly the same level of homosexual speculation that Holmes and Watson do—Moriarty and Holmes's possible romantic subtext is mostly relegated to slash fan fiction—but *Elementary* takes any relationship that prior could have been considered subtextually homosexual—even if it was by a smaller subset of fans—and erases the possibility for that interpretation in the name of normalizing the relationship and shocking a loyal fan base.

To examine knowledge barriers or twists aimed at shocking in-group fans is to study the epistemology of the remake, or the level of knowledge expected or required of the original to fully understand the new version. If one watches *Elementary* having never heard of Moriarty before, the gender twist is not exactly earth shattering; however, that is not for whom this twist is intended. Those in control of the newest Holmes narrative encourage the eternal return of the same by positing Holmes as forever relevant and defining our mediated nostalgic pasts, as well as "idealizing" the narrative in an ideologically hegemonic manner. Fans are even given the requisite, jealousy-laden conversation between two romantic rivals, now female, where Moriarty asks Watson whether she wants to sleep with Holmes. What once might have been considered a transgressive conversation is now forced into a hegemonic conception of "normal" and the remake then serves to simplify and de-radicalize the past.

B. REMAKE CHANNELS?

Remakes like *Elementary* can be refuges for those constructed as televisual nostalgics, but there is also a US channel called The Hub that provides a veritable nightly haven of media-defined history, housing a great many series remakes like *Transformers: Prime* (2010–present), *G.I. Joe: Renegades* (2010–present), and *My Little Pony: Friendship is Magic* (2010–present). This channel consists of children's programming during the day and at 8 p.m. changes into nostalgic content, much in the same way Nickelodeon becomes Nick at Nite in the evening and often includes many remakes of cartoons past. The ratings for these nostalgic programming blocks "experienced sequential gains each month" culminating in "record audience deliveries" when they previewed summer nostalgic programs.[19] Similar ratings records have been noted for other channels' nostalgic programming, such as TeenNick's "The 90s Are All That" programming block, which garnered the "highest late-night viewership levels ever" for the network and propelled it into number six among 12-to-34-year-olds for its time slot in the summer of 2011.[20]

The Hub's nightly lineup of shows like *Batman* (1966–68), *Happy Days* (1974–84), *Mork and Mindy* (1978–82), *Doogie Howser, M.D.* (1989–93), and *The Wonder Years* (1988–93) creates an evening of nostalgia that does not end until early the next morning. This kind of programming not only mimics other networks like Cartoon Network's "Adult Swim" lineup in marketing to specific generations who might be awake at three in the morning, but also serves to highlight possible alternative economic motivations for this channel other than the creation of child-friendly programming. By relying on insider knowledge of the remake's ancestors, shows that appear aimed squarely at contemporary children reveal their dual purpose as fostering nostalgia in those who loved previous iterations. For instance, in the pilot for *Transformers Prime*, a remake of the original *The Transformers* series (1984–87), there is little to no explanation of the robots in disguise, coupled with a complex, bloody, and difficult-to-follow plot. In the pilot episode, references to characters familiar to seasoned fans of the original series, along with inside jokes about the rich back stories between characters, do not speak to a welcoming environment for the uninitiated. This remake erects barriers of knowledge as it speaks primarily to those who are already in the know about Optimus Prime and his dealings with the Decepticons. A small child in the pilot of *Transformers: Prime* wonders aloud, "What did we just see?" This appropriate reaction is probably shared by many children watching this series with no prior Transformers experience, which signals that the primary purpose of The Hub's reliance on the collision of a retro series with its remake iteration, a technique it employs often with the Batman and G.I. Joe brands as well, is to erase a radical past and provide for a false continuity of these texts/brands as cultural markers.

The Hub channel's nightly programming focuses all of its viewers' attention eternally backwards and asks them to consider the past as all important and melancholic in its refusal to relinquish past objects, and as such uncritically defined by the longed-for media texts. Constructing this nostalgic subjectivity means adhering to automatic nostalgic triggers, including the voice of the announcers on this channel that seem to speak to the child in all of us with their Saturday Morning Cartoon tone. One key nostalgic trigger is The Hub brand bumpers that occur before and after commercials, making them reminiscent of children's shows where "bumpers between programs and commercials are required."[21] A *Laverne and Shirley* (1976–83) episode at 11 p.m. is not aimed at a child demographic, but the bumpers sure make it seem that way. This dynamic becomes all the more pronounced when considering The Hub's late night programming called "Huboom!" consisting of *Batman, Transformers,* and *G.I. Joe* (1983–86) episodes every weekday night at 11:30 p.m. This consistent nostalgic programming not only contains the aforementioned Hub bumpers, but also original bumpers from the vintage shows. As each show progresses in its original sequential order, the attempt to construct nostalgia as concerning the perpetual recreation of a lost object is well executed. To see what happens next to Batman or Optimus Prime, viewers must continually revisit their pasts nightly and further reify their nostalgia. The conflation of multiple time periods also continues during the Huboom! portion of The Hub's nightly lineup as *Batman* and its two animated series remakes originally aired two decades apart, yet exist side-by-side today. Multiple pasts conflate with each other and with the present in this remade and recreated nostalgic media-defined history.

C. EVEN COMMERCIALS ARE REMADE?

Televisual nostalgia works as a feedback loop including advertisements, with ads continuing the uncritical content and problematic temporality of the shows themselves—a repetition beneficial for advertisers who wish to maintain a consistent buying mood. As commercials represent the "most consistent and pervasive genre of television content," their automatic nostalgic triggers become all the more significant to explore. [22]

Television commercials can be nostalgic in a few key ways: through specific referencing of texts from the past, or through a historically located temporal tone. Whereas a Guinness commercial that features Etta James's "At Last" triggers nostalgia through its connection between this product and a song that transports those in the commercial to a more simple romantic time, an Enzyte commercial campaign might contain a whole 1960s nostalgic *mise-en-scène*. The tone set for a nostalgic commercial is many times determined by the choice of a vintage song. Countless examples exist, such as the 2005 Diet Pepsi commercial where soda cans danced to The Ramones' 1976 song "Blitzkrieg Bop" and the tone set is a mix of nostalgia and rebellion, but in the form of a commodity. The commodification of rebellion is a common marketing tactic that serves to reaffirm the dominant power structure through incorporation of opposition, or what Dick Hebdige sees as a "continual process of recuperation" through which the "fractured order is repaired." [23] Cotten Seiler describes this common dynamic prevalent in music from concerts to records as those in power in the music industry have "always cohered around those images and models of disaffiliation and rebellion, whose threat had been neutralized or subsumed" from Elvis to Kurt Cobain. [24] The Diet Pepsi cans are shown to love The Ramones while "unhip" Diet Coke cans complain that the music is "so annoying." Music that claims to resist the establishment is featured in a giant corporation's commercial asking the audience to both focus on the past and simultaneously "rebel" by buying the "cooler" diet soda. Most significantly, "rebellious" nostalgic memory triggers are used to sell commodities and not to engage in comparative and adaptive historical discourses.

Music is not the only kind of referencing utilized to maintain nostalgia in commercials, as other pop culture texts from the past consistently make their way into contemporary television commercials. Here, like in so many other examples of nostalgia that lack a radical edge, the past is defined by the media texts themselves at the expense of a collective and adaptive history. Volkswagen often employs nostalgia in commercials for throwback-style Beetles and sound systems that play oldies like "Rocket Man" with higher fidelity, as shown in a 2011 commercial. VW serves as nostalgic exemplar in its 2012 "The Force" commercial that depicts a child attempting to use *Star Wars* "force" powers on household objects, complete with Darth Vader costume and music. The past is present in music, *mise-en-scène*, and tone, but most pertinent is the reference to the *Star Wars* series (1977–present) itself. The Darth Vader child reminds grown-ups of their love of *Star Wars*, a point made stronger by the imitation of a version of a character that may not be as familiar to current generations who only know Anakin Skywalker from the prequel films or the animated series *Star Wars: The Clone Wars* (2008–13). Those in the market for a Volkswagen are made to feel nostalgic for the original *Star Wars*; this feeling is parlayed into a car commodity.

Some commercials even trigger referential nostalgia by remaking other commercials. The 2011 Motorola Xoom ad that aired during the Super Bowl parodied the famous "1984" Apple ad by making fun of the contemporary "cult of Apple." This critique is achieved through images of uniform-clad workers moving in lockstep, wearing iconic Apple headphones, alongside images of the lone "non-conformist" reading the very literary text the commercial is using to critique what Apple had claimed to fight against. In a 2011 Wendy's commercial, the burger chain resurrected its 1984 slogan "Where's the Beef?" through two new commercials that acted as exemplary automatic memory triggers for nostalgic television viewers. The first commercial briefly depicted the iconic 1984 footage of the old women standing over the tiny burger in a large bun, and told audiences that something big was coming soon. In the second "Here's the Beef!" commercial, the automatic memory trigger becomes exponentially more salient. A young man sifts through a vintage t-shirt bin at a clothing store, and stumbles upon a shirt that simply says, "Where's the Beef?" He puts this shirt on and begins to stroll down the street, where every single person he passes, young and old, throws the catchphrase back at him in a knowing manner. The t-shirt triggers the memories in the fellow passersby, much like it is triggering nostalgia in the viewers. Similarly, Kraft released a 2013 remake of its classic Grey Poupon commercial in which rich men ask for the condiment through fancy car windows. Tellingly, Kraft entitled this commercial "The Lost Footage" and feigned it was simply an extension of the 1980s version, developing a false continuity between these time periods and its commodities. These commercial remakes index a powerful connection between the past and the present while reinvigorating the brand in the present. These remakes give the illusion of a shared past, but one based on artificial mediated nostalgia that has been contemporized and idealized.

As a caveat, like nostalgic programming, the past-centered advertisement is an increasing phenomenon, but is certainly not an all-encompassing norm. A content analysis was conducted in 1991 of over 1000 commercials with 10 percent "assessed as nostalgic," and while this number appears to be much higher today, it is far from 100 percent.[25] An opportunity exists for updated research in this area of study. As a second caveat, advertising has some inherent friction with the nostalgic mode, as so many ads are designed to introduce the "newest" products available. Ads for electronics appear to reject the nostalgic mode more often than not, as the celebration of the new is the crux of this industry. What these caveats hint at is that the nostalgic commercial may contribute to the television's construction of nostalgia, but this must be understood as still determined by the constraints of the advertisers, whose goals are to sell the newest products. What can be said, however, is that the commercial mindset is one that thrives on uncritical viewing that preserves consumptive thinking.[26] Even if a commercial is not nostalgic, the system of advertising in place in the television medium "asks" the content producers to avoid controversy as well as "ideas that are too complex" and promote "critical thinking," all goals that are accomplished through nostalgic programming.[27] The symbiotic relationship between nostalgic programming and its commercials benefits from this avoidance of a radical, critical, and comparative past that would question the status quo.

D. *HOW I MET YOUR MOTHER* AND THE IMPLICITLY NOSTALGIC TELEVISION SHOW

Remakes and explicit nostalgic programming/advertising do not fully explain the pervasive nature of longing for the past within the television medium. In fact, if viewers were only dealing with clearly demarcated moments of triggered past-focus, there would be less of a concern for the uncritical and melancholic nature of the constructed compulsive drive to recreate and retain an individual lost object. Additionally, the implicitly nostalgic televisual text triggers nostalgic memories on a level closer to what Proust had in mind when he described the involuntary remembering associated with eating madeleine cookies. One cannot know what will trigger the memory, which presents misrecognition that a memory can fully be recovered (for the more one chases the memory, the more it recedes). The implicitly nostalgic television text does not come right out and say "it is time for you to long for your lost childhood," but instead reinforces the act of remembering through character traits and narrative flashbacks. For the implicitly nostalgic television text, the focus is less on vintage clothing, retro coloring, and referential music—though these elements surface often in flashbacks—and more on the validation of the remembering act itself, which is dramatized by the narratives and, subsequently, triggered in viewers. Characters are shown to be continuously reliant on their pasts, triggering a sympathetic nostalgic reaction among viewers. The implicitly nostalgic show raises focus on the individual past to a status of extreme importance, even in shows that may seem to be far from nostalgic. Examples of shows that long for the past despite their present/future veneers are *Fringe* (2008–13), *Flashforward* (2009–10), *Lost* (2004–10), and *Revenge* (2011–present), which all encourage a consistent focus on personal pasts, implicitly validated through fixation on main characters' histories.

One of the most clearly observable examples of a television show that validates perpetual nostalgia is only implicitly nostalgic itself because of its future/present setting. Technically set in the year 2030—a time that looks blandly like our present — *How I Met Your Mother* (*HIMYM*) chronicles the retelling of a parental meeting by a father to his children. The children in 2030 are seen in the beginning of some of the episodes accompanied by an offscreen father's voice, but the primary setting of the show is present day. The show debuted in 2005 and as each year passes the narrative moves forward at the same pace. Viewers of this show occupy an odd relationship to the past on the screen, as it is their present. The narrative structure of this show proves to not only create nostalgia about a time that has not even passed yet, but also validates individualized nostalgia as one of the most important activities in one's life. *HIMYM* is the perfect text for dramatizing how media constructs and validates subjects who are perpetually nostalgic, even if it is technically an implicit nostalgia for the present.

The past, and significantly an individual's past, is of the utmost importance to the characters of *HIMYM*. The main character, Ted Mosby, who is in search of the eventual mate who will be the 2030 mother, recounts a tale that is anything but brief. Instead, the narrative meanders to minutiae about him and his best friends Marshall (his college roommate), Lily (Marshall's wife), Barney (his philandering friend), and Robin (his on-again, off-again girlfriend). When the producers of the show decided on a title, they ensured that continued success would mean adding more tangents and plotlines before the introduction of the mother. Like many serialized shows, producers claim to "have an idea of where [the series] will end up" asking only for audiences' continued trust.[28] Here the very point of the show, the introduction of the mother figure, was delayed in a manner that suggested that once the reveal was made the show may be over or at the very least in its endgame. Viewers were given a visual introduction at the end of the season eight finale as a way to propel the narrative to conclusion in its final season, though Ted has not yet fulfilled the titular requirement of actually meeting her. Analogs can be drawn to the figure of Scheherazade who, knowing that she is to be killed each morning, creates an exciting cliffhanger at the end of each night to ensure her survival for one more day, or in the case of *HIMYM*, one more episode. Nostalgically, this functions to validate an eternal concern with every minute detail from the past. The 2030 children have remarked that their father has been telling the story "forever," and in a 2013 Internet video parody the actor and actress who played the children (but had aged considerably since) joked that the father had literally been telling the story for eight years. Alternatively, in the season two episode "Brunch" (2.03), Ted's parents tell him the story of how they met by simply saying, "Oh, great story, at a bar." Despite this gentle ribbing about the length of the show's overarching "story," individual nostalgia is ultimately validated as all-important.

The past is so important to the characters of *HIMYM* that many episodes are based around stories being told within the main 2030 story.

Episodes like season two's "The Scorpion and the Toad" (2.02), season three's "How I Met Everyone Else" (3.05), and season five's "Perfect Week" (5.14) all revolve around nesting stories that evolve into multi-layered retellings. The most over-the-top example is the season three episode "The Platinum Rule" (3.11), where Ted is recalling a story to his children about Barney telling him a story about when Lily and Marshall told Robin a story about when Barney told her a story. It is quite the complex episode. The main character is waxing nostalgic about being nostalgic to his kids. As noted in some of these examples, the teller of the story within a story is not always Ted, which leads to a further validation of the personal account as important with future Ted relaying second-hand information to his children as historical fact.

HIMYM does, however, complicate some of these issues along the way, especially as they relate to the inherently faulty nature of human memory. Ted Mosby is talking to his children in 2030, which represents a mitigating factor when considering the relative "accuracy" of this fictional oral history. In many episodes, future Ted is either wrong about how something happened, unwilling to present the entire story to his children, or lacking in the whole truth (due to lie or omission by one of his friends, especially Barney). Sometimes the information about the past is unavailable, such as in the season five episode "Zoo or False" (5.19) where Marshall has been mugged and after multiple versions of the story it is unclear whether he had his wallet stolen by an armed assailant or a monkey. Because of Marshall's unwillingness to reveal the truth in 2010, Ted is unable to say with confidence what happened when telling the story in 2030. Series co-creator and show runner Craig Thomas describes this somewhat unreliable narrator as "a guy who is telling the story so many years in the future, and he jumbles it up in his memory a little bit." [29] Though the accuracy of the narrator's remembrances is less important as criteria for the validation of an implicit nostalgia, it does point to the potential contained in addressing the past as more complex. However, though the unreliable narrator and memory questioning in *HIMYM* border on a more nuanced look at history's contradictory and complicated interpretations, the overpowering effect of personal nostalgia as supremely validated creates a text that is more uncritical than comparative.

E. CONCLUSION

Nostalgia as an adaptive and progressive influence "can become available and advantageous under specific social, historical, cultural, and performative circumstances," [30] but this assumes the longing for the past is used as a way to make social progress. Looking at the television lineups in recent years, it quickly becomes evident that the industry believes shows that trigger or reify a nostalgic view of the past are a safe bet for programming, but not to encourage an adaptive and critical mindset. When comparative history involves the differences between the original *Transformers* and its remake, what is lost are comparisons about the eras in which each text was made. With planned remakes of *The Flintstones* (1960–66), *Thunderbirds* (1965), and even *The Exorcist* (1973) set to join shows like *Hawaii Five-0, Nikita, Dallas* (2012–present), and *Parenthood* (2010–present), there is no shortage of rebooting on television. However, it is not enough to simply look at the line-up and point out the obvious remakes and shows centered on historical representations. Television nostalgia, instead, burrows itself much deeper into every content area of this medium in a way that matches the pervasive and convergent nature of contemporary media. Television may be a fractured medium with countless idiosyncratic ways to consume its content, some that are important to the development of nostalgia in digital access outlets, but individualized and idealized nostalgia holds because a dominant aesthetic/mode of this medium is one that de-radicalizes and triggers past yearning no matter the content or viewing situation. Whether it is the idealized and normalized gender hegemony of *Elementary* or the affirmation of the eternal individual nostalgic in *HIMYM,* the common denominator is a predictable nostalgia that can be triggered or evoked in televisual content and advertising. Nostalgia exists throughout the television medium, and asks viewers to examine the past on a cursory level at the expense of significant critical engagement.

FILMS AND TV SHOWS

Batman. ABC, 1966–68.
Battlestar Galactica. The Sci-Fi Network, 2004–09.
Charlie's Angels. ABC, 2011.
Dallas. TNT, 2012–.
Doogie Howser, M.D. ABC, 1989–93.
Elementary. CBS, 2012–.
The Exorcist. Directed by William Friedkin. 1973. Warner Bros.
Flashforward. ABC, 2009–10.
The Flintstones. ABC, 1960–66.
Fringe. Fox Network, 2008–13.
G.I. Joe. Claster Television, 1983–86.
G.I. Joe: Renegades. The Hub, 2010–.
Happy Days. ABC, 1974–84.
Hawaii Five–0. CBS, 2010–.
House M.D. Fox Network, 2004–12.
How I Met Your Mother. CBS, 2005–.
La Femme Nikita. USA Network, 1997–2001.
Life on Mars. ABC, 2008–09.

Lost. ABC, 2004–10.

Mork & Mindy. ABC, 1978–82.

My Little Pony: Friendship is Magic. The Hub, 2010–.

Nikita. The CW, 2010–13.

Nikita. Directed by Luc Besson. 1990. Gaumont.

The Office. NBC, 2005–13.

Parenthood. NBC, 2010–.

Point of No Return. Directed by John Badham. 1993. Warner Bros.

Revenge. ABC, 2011–.

Sherlock. BBC, 2010–.

Star Wars. Directed by George Lucas. 1977. Twentieth Century Fox.

Star Wars: The Clone Wars. Cartoon Network, 2008–.

Thunderbirds. ITC, 1965–66.

The Transformers. Claster Television, 1984–87.

Transformers: Prime. The Hub, 2010–.

The Wonder Years. ABC, 1988–93.

NOTES

1. Matthew Jordan, "Mourning, Nostalgia, Melancholia," in *Henry James Goes to the Movies*, ed. Susan M. Griffin (Lexington: University Press of Kentucky, 2002), 89.

2. Todd Gitlin, *Inside Prime Time* (Berkeley: University of California Press, 1994), 77.

3. Fredric Jameson, *Postmodernism, or, The Cultural Logic of Late Capitalism* (Durham, NC: Duke University Press, 1991), 6.

4. Aurélie Kessous and Elyette Roux, "A Semiotic Analysis of Nostalgia as a Connection to the Past," *Qualitative Market Research* 11, no. 2 (2008): 194.

5. Svetlana Boym, *The Future of Nostalgia* (New York: Basic Books, 2001).

6. Tim Wildschut et al., "Nostalgia: Content, Triggers, Functions," *Journal of Personality and Social Psychology* 91, no. 5 (2006): 975.

7. Michael S. Roth, "Remembering Forgetting: Maladies de la Mémoire in Nineteenth-Century France," *Representations* 26 (1989): 50.

8. Boym, *Future of Nostalgia*, 54.

9. Alastair Bonnett, *Left in the Past: Radicalism and the Politics of Nostalgia* (London: Continuum, 2010), 3.

10. Jameson, *Postmodernism*, 24.

11. Marcel Proust, *Remembrance of Things Past, Volume 1*, trans. C.K. Scott Moncrieff (Ware, Hertfordshire: Wordsworth Editions, 2006), 61.

12. Proust, *Remembrance*, 61.

13. Ibid., 61.

14. Ibid., 63.

15. Ibid., 62.

16. Michael Wood, "Proust: The Music of Memory," in *Memory: Histories, Theories, Debates*, ed. Susannah Radstone (Bronx, NY: Fordham University Press, 2010), 110.

17. Jonathan Gray, *Television Entertainment* (New York: Routledge, 2008); Henry Jenkins, *Convergent Culture: Where Old and New Media Collide* (New York: NYU Press, 2006); John T. Caldwell, "Welcome to the Viral Future of Cinema (Television)," *Cinema Journal* 45, no. 1 (2005): 90–117.

18. Tim Walker, "Sherlock is the 'gayest story in the history of television,' says Martin Freeman," *The Telegraph*, May 24, 2011, accessed April 22, 2013, http://www.telegraph.co.uk/culture/tvandradio/8531671/Sherlock-is-the-gayest-story-in-the-

history-of-television-says-Martin-Freeman.html; Alyssa Rosenberg, "The Sexual Tension Between Sherlock Holmes and John Watson," *Think Progress*, March 2, 2012, accessed April 22, 2013, http://thinkprogress.org/alyssa/2012/03/02/433781/the-sexual-tension-between-sherlock-holmes-and-john-watson; Barbara Barnett, "*House, MD's* House and Wilson: A Fine Bromance," *Blogcritics*, September 3, 2008, accessed April 22, 2013, http://blogcritics.org/video/article/house-mds-house-and-wilson-a/

19. Georg Szalai, "Analysts Defend Early Ratings for The Hub as 'Decent,'" *The Hollywood Reporter*, January 13, 2011, accessed December 7, 2011, http://www.hollywoodreporter.com/blogs/live-feed/analyst-defends-early-ratings-hub-71543; Discovery Communications, Inc., "The Hub TV Network Generates 'Truly Outrageous' Record Ratings With Holiday Weekend Sneak Peek Preview of Summer Programming," *Discovery Press Web*, June 1, 2011, accessed December 7, 2011, http://press.discovery.com/us/hub/press-releases/2011/hub-tv-network-generates-truly-outrageous-rec-1344/

20. Robert Seidman, "TeenNick Proves the '90s Are 'All That' as New Late-Night Retro Block Reaches Record Ratings," *TV by the Numbers*, July 27, 2011, accessed December 7, 2011, http://tvbythenumbers.zap2it.com/2011/07/27/teennick-proves-the-90s-are-all-that-as-new-late-night-retro-block-reaches-record-ratings/99022/

21. Matthew P. McAllister, and Matt J. Giglio, "The Commodity Flow of U.S. Children's Television," *Critical Studies in Media Communication* 22, no. 1 (2005): 31.

22. Matthew P. McAllister, "Television Advertising as Textual and Economic Systems," in *A Companion to Television*, ed. Janet Wasko (Malden, MA: Blackwell Publishing, 2005), 217.

23. Dick Hebdige, *Subculture: The Meaning of Style* (New York: Routledge, 1979), 94.

24. Cotten Seiler, "The Commodification of Rebellion: Rock Culture and Consumer Capitalism," in *New Forms of Consumption: Consumers, Culture, and Commodification*, ed. Mark Gottdiener (Lanham, MD: Rowman and Littlefield Publishers, 2000), 217.

25. Lynette S. Unger, Diane M. McConocha, and John A. Faier, "The Use of Nostalgia in Television Advertising: A Content Analysis," *Journalism Quarterly* 68, no. 3 (1991): 350.

26. Matthew P. McAllister, "Television Advertising as Textual and Economic Systems," in *A Companion to Television*, ed. Janet Wasko (Malden, MA: Blackwell Publishing, 2005), 227.

27. Ibid., 229.

28. Vlada Gelman, "'How I Met Your Mother' shocker: Season 6 kicks off with 'game-changing moment,'" *Entertainment Weekly*, July 29, 2010, accessed June 2, 2011, http://insidetv.ew.com/2010/07/29/how-i-met-your-mother-scoop-2/

29. Korbi Ghosh, "'How I Met Your Mother's' Craig Thomas on Ted & Barney's Breakup, Eriksen Babies and The Future of Robarn," *Zap 2 It*, May 18, 2008, accessed June 2, 2011, http://blog.zap2it.com/frominsidethebox/2008/05/how-i-met-your-mothers-craig-thomas-on-ted-barneys-breakup-eriksen-babies-and-the-future-of-robarn.html

30. Bonnett, *Left in the Past*, 42.

FOUR

Multiverses and Multiversions

Meditations on the Rebootings of Fringe

Heather Marcovitch

The Fox television show *Fringe* (2008–13), created by J.J. Abrams, Alex Kurtzman, and Roberto Orci, has recently completed its five-year, 100-episode run and in the process created a truly remarkable television narrative.[1] It began as, to some early viewers' skepticism, what seemed to be a paranormal mystery show along the lines of *The X-Files* (1993–2002), with elements of Ken Russell and Paddy Chayefsky's *Altered States* (1980) thrown in for good measure. But while the show suffered from low ratings over the years, likely occasioned by its position in Fox's Friday night "death slot," it garnered critical accolades and a devoted cult following.[2] The reason for this high praise, *New York Times* television critic Mike Hale surmises, was the writers' unwavering focus on the central characters and premise of an alternate universe, populated, as John Noble's character Walter Bishop reminds us, by "versions of us" (1.20, "There's More Than One of Everything").[3] This degree of focus, unusual in shows that promise complicated myth arcs, allowed the writers to structure *Fringe* as a meditation on parallel universes, character, and the functions of television narrative. This chapter will explore these meditations, from the quantum mechanical theories about the existence of parallel universes to the narrative possibilities such theories suggest. *Fringe* is a show with a narrative, but it is also a show *about* making television narratives, and I argue that within this show is an exploration of television shows as texts that inherently reboot themselves; in doing so, they create alternate universes with each reboot. *Fringe*, as we shall see, remakes itself with every season and, in doing so, makes plain that its constant refashioning and revisioning is in the very nature of television shows.

Every season of *Fringe* reimagines the central premise and narrative as variations on a questionably core universe. I qualify this statement because *Fringe* deviates from a conventional science fiction narrative structure: if the science fiction story is about travelling through time, or encountering different universes, one world is usually positioned, textually or hermeneutically, as that which is authoritative, and from which we see the differences in time and place unfold. One example is the recent reboot of *Star Trek* (2009), directed by J.J. Abrams and written by all three of *Fringe*'s creators, which, despite its reboot of characters and timeline, still looks to the original series as its authority. Kirk and Spock, in both story and performance, are read in light of the original characters; Leonard Nimoy's character is even listed in the credits as Spock Prime, to distinguish him from Zachary Quinto's character. In *Fringe*, though, the writers pose the question about whether the initial world we encounter is indeed the core or prime world or whether each season contributes as a sort of free-floating signifier without any authoritative status. In this chapter I use, for clarity's sake, the term "original" or "prime" to speak of the universe that is postulated as "our" universe. However, the show complicates this idea by displacing characters and timelines so that, in later seasons, the seeming authority that the original world possesses in terms of narrative structure has vanished.

The first season introduces us to our leading trio of characters, FBI agent Olivia Dunham (Anna Torv), Dr. Walter Bishop (John Noble) and his estranged son Peter (Joshua Jackson), as well as the recurring supporting cast: Astrid Farnsworth (Jasika Nicole), the FBI agent who becomes the Fringe team's assistant; Lieutenant—later Colonel—Broyles (Lance Reddick), the team's commanding officer; Nina Sharp (Blair Brown), the president of the scientific research and development company Massive Dynamic; and, intermittently, the company's enigmatic owner and Walter's former partner in science, William Bell (Leonard Nimoy). In the first season, we learn that Walter and William discovered the existence of an alternate universe which contains different versions of Olivia (called Faux-livia or Bolivia on fan sites), Astrid, Broyles, Nina, Lincoln Lee (Seth Gabel, who joins the cast in the third season), and the man Walter whimsically names his Walternate.[4]

At the heart of the first four seasons is the central tragic action of *Fringe*—that, in 1985, Walter's young son Peter succumbed to a mysterious illness. While watching the alternate universe through a specially designed window, Walter not only learns that another version of Peter is also dying of the same illness on "the other side" (as the alternate universe is called in the show), but he deduces the cure from watching Walternate's efforts—too late for his own son but in time to save the other Peter. In a desperate attempt to save the other version of his son, Walter crosses over into the other universe, kidnaps Peter, and brings him over to his world in order to administer the treatment. In this world, father and quasi-son fall through the lake where the opening between universes is located. They nearly drown, but a mysterious bald man suddenly appears and saves them both (2.16, "Peter"). Walter cures Peter but is unable (and unwilling) to return him, and he and his wife Elizabeth brainwash Peter into believing that his memories of having lived in a different world are illness-induced delusions (3.15, "Subject 13").

The consequences of this action, one which showrunners J.H. Wyman and Jeff Pinkner keep emphasizing were based out of the desperate act of a grieving father, provide both the backstory and the thematic foundation of *Fringe*, one which is deepened as the series progresses.[5] Elizabeth Bishop, guilt-ridden because of her complicity in Peter's kidnapping and brainwashing, commits suicide. As a result, Walter suffers a severe mental breakdown and is hospitalized for nearly twenty years. And Peter, estranged from his father and feeling like a misfit for reasons he can no longer remember, becomes a con artist. He is recruited by Olivia to act as caretaker for Walter who, despite the mental and emotional scars of his breakdown, still possesses a vast knowledge of paranormal science research necessary to solving the episodes' mysteries. Olivia's connection to the Bishops is also revealed: as a child, she was experimented on by Walter and William Bell and was given massive doses of a drug called Cortexiphan, designed to engineer children who could cross between universes.

On a larger narrative scale, the action of 1985 produces what Slavoj Žižek, borrowing from both Derrida and theoretical physics, calls an Event. Žižek cites Heidegger in defining an Event as "the epochal disclosure of a configuration of Being," where a moment in time constructs not only future events but reconstructs memories of the past.[6] Walter's initial crossing in 1985 caused a rip in the fabric separating universes and, like an unraveling piece of cloth, began the destruction of the other universe, which in turn causes Walternate's intent to destroy the "prime" universe. When we first see the other universe, the evidence of this destruction is made clear: street signs flashing for oxygen masks to be donned, dead forests lining the highways, and vortices that must be plugged up with a mixture of amber resin. As William warns Olivia, "There is a war coming" and he fears that, with Walternate's superior technology and fury, "our side will lose" (2.04, "Momentum Deferred"). Like the traumatic events of 9/11 which inform the show's subtext, one Event creates a new paradigm in our perception of the world. As far as the narrative of the show is concerned, the rip in the fabric of the universe opens up not only the dramatic conflict but the questions of narrative stability and character identity which recur throughout the series.

With the introduction of the alternate universe, the central conflict of seasons two and three plays out, in which Peter becomes entangled in a triangle involving the Olivias from both universes. The third season is structured as a treasure hunt involving finding and assembling pieces of a doomsday machine. When Peter turns the machine on, he is transported to the year 2026 where Walternate, the last survivor of the other universe, engineers the destruction of the "prime" universe. In an effort to save both worlds, Peter returns to the present and declares that cooperation between the two sides is necessary in order for both worlds to survive. An uneasy alliance is struck and Peter, in an instant, vanishes from the screen; the other characters seem to have instantaneously forgotten him.

It is here, in season four, where the show starts to focus heavily on questions of remaking a narrative. Peter's sudden cessation of existence creates a new set of universes. In the original universe, the Fringe team is still operating, and is indeed cooperating with the alternate universe, but the core team is Olivia, Walter, and Astrid. In this incarnation, Walter, though he had crossed over to the other universe in 1985 to save that version of Peter, had been unsuccessful in this altered timeline, and so had lost both boys. He still suffered a mental breakdown and we see that without the presence of his son, he is much slower to recover. Olivia, without her lover, is still guarded and distrustful of people, with the exception of Nina Sharp who, in this timeline, has acted as her foster mother after Olivia ran away from the drug trials and her abusive home. But in this version, Walternate, whose son died rather than disappeared, is no longer the agent of vengeance he was in earlier versions. The antagonist in season four is William Bell, who is now a Dr. Moreau-like mad scientist. Likewise, the alternate universe also enters a different timeline. Faux-livia, for instance, had slept with Peter in season two and had given birth to their son; in the new timeline, neither the affair nor the child ever existed. And the alternate Broyles, who died in season three, is resurrected, as is villain David Robert Jones (Jared Harris).

I've included this fairly lengthy and complicated synopsis by way of introduction into the rich narrative of *Fringe*. Despite the multiple universes and versions of characters, the show is actually much less convoluted than the sprawling, untethered myth arcs of shows like *The X-Files* and *Lost* (2004–10), where it eventually became apparent that trying to locate a logical narrative structure in mythologies riddled with inconsistencies and tangents was a futile endeavor. Mike Hale describes *Fringe* as a narrative that expands vertically, rather than the horizontal sprawl of other myth-based shows.[7] That is, the addition of variations, new possibilities, and alternate timelines allows us to look at the universe of *Fringe* as a world that is decidedly unfixed and unstable, a Ray Bradbury-inspired world where one misplaced step on an insect could fundamentally alter timelines. The concept of parallel and multiple universes is a familiar trope in science fiction narratives but the *Fringe* writers invoke the writings of theoretical physics to construct their alternate universe.

This interweaving of multiverse theory is present not only in the overall premise of the show but also in important narrative details.

The theory of parallel universes belongs to both the field of quantum mechanics and to speculative fiction. While the theory itself is not universally accepted by physicists, its metaphorical possibilities invite questions of metaphysics and ethics, and it is these questions that *Fringe* explores far more than the hard science. Nonetheless the show's writers use some basic theories about multiple or parallel universes disseminated for the popular audience. One of the most prolific of the physicists who subscribe to the multiverse theory is Alex Vilenkin, who describes it as such: following the Big Bang, universes—which Vilenkin does not define in a philosophical sense of everything that is knowable, but rather, following the discourse of physics, as "completely disjointed, self-contained space-times"—exist within a space always expanding, or undergoing inflation.[8] As Vilenkin explains,

> Regions like ours, where inflation has ended, are also constantly being produced. They form "island universes" in the inflating sea. Because of inflation, the space between these islands rapidly expands, making room for more island universes to form. Thus, inflation is a runaway process, which stopped in our neighborhood, but still continues in other parts of the universe, causing them to expand at a furious rate and constantly spawning new island universes like ours.[9]

In other words, Vilenkin describes an infinite number of universes, all variations of one another. Some, he claims, would be virtually identical to our universe, while others would deviate from ours ranging in degrees from barely perceptible differences to ones so profound as to make the worlds unrecognizable to each other. Like the premise of *Fringe*, Vilenkin postulates that some other universes would have similar evolutionary patterns and similar histories, and therefore would have versions of ourselves living in them. As he and Jaume Garriga explain in their essay "Many Worlds in One,"

> Whenever a thought crosses your mind that some terrible calamity might have happened, you can be assured that it *has* happened in some of the O-regions [other universes]. If you narrowly escaped an accident, then you were not so lucky in some of the regions with the same prior history. . . . On the positive side . . . there are infinitely many O-regions where Al Gore is President and—yes!—Elvis is still alive.[10]

This idea takes shape in *Fringe* on both an exemplary level and on a level that questions the development of character. For instance, William Bell in the alternate universe died in a car accident; moreover, he never met Walter Bishop and therefore they never pursued their gonzo science to the point of crossing universes or injecting children with mind-altering drugs. The original Walternate therefore is a more sober and sane individual than Walter, not any less a visionary, but—not having committed such unethical acts in the pursuit of knowledge—he is not governed by a sense of remorse and, therefore, seems to lack that element of pathos that makes Walter so poignant a character.

While I would personally prefer to imagine a living River Phoenix or Kurt Cobain rather than Elvis, what intrigues me in Vilenkin's argument is its potential for speculative narrative and how it resonates in our current cultural moment. One of the most appealing ideas about alternate universes is the possibility of the "do-over": to have the chance to rectify mistakes or change the vagaries of fate, to have a refusal turn into an acceptance or that road which was previously not taken now journeyed upon and its destination met. In our society with its fear of finalities or of irreversible decisions, the idea that, when faced with an array of life choices, one might have the potential to choose *all* of them resonates in *Fringe*. We see, for example, that the alternate universe Olivia, not having experienced either an abusive stepfather or the ordeals of the Cortexiphan drug experiments, is self-confident, gregarious, and, one assumes, much better adjusted than the fearful, guarded Olivia of the original universe. Astrid's intelligence and attention to detail, traits which she uses to great effect in the Fringe Division's lab in the original universe, are transformed into Asperger's Syndrome in the alternate universe.[11]

Despite the changes between seasons and universes, the one set of characters that remains constant is a group of mysterious bald men who speak and move in a stilted fashion and who provide Hitchcock-like cameos in every episode. In late season four, we learn that these men, called the Observers, are in fact *us*; this is true not only in terms of the show's narrative, which postulates humans' eventual evolution by the twenty-seventh century into a transhumanist, limbically inhibited species, but also in terms of the phenomenon of observing in quantum mechanics—simply put, that which is observed will change because of the act of observation. In fact, *Fringe* makes this basic tenet of quantum mechanics a narrative point when the Observer named September (Michael Cerveris) hints about the dizzying array of alternate futures and pasts created by his "interference" in the events he witnessed, such as distracting Walternate in 1985 so he does not see that he has discovered a cure for his son's illness, and by saving Walter and Peter from drowning in Reiden Lake (2.16, "Peter"), to name but two examples.

Until season five, when they become the antagonists of the show, the Observers play a role that falls somewhere between a Greek chorus and the Delphic oracle, in that they alternately comment on the action and utter ambiguous statements that foreshadow future events. The two competing theories of time that the Observers refer to—that events are fixed but for the ones that can be changed by human choices—can be traced back through literature to tragedy, both classical and Shakespearean, which, more so than science fiction or investigative narratives, is the major literary influence on *Fringe*.

Peter and Walter's relationship is not unlike the story of Oedipus Rex, but is more akin to Freud's interpretation—which emphasizes the struggle and competition between father and son—than to Sophocles' drama. The writers extend this metaphor of struggle to include virtually all parent-child dyads, from William Bell to Olivia, to Nina and Olivia in season four, to the alternate Olivia's subversive investigations of her superior officers Broyles and Walternate in season four. Olivia, in fact, is far more of an Oedipal character than Peter in this respect, which is why she, as well as Peter, is attached to the Greek phrase recurring throughout the series, translated into English as "Be a better man than your father." The phrase is spoken by Hector on the eve of his death in Book VI of *The Iliad*, another epic about a decisive war, and it is a sentence that the show treats both seriously and ironically, especially when we take into consideration the multiple father and authority figures who act as foils to the Fringe team's efforts.

The recurrence of this philosophical phrase cannot help but evoke the trace of tragedy and so one of the main themes in *Fringe* is a very old one: the question of fate versus free will. Walter is the character through which this question becomes disseminated. In possibly every version of him we encounter, Walter is a man who, even in a fragile emotional state, is governed by both a genius imagination and the hubris that has been associated with characters from a Greek king to the mad scientist of B movies. But he also is a character whose greatest error stems from a desire to save his dying son, and so the unforgivable action rises out of one of the most forgivable motives.

While there may be several universes operating in this show, there are only two distinct realities, both predicated on a sense of loss. *Fringe* builds universes based on the related imaginary constructions of nostalgia (in which there is an imaginary reclamation of that which has been lost) and melancholy (in which the loss dominates the imagination). From Walter's lost son, to the return of Olivia and Peter's absent mothers, to a more broadly cultural nostalgia represented by the Twin Towers still standing in the alternate universe, a sense of loss structures both the main narrative and its secondary stories. The holes in the universe that must be plugged up with amber are not just structural threats; they are also the Real as Lacan defines it, the void of loss and nothingness that must be hidden and built over in order to avoid the disintegration of personality.

In fact, early speculations on alternate realities coincided with the development of psychoanalysis and the formal articulation of the presence of an unconscious governed by irrational drives such as grief and desire. The first coinage of the term "multiverse" is by William James in 1895, but his definition is connected to the psychological and the philosophical, rather than to the then-nascent field of quantum mechanics.[12] James conceived of the world as containing various universes, embodying the different levels of reality (something Walter and William explore in their many LSD trips). "Visible nature," he writes, "is all plasticity and indifference—a moral multiverse, as one might call it, and not a moral universe."[13] For James, living in a particular universe is a matter of a moral choice, and this is a fitting description for *Fringe* since ultimately the two universes stand based on the balancing of moral behavior against the grieving of a loss. In the *Fringe* universe—or in the prime one, at least—loss can only be recovered by truces, alliances, and collaborative work, all things that comprise James' exhortation to reside in a moral universe. In emphasizing a relationship between morality and experience, *Fringe*'s narrative repeatedly refutes the Manichean structure that dominates so many science fiction and fantasy narratives. As Ken Tucker notes, *Fringe* "is, at its center, an optimistic, positive, we-can-change-the-world(s) show. Whereas everything from *The X-Files* to *Battlestar Galactica* was essentially doom-struck, a constant battle against conspiracy or malevolent fate, some *Fringe* characters have arrived at the idea that there is 'another way,' that this doesn't need to end up with one world destroying the other."[14] We see this sensibility at work at various points during the show, most notably at the end of season three when Peter insists that the two worlds can work together to avoid a double apocalypse (3.22, "The Day We Died"). This deep optimism that Tucker describes makes *Fringe* a rarity in science fiction television in that its continual remakings in each season are following a larger progressive, rather than degenerative, narrative. In part, *Fringe*, in arguing that universes are created out of personal choices, keeps returning to James' idea that reality is governed by the moral sense; on a psychological note, the optimism of *Fringe* and its insistence on finding better alternatives and focusing on new futures combats both the nostalgia and melancholy that are the roots of the dramatic conflict.

It is film that is generally seen as the medium through which to explore the unconscious. Thus films like Alfred Hitchcock's *Spellbound* (1945), featuring Salvador Dali's surrealist backdrops for the famous dream sequence, or Fritz Lang's *Metropolis* (1927), with its nightmare proletarian sets, are analogues to James' multiverse or to psychoanalytic theories. But television too has worked with trying to recreate the unconscious, such as Tony Soprano's extended dream sequences or the musical numbers that express characters' desires in *Six Feet Under* (2001–05). These depictions are inserted into a realist narrative, however, and their deliberate non-mimetic structures end up underscoring the realism of the core narrative. *Fringe*'s narrative structure allows for the episodes to depict more elaborate dream settings where both cultural musings and characters' inner desires, both positive and negative, are made manifest.

On the cultural front, the alternate universe of *Fringe* is a treasure trove of technological prototypes made real and a slew of what-ifs surrounding technological development. As Noel Murray of *The A.V. Club* remarks, "The *Fringe* folks have always had a fascination with outmoded tech; they're like steampunkers, but a century later. Theirs is a dot-matrix rendering of the future."[15] In the alternate universe, tablets have been necessary tools for people since the 1980s and are so endemic that the ballpoint pen has been rendered as obsolete as the quill. Smart cards are also ubiquitous and the general form of identification, whimsically termed the Show Me, seems to be a card accessing both one's personal information and one's bank accounts. *Fringe* repeatedly plays these games with different technologies; for instance, Walter, after spying on the alternate universe in 1985, brings to the government a prototypical cell phone.[16] In addition to the technology, we see the alternate universe as a representation of changed histories, of the sort that Vilenkin describes, in that Richard Nixon's face is on the head of a quarter; the tiny Caribbean island Aruba, not Vietnam, was the site of a drawn-out war in the 1960s and 1970s; and Secretary Bishop has a photo of an elderly John F. Kennedy on his wall. These changes function as curiosities rather than significant plot points, allowing the audience to play seek and find with all of the changes—some of them quite detailed—found in the alternate universe. They also end up contributing to a dreamscape of sorts, as if each change functioned as a visual paralepsis, a manifestation of an unconscious wish or fear.

I conclude this chapter by speaking of *Fringe* in a more metaphorical sense. A show that constantly reboots itself provides insight into the nature of television narratives regardless of genre since, often because of production exigencies, they are also remade and reinvented mid-run. As viewers, we tend to accept television storylines that sometimes stretch credulity because of a change in writing staff, the departure of a lead actor, or any number of reasons. Whereas conventional dramas, including the naturalist science fiction shows of the past decade, try to avoid such breaks in the fourth wall, non-realist shows, such as sitcoms and soap operas, tend to integrate their changes directly into the narrative. In constantly remaking its narrative, *Fringe* bears a stronger resemblance to nighttime soaps like *Dynasty* (1981–89) than to science fiction television. For example, during its run, *Dynasty* recast two of its main characters. One recasting, when Jack Coleman replaced Al Corley as Steven Carrington in 1982, was given a narrative explanation involving some truly impressive facial reconstruction surgery purportedly done in a secret Central American clinic; the second introduced Emma Samms as Fallon Colby after the departure of actress Pamela Sue Martin without any mention in the show of Samms and Martin bearing no resemblance to one another. In that case, entertainment journalism did that narrative work for the show; Samms's casting was heralded months in advance and the actress already was recognized for her work on *General Hospital* (1963–present), then in its ratings heyday. Explanations within the narrative, unlike with the relatively unknown Jack Coleman, were not needed.

Such changes do not only occur in writing and casting decisions. Even a change in production venue can alter the visual look of the show, and therefore the world in which it is set, in sometimes drastic ways. For example, *The X-Files'* move from overcast Vancouver to sunny Los Angeles in its sixth season meant a loss of the misty, eerie cinematography that served as a backdrop for Mulder and Scully's paranormal investigations. *Fringe* changed its location *to* Vancouver from New York in its second season, which ended up reinforcing on a visual level the strangeness of its universes, since Vancouver was substituting for both Boston and New York. Not only did we encounter some of the aforementioned prop changes, but this was an American East Coast setting that obviously did not look like one. The strangeness of these new universes ended up being doubly emphasized, albeit probably unintentionally, to the Canadian viewers familiar with the layout and signage of Canadian supermarkets or the design of Vancouver public transit vehicles. But *Fringe* also played with these differences, defamiliarizing even our own culture, especially in a flashback to 1985 when the child Peter is taken to a toy store and we see an array of toys and games in packaging that now seems alien to us (3.15, "Subject 13").

For *Fringe's* final 12 episodes, the show reboots itself one last time, but this time it is a radical reboot both in terms of plot and tone. The fifth season transforms the series into an Orwell-inspired dystopia. Replicating season three's search for machine parts, season five's plot involves an even more elaborate treasure hunt for machine parts to construct a device that vanquishes the Observers and reboots the season one last time to a moment of family bliss—Peter, Olivia, and their young daughter Henrietta playing in a park. The final season's overplotted nature (another episode, another videotape to watch, another machine part to find) gives it the feeling of an elaborate video game. In this respect, it betrays the narratives of previous seasons. Whereas compromise and change from within formed the ethics of the series, articulated by the repeated phrase "There has to be another way," in season five the threat of mind-reading, omnipresent Observers, complete with heavyhanded Big Brother imagery, is so totalizing that the only means of victory is to activate the ultimate reset button. What is regrettable with this change is that the totalitarian narrative of season five ends up negating the interesting thought experiments of alternate universes and timelines of the first four seasons. In the previous seasons, little changes and choices marked the differences between universes, and thus raised possibilities of events being flexible and universes being shaped by the people who live in them. Previous seasons also showed the consequences that arose from these choices and as a result the characters of *Fringe*, from Walter to Walternate, Alt-Broyles to Faux-livia, Peter to William Bell, became complex, morally ambiguous constructions. The last season gives us a Fringe team indisputably on the side of the angels, the Observers as unrelenting villains, and a conflict so insurmountable as to render the heroes powerless unless they obliterate the entire future. In season five, the premise of different universes created by different choices seems unlikely when the choices have been reduced to do over or die.

To recap, here is the breakdown of all of the levels of rebooting that occur in *Fringe*. By the end of the series' run in February 2013, viewers had seen no fewer than six different universes and timelines—the original one of the first season, the original alternate universe introduced at the end of season one, the apocalyptic future of the season three finale, the reset timelines of both prime and alternate universes of season four, and the dystopic Observers-run future of season five. We must add to this list September's comment to Olivia in season three about all of the possible futures he has witnessed, as well as his comment to Peter about all of the possible timelines he has altered, as well as the Episodes 19 in seasons two through four that became signature stand-alone episodes. These episodes ranged from season two's Dennis Potter-inspired musical film noir episode (2.19, "Brown Betty") to season three's *Inception*-inspired animated journey into Olivia's damaged psyche (3.19, "Lysergic Acid Diethylamide ") to season four's prologue to the following season's narrative arc (4.19, "Letters of Transit"). Related to the ongoing narrative, these episodes broke with the narrative structure and as a result became the signifieds of the show, expressing the playful relationship between the fantastic and the real that the writers were deeply committed to. Above all, what *Fringe* shows us is a classic lesson in deconstruction: not only that the assumed structure of narrative in television can be destabilized through a series of alternate versions, retellings, and reboots, but that it has, to use the jargon, "always already" been destabilized. But it also gestures beyond the narrative of a science fiction show to the physicists who are narrating the history and development of the universe. In that sense, there is something quintessential about the whimsical, poignant, personal, and generalized universes of *Fringe*.

FILMS AND TV SHOWS

Altered States. Directed by Ken Russell. 1980. Warner Bros.
Battlestar Galactica. Sci-Fi Network, 2004–09.
Dynasty. ABC, 1981–89.
Fringe. Fox Network, 2008–13.
General Hospital. ABC, 1963–.
Lost. ABC, 2004–10.
Metropolis. Directed by Fritz Lang. 1927. Universum Film.
Six Feet Under. HBO, 2001–05.
Spellbound. Directed by Alfred Hitchcock. 1945. United Artists.
Star Trek. Directed by J.J. Abrams. 2009. Paramount Pictures.

The X – Files. Fox Network, 1993–2002.

NOTES

1. Abrams, Kurtzman, and Orci are listed as *Fringe*'s creators and executive producers. The day-to-day running of the show, however, was handled by Jeff Pinkner (who left the show in season five) and J.H. Wyman.

2. The Nielsen ratings for the series finale only showed a viewership of 3.2 million and a 1.0 share in the coveted 18-to-54-year-old demographic. But, as James Hibberd reports, *Fringe* gained an additional 60 percent of viewers through DVR recordings. Its loyal fan base, plus the ability of its creators to strike syndication deals with Warner Bros., helped keep the show on the air despite its low ratings. James Hibberd, "'Fringe' Ratings Up for Finale: How the Show Survived," *Inside TV with James Hibberd & Lynette Rice, E.W.com.*, January 29, 2013, accessed May 27, 2013, http://insidetv.ew.com/2013/01/19/fringe-series-finale-ratings/.

3. . Mike Hale, "Taking a Time-Bending Leap into a Final Season," *New York Times*, September 27, 2012, accessed May 15, 2013, http://www.nytimes.com/2012/09/28/arts/television/fringe-begins-final-season-on-fox.html?_r=0.

4. While the first season focused on random inexplicable events that were purported to be loosely connected by a series of phenomena called "the Pattern," that idea was abandoned by season two to focus exclusively on the parallel universe.

5. In an interview on *Entertainment Weekly*'s website, Pinkner asserts: "We have said from the beginning that *Fringe* is a family drama masquerading as a science fiction/investigation show. . . [I]t's about three characters that live on the fringe of life and society and have a hard time dealing with their own emotions, but who find each other and find connection with each other. We will remain true to that." Jeff Jensen, "'Fringe': Exec producers Jeff Pinkner, J.H. Wyman answer fan questions about the finale—Exclusive," *Inside TV with James Hibberd & Lynette Rice, E.W.com*, May 13, 2011, accessed January 10, 2013, http://insidetv.ew.com/2011/05/13/fringe-finale-exec-producers-answer-questions/.

6. Slavoj Žižek, *The Parallax View* (Cambridge: MIT Press, 2009), 165.

7. Hale, "Taking a Time-Bending Leap into a Final Season."

8. Alex Vilenkin, *Many Worlds in One: The Search for Other Universes* (New York: Hill and Wang, 2006), 133*n*.

9. Ibid., 81–82.

10. Jaume Garriga and Alex Vilenkin, "Many Worlds in One," *Physical Review* D64 (2001): 043511. Qtd. in Vilenkin, *Many Worlds in One*, 113.

11. That the alternate universe's Astrid has Asperger's Syndrome is mentioned in several interviews by Jasika Nicole, the actress who plays the character. "Jasika Nicole Reveals 'Fringe' Season 3 Twist," *Crave Online*, August 4, 2010, accessed May 17, 2013, http://www.craveonline.com/tv/articles/136114-jasika-nicole-reveals-fringe-season-3-twist.

12. William James, *The Will to Believe and Other Essays in Popular Philosophy / Human Immortality* (New York: Dover, 1956 [1897–98]).

13. Ibid., 43–44.

14. Ken Tucker, "'Fringe' recap: 'Entrada' and exits, lives saved and lost," *Ken Tucker's TV*, Dec 2, 2010, accessed January 8, 2013, http://watching-tv-ew.com/2010/12/02/fringe-entrada-season-3-episode-8/#more-13648.

15. Noel Murray, "Fringe: Peter S2/E16," *The A.V. Club*, April 1, 2010, accessed January 10, 2013, http://www.avclub.com/peter, 39772/.

16. The reference is amusing but not accurate, since prototypical cell phones have existed since the 1970s.

FIVE

Look—(Stop Me If You've Read This One) But There Were These Two Spies

The Avengers *Through the Swinging '60s*

James W. Martens

On January 7, 1961, *The Avengers,* a gritty street drama, premiered in the UK. In the episode, "Hot Snow," the talented Dr. David Keel (Ian Hendry) sees his fiancée murdered by villains. Keel reluctantly teams up with a street-wise young "gentleman" of sketchy pedigree, John Steed (Patrick Macnee), to solve the murder and cement an alliance based on a shared sense of social responsibility.

> Steed (to Keel): We could use you and you could use us. Crime is a disease. Work with us. There is not so much good in the world that we can't use a little more. We'll only call on you when you're needed—really needed.[1]

The show featured the raw jazz of Johnny Dankworth played over moody, shadowy credits, and cultivated a sense of realism similar to the "kitchen sink" style of films of the period. *The Avengers* first appeared as a post-war drama for the "managed state," easily identified with Cold War crime and espionage. In the series finale, which aired nine years later, Tara King (Linda Thorson), a mid-Atlantic sex symbol, sips champagne with her mentor, the suave John Steed, after seeing off a chorus line of handcuffed baddies. The pair is inside a four-stage rocket that Steed has built in his garden, from a kit. Decked out in a high-collared white lace minidress, poor Tara accidently pushes the button that launches the rocket skyward. Fear not: their "governor," the corpulent, wheelchair-bound "Mother," assures us Steed and King, *The Avengers*, will be back. (They never were.)

So how did a serious drama evolve into a weekly spy-fi comic romp? Certainly remade television shows and films are often quite unlike the originals that had inspired them. What is curious about *The Avengers* is that the remaking seemed to occur on the fly. The fact that *The Avengers* lasted almost 10 years was remarkable in the decade of the 1960s, a time of relentless readjustments to the post-war era. The show's ability to respond to the insatiable appetite for things new kept the series fresh and alive, until it too fell victim to the desire for more and different.

In retrospect, *The Avengers* established itself as an important element of the autobiographical memory for many of the post-war generation. Jerome Schulster asserts that those events that occur in a life between the ages of 16–24 years are "especially important" in developing a personal biography, as these events often happen to the maturing young adult for the first time.[2] This is not to say *The Avengers* itself defined the generation, but rather it complemented the shifting attitudes developed across the 1960s as England evolved from a war-weary managed state to an era of liberal individualism.

Across the span of nine years, if one loose element might be identified as defining the series, it was the demise of the Victorian Age. Likely, this was not a conscious strategy, but the pace of post-war modernization and its ambiguities were mirrored on *The Avengers*, in a post-modern parallel universe embracing all the latest trends. The series reflected the socio-cultural developments of the post-war, and delighted in the presentation of a 1960s Britain more imagined than real.

The original idea for *The Avengers* is credited to Canadian Sydney Newman, who had developed *Police Surgeon* (1960) for ABC-TV in England. Newman's idea for *The Avengers* was a high-quality, "genuine, action adventure series."[3] *Police Surgeon* star Ian Hendry was cast as Dr. Keel, the young professional, and unknown Patrick Macnee was to play John Steed, the "amoral sophisticate." Macnee conceded that in these early episodes he was to be second fiddle. The character was so underdeveloped that he was told to create a personality and a clothing style for Steed, or be replaced.[4] Thus began the evolution of John Steed from a fashion-conscious "regency fop" into the paragon of upper-class sartorial splendor, replete with bowler and umbrella, by 1969.

The first series reflects an atmosphere of late 1950s and early 1960s England, referred to by Mark Donnelly as a "dull ache."[5] The turn-of-the-century Fabian dream of a bureaucratized state was seemingly coming true. Arthur Marwick christened the 1950s state-sponsored architectural style "The New Brutalism."[6] Industrially, post-war governments concentrated on chemicals, engineering, and telecommunication, and education was directed toward these areas of national renewal, as well as medical science.[7] Years prior to Harold Wilson's announcement that the nation's future would be forged by the white heat of technology, politicians understood that education, science, and innovation would rescue a war-ravaged nation still wrestling with bombed-out urban landscapes and the rationing of chocolate. British social historian Peter Bailey calls life in Coventry of the late 1950s and early 1960s an engineered life: "orderly modernity, devoid alike of any risk and romance."[8] This post-war populace sought adventure in movies, television, and music.

The nation also wrestled with the right of the state to make moral decisions for its citizens.[9] The much employed example of *Lady Chatterley's Lover*'s obscenity trial in 1960 was only one case. The censorship issues surrounding the emergence of commercial television became a concern after the 1954 *Television Act* and the Tory anti-monopoly legislation sympathetic to "independent television." The social engineers of the liberal left feared that commercial television would create mind-numbing trash in its search for profit. Instead, they got *The Avengers.*

Finally, *The Avengers* came into existence amid a string of spy scandals, the Cold War, a nuclear arms race, political assassinations, and a widespread ambivalence concerning the future. In 1946, British scientist Alan Nunn was arrested as a Soviet spy. In 1950, atomic scientist Bruno Pontecorvo defected to the USSR. The fact that the country's best and brightest were not all committed to Queen and country became clear when university scholars and graduates dubbed the "Cambridge Five" began disappearing, and by 1956 it was confirmed that two—Guy Burgess and Donald Maclean, Soviet moles in the civil service—were now in Russia (arriving only one step ahead of the Secret Service). Russian spies Harry Houghton and Gordon Lonsdale were arrested in 1961, about the time that the Profumo Affair (combining that always riveting troika of spies, sex, and dirty politicians) began to dominate the world press. These were the early days of James Bond novels. The search for the remaining members of the "Cambridge Five" inspired John le Carré's fictional Smiley series.[10] Any discussion of *The Avengers'* first series must include David Buxton's observation that these types of television drama series were based on "widespread social fears."[11]

The Keel series was twenty-six episodes long, featuring mad scientists, extortionists, drug and diamond smugglers, white slavery, sociopathic doctors, "trick cigarettes," an evil circus clown, a frozen fascist, and of course spies. If "The Frighteners" (1.15) is any indication, in true Sherlock Holmes fashion, Steed made use of his own streetwise "irregulars" (e.g., a flower girl and a cabbie) to stay in the know, explaining his remarkable ability to be only a step behind the evildoers. The Dr. Keel episodes have not withstood the rapid pace of change, as now only two full shows and part of another still exist. The series was truncated by an Actor's Guild strike in November 1961, during which Hendry chose to pursue a career in film and left the show.

Originally, the second series featured Jon Rollanson as Dr. Martin King, a thinly veiled replacement for Dr. Keel. After filming three episodes, Rollanson took a role in *Coronation Street* (1960–present). The role of the "amateur" agent eventually fell to Honor Blackman, hired as a second choice by Newman to complete six episodes originally scripted for a male character. Dr. Cathy Gale was constructed around a real widow who had lost her husband in the Mau Mau uprisings and then returned to England to continue work as an anthropologist.[12] She supplied the duo with skills that Steed did not have: academic training and sex appeal. A third new cast member in series two was jazz singer Venus Smith, fronting a real band, The Kenny Powell Trio.

It is obvious that the one-time second banana was to be the linchpin of the second season. In the credits, Macnee was given top billing. The earnest Keel and cheeky Steed working the back streets of the Big Smoke were replaced with hip jazzers, sipping cocktails in a 1950s James Bond styled "world." Steed could now draw on the specialized skills and social acumen of Gale, King, and the very hip young Venus as scripts dictated, giving the writers a wide range of options for story development.[13] Venus Smith was an early nod to the emerging "youth culture" of England, but it was Cathy Gale who captured the audience's attention. She was a modern woman with a university degree, field experience, and leather outfits that allowed her to wrestle with the villains (judo was the martial art most to her liking). She carried a gun in her stocking top and wore a black bra.

Gale's fetish gear becomes a feature of the series beginning in the episode "Mr. Teddy Bear" (2.01). It has been explained that leather was more resilient for the action scenes, and "filmed" better than suede. Much later, in a BBC Radio 3 talk show, *The Avengers* writer, and later producer, Brian Clemens offered an explanation of the fashion choice which, while supporting the durability of the "biker gear," also conceded its obvious fetish appeal, as well anticipating it as the "in" thing in European fashion the next year.[14] In the same roundtable discussion, writer Sarah Dunant notes that Dr. Gale was like the attractive, confident friend of your family that your coming-of-age younger brother "had a mad crush on," those first sexual stirrings prominent in a young man's autobiographical memory.[15] Gale was revealed to have been born October 5, 1930 (2.18, "Warlock"), well before the Swinging '60s. She was not the "dolly bird" of the nascent Swinging London; she was more typical of the 1950s "jazzy" liberated crowd, "the symbol of the jet set woman" of the 1950s.[16]

Steed was by the second series developing a more overtly conservative look, tending increasingly toward an overcoat, bowler hat, and well-cut suits, and a softer, less street-smart personality—a modern-day Beau Brummell. Also in the second series, Steed and Gale took direction from "One-Ten" (Douglas Muir), but never seemed to answer to anyone.

Quoted in *From The Avengers to Miami Vice,* Kingsley Amis said of the series:

> Whenever anyone sets about poisoning off most of the human race or blowing up London, Steed and Cathy (Gale) are sure to turn up; often it seems by the merest chance. This on-the-spotness is often a snag in thriller series; *The Avengers* cleverly turns it into a virtue, something to enjoy.
>
> These are a pair of heroic free lancers [sic], inspired amateurs, who knock off a couple of world-wide conspiracies in the intervals of choosing their spring wardrobe. All this is, so to speak, a wink at the audience, a joke to share with them.[17]

It could be understood that Steed represented traditional British values, while his "amateur" female partners reflected the forward-facing, modern England. The idea that tradition and modernism could coexist for the betterment of all was a theme increasingly observable throughout *The Avengers.* By the time the second season had finished, and England remained secure under the watchful eye of "the ministry," the country itself was changing.

In late 1962, the Beatles had recorded "Love Me Do," and the Rolling Stones prowled the streets of Soho. Working-class realism in British cinema had peaked with *The Loneliness of the Long Distance Runner* and *This Sporting Life.* By contrast, the Bond franchise released its second installment, *From Russia With Love,* in 1963. Must reading was le Carré's *The Spy Who Came in From the Cold.* Youngsters in Liverpool were checking out of work at lunch to catch their favorite beat groups. While realism still remained popular, filmgoers also enjoyed *Cleopatra* and *The Pink Panther.* There seems to have been a cautious loosening of Cold War anxieties. Many elements that would liberate England from its war-weary past were now in place: Mods in the West End of London, Mary Quant's fashion line for High Street boutiques, and of course the Mersey Beat sound. Television remained a reflection of social reality and by 1963, humor appeared on the small screen as well as in film. *Steptoe and Son* was on television, and Peter Sellers starred in *Dr. Strangelove.* Reaction to social concerns appears to have become more manageable, and more fun.

The third season of *The Avengers* saw the departure of Venus, leaving the safety of the nation in the hands of Steed and Cathy Gale. Creator Sydney Newman had defected to the BBC, loosening control on the direction of *The Avengers.* Early in the third season, the show had reached new heights. The "Nutshell" episode (3.04), written by novelist Phillip Chalmers, is still rated as one of the best ever.[18] Steed is suspected of revealing secrets about the underground bunker designed to protect the government in case of nuclear attack. The episode of course includes a leather-clad Cathy Gale who must clear Steed, as she also did in "The Man With Two Shadows" (3.03). "Nutshell" obviously plays to the reality of the

"Cambridge Five," moles and defections to the other side, but stands out because it is Cathy Gale who takes control of the situation—a hint of an emerging feminism many have debated as it relates to the series.[19]

However, the show also abandoned the seriousness of the Keel episodes and became more playful, with a modern-day Julius Caesar who plots world domination by poisoning the food supply (3.10, "The Grandeur That Was Rome"). In "Build a Better Mouse Trap" (3.21), Cathy joins up with a motorcycle gang for a party in a rural pub. The publican reminds a disapproving Steed, "You've got to move with the times," and the episode does so with rock music, dancing bikers, and a young lad who tells Gale that "anyone over 20 is ancient." Throughout season three, Gale gave the viewers what they wanted; leather was featured often, and her wit and cunning became as important as her judo. As a consequence, and to no great surprise, she began getting "naughty" fan mail. Clemens claims he was asked by his friends to bring along Mrs. Gale's fetish gear to social occasions. There was surely a growing devotion to this feminist symbol of modern Britain.[20]

Throughout 1963, *The Avengers* had quietly evolved as "younger" and more fun, and at least aware of the pop cultural changes happening around it. Clever promotions had Macnee and Blackman record a pop song for the teen television show *Top of the Pops*, exposing the duo to a younger audience. "Kinky Boots" was a celebration of the fashion Cathy Gale had made so popular.[21] The lyrics suggest the footwear was fashionable with everyone: "sweet girls, street girls, grumpy little beat girls" (thankfully the song proved less enduring than the fashion trend) and there is even a reference to Steed's aunties wearing them. The flipside of the record made reference to the Gale/Steed relationship with "Let's Keep It Friendly." Or perhaps it was a comment on the fact that by late 1963, everyone involved in the show was aware that Blackman was leaving, seduced by the charms of James Bond and a film career.

The Blackman series ended in March 1964. Again, the opportunity to recast and retool presented itself. Dominic Sandbrook notes that until the fourth series, *The Avengers* was really an older person's show.[22] A year and half after Blackman's departure, the series would re-emerge more hip, funnier, and very much a part of the self-confident New Albion.

In 1963, England was itself retooling from a dull, grey bureaucratic state into new "rock and roll" culture led by a Pop Aristocracy of Lennon and McCartney, TV presenter Cathy McGowan, photographer David Bailey, fashion designer Mary Quant, and Twiggy. Mod fashions were the style of the day with dots, stripes, bright colors, and patterns. Addresses like Carnaby Street, Matthew Street (The Cavern Club), Saville Row, Menlove Avenue (Lennon's childhood home), Soho, and Abbey Road were replacing Buckingham Palace, The National Gallery, The Tower of London, and the Houses of Parliament as must-see English destinations. Time spent being "fab" or "gear" had replaced job training, worrying about The Bomb, or lamenting that England's post-war pop culture had been a sad imitation of America's.

In 1964, kitchen sink realism was waning as moviegoers yearned for *A Hard Day's Night, Goldfinger, My Fair Lady,* and *A Fistful of Dollars.* While there were still struggles with those resistant to change, England was embracing a homemade modernism, celebrating everything new, and adding a great deal to the notion of the Swinging '60s.[23] After the Beatles appeared on *The Ed Sullivan Show* in early 1964, Beatlemania and those things British became the rage in the United States, and worldwide. The *Billboard* Top 50 for 1963 had not a single UK artist, and in 1964 the same chart had 18 British singles.[24] A host of young, gifted film stars was emerging as part of England's youth movement, including Michael Caine, Julie Christie, and Terence Stamp. With the Tories swept from office in October 1964, it might have seemed that a new "re-branded" England was ready to take the final thrust into the Modern Age.

During the 1964–65 "long weekend," Brian Clemens told a concerned Macnee to stop worrying; when *The Avengers* folded with one approach, it would start up again with another—surely the modernist view.[25] This self confidence and faith in the future has led Dominic Sandbrook to note that the series "never wallowed in declinism," but always pushed forward.[26] Major technical changes were made possible in season four as the switch from tape to film accommodated more realistic outdoor action, easier scene reshoots, over-dubbing, and generally better sound quality. Beth Sheppard was hired to replace Blackman, but after filming a version of "Town of No Return," she was dismissed, and replaced with Diana Rigg as Mrs. Emma Peel.

Season four, which premiered in England on October 7, 1965, featured new graphics which included a long slow pan of Rigg's leather-clad arm, and then some martial arts poses in full leather, backed by a more contemporary jazz theme. Emma Peel was the amateur agent that most of North America associates with *The Avengers,* because American Broadcasting Corporation in the United States bought and debuted the series in 1965. Mrs. Peel was athletic and well versed in the arts, independently wealthy, and upon first glance seemed more delicate than her predecessor. More importantly, she had the hair, makeup, and fashions of the new Swinging '60s.

Unlike the Keel episodes, which were dark and earnest, the Peel years were fun and "off the wall." Clemens noted that the switch to film allowed him "to flex his surreal and sexual muscle," and Macnee notes that after 1965, "Disbelief was suspended at the perimeter gate [of the studio]" under producer Roger Marshall.[27] Emma Peel now came to personify "the spirit of British modernism."[28] Meanwhile, Steed became even more conservative and stereotypical of old-style British resolve. Again, intentional or not, the subtext of season four was the ability of the modern and the traditional to unite in common cause against a list of strange villains and unthinkable national threats. The umbrella, bowler, and top coat remained symbolic of British tradition, while miniskirts, floral patterns, and form-fitting cat suits were of the new age. While episodes varied in their seriousness, all were much more playful than in the early years, fitting perfectly into the apolitical pleasure of the mid-'60s Swinging London.

In season four's first episode, "The Town of No Return," Steed appears at Emma's flat while she is practicing her fencing (wearing leather). Through a playful "duel," Steed convinces Mrs. Peel to join him for a train trip to the seaside to examine the apparent disappearance of agents. This of course appeals to Emma, and the pair take off on their first television adventure. In this episode, Mrs. Peel is immaculate in her 1960s fashions, turtlenecks, pantsuits and even John Lennon–style NHA glasses. Finally with all the baddies under wraps, the pair escapes the seaside village on a Vespa (another symbol of England in the modern age). This tag theme continued throughout the series with the pair departing in/on any manner of transportation: bicycles, an amphibious car, and a flying carpet, to name a few. It was all part of the revamped *Avengers* and the very "fab" Peel Years.

Season four was delightfully new, at times reminiscent of *A Hard Day's Night*. In "The Girl From A.U.N.T.I.E." (4.17; an obvious nod to *The Avengers'* US competitor *The Man From U.N.C.L.E.)*, the quartet of victims is John, Paul, George, and Fred, one of the few rock-and-roll references in the entire series. In "Castle De'ath" (4.05), awful Scottish jokes abound in a story built around the real-life issue of converting castles into tourist attractions. Perhaps the silliest of all season four episodes involves Mrs. Peel infiltrating a university group led by a fascist radical planning to rewrite history. As a backup to Mrs. Peel, Steed camps out in the woods still dressed in his bowler and top coat. A jab at those who resisted the current trends of the 1960s occurs when the modernist students critique their elderly professor with the observation "he lives in the past" (4.24, "A Sense of History").

No doubt the most talked about episode of season four was the highest rated episode in the series' nine-year run: "A Touch of Brimstone" (4.21). This episode deals not with spies, but rather seemingly apolitical "social" misfits, out to destroy the Cabinet using explosives. The show had trouble with UK censors, and was initially banned in the United States, because of the word "hell" in The Hell Fire Club, the cover for these dastardly deeds. Mrs. Peel, under the guise of canvassing for charity, arrives at the millionaire John Cartney's home shortly after a series of diplomatic disasters. Emma says to the leering Cartney, "I've come to appeal to you," and he responds, "You certainly do that" (nudge, nudge). Emma leaves with the compliment, and a lead to the hedonistic doings of an aristocratic "lad's club," with gambling, drinking, boxing, and sex. As usual, all goes momentarily pear-shaped and Emma's true identity becomes known. She is drugged, and much to Steed's shock, she appears at the Night of All Sin celebration in a bustier, black boots, and shovel loads of mascara, wearing a studded collar and holding a python. Cartney tells his guests that she is the Queen of Sin, there for their pleasures. To the viewers' relief, Mrs. Peel recovers quickly enough to discover the plot and vanquish some baddies before the whip-wielding Cartney plunges to his end.

It was a fine example of Clemens flexing both his surreal and sexual muscle. It was the most overtly sexualized episode since the chaste days of 1961. It was loaded with gags as campy as exploding cigars and collapsing chairs. Who would not have known things were about to go bad as soon as Mrs. Peel tells Steed that the club seems "innocent enough"? Clemens was impressive, mixing Marx Brothers hijinks with sadomasochism. Rigg called the episode "high camp."[29] Ratcheting up the eroticism of the fourth series, in the final episode (4.26, "Honey for the Prince"), Emma appears doing the dance of the seven veils and then smoking a hookah while talking of her fantasies.

This series and the changes to come were praised for their "absolute unreality."[30] *The Avengers* existed in an England that was an imagined space. There were no workers and no poor people—in fact, the city seemed to be very sparsely populated. At times only Steed and Peel and the heavies tailing them seemed to be in the city. In series four, the city—the modern urban space—seemed safe and manageable, while the bucolic rural regions were unpredictable and dangerous and often eerily unmodern.

In *From The Avengers to Miami Vice,* David Buxton observed that the spy genre became "coded with discourses pertaining to tourism."[31] With the success of the show in the United States after series four, ABC in America pushed for a number of changes, the most important being color film. Steed was now decked out in Pierre Cardin (the same designer as collarless Beatles suits), and theatrical designer Alan Hughes was brought in to dress Rigg.[32] The England of the fifth series was the England of the American imagination, similar to the mythical urban utopia found in Roger Miller's pop anthem, "England Swings." There were red phone boxes, open double-decker buses, and all the symbols of historic London, as well as Swinging '60s signifiers such as High Street boutiques, miniskirts, and sporty cars (Mrs. Peel drove a Lotus Élan). Scenes were set at country estates, King's Cross Station, and Wembley Stadium (scene of England's 1966 World Cup victory). The show was broadcast in over 70 countries by 1967, delivering a wholesome, fun, fanciful, modernist England to the viewing world.[33]

Series five begins with a bongo-heavy version of the theme music and Steed and Peel in a variety of outfits. Holding a pistol in one hand, Mrs. Peel pulls her hair away from her eyes with the other, ready for action. While in the previous season, the tag played on the gag which had our heroes leaving in various modes of transportation, series five introduces the message "Mrs. Peel, we're needed" (a nod back to the first series) in various ways. Steed appears on television (which Emma is watching) to tell her they are needed in "Never, Never Say Die" (5.10). At the start of "The Living Dead" (5.07), the message is flashed on the traffic lights as Mrs. Peel waits for red to change to green. *The Avengers* in color, new again, was to be very different than that of black-and-white season four, reaching for appeal beyond the limits of the shores of "the green and pleasant land."

On-line *Avengers* fan site *"The Avengers* Forever" notes of the first color episode "Fear Merchants" (5.02, aired January 20, 1967) that aspects of it had "no believable motivation..."[34] It seems a bit late to go looking for anything "believable" on *The Avengers* when in series four "Man-eater of Surrey Green" (4.11) featured carnivorous plants from outer space that wanted to take over the world (*Little Shop of Horrors*?). The days of Blackman and Hendry, when believability mattered at least a little, were long gone by 1967. Much of season five resembled *The Monkees* television show with slap stick gags, witty asides, and laughable villains. Where the early series had been popular with young adults, this series was redirected toward the younger teen audience. It was driven by fashion and gags as much as by social commentary or clever plots. In the "Winged Avenger" (5.06), a "super hero" frees the nation from greedy businessmen. He walks on roofs and up walls, reminiscent of Adam West's Batman (both *The Monkees* and *Batman* debuted in 1966). In "Never, Never Say Die" (5.10), the straight-faced android, Christopher Lee, tells the Avengers "we are programmed to take over"; comic book science-fiction, not science, was now a major theme. "Something Nasty in the Nursery" (5.14) broadly hints of LSD when Mrs. Peel takes a mind-altering drug which carries her back to her childhood. In "Dead Man's Treasure" (5.20), a car rally similar to the film *It's a Mad, Mad, Mad, Mad World* (1963) is the theme, and predictably features wonderful cars, including the Jaguar XKE, and ends with a villain named Needle, found in a haystack. This series was playful, but in an increasingly cartoonish manner. The show had become very much about mod fashion and giggles, not plot and development.

If the music used on radio broadcasts (5.10, "Never, Never Say Die") or at dance parties (5.16, "Who's Who???") was laughably "square," Mrs. Peel's fashions were always spot on. She was often decked out in one-piece cat suits, with industrial-sized zippers. Miniskirts were a staple in season five, appealing to a younger, fashion-savvy audience. In "You Have Just Been Murdered" (5.21), Peel sports a one-piece PVC jumpsuit that she manages to get wet, but there was no leather gear. It is generally understood that Diana Rigg did not enjoy wearing the fetish costumes that to this day remain part of the mythology of the show.[35] Series five appears to have been geared to younger consumers, making Carnaby

Street fashion more a part of the series than leather, and identifying *The Avengers* as part of the youthful Swinging '60s.

In series five, there was a torrid pace of shoot and show. Episodes filmed only a few months earlier aired soon after.[36] The result of this rapid turnaround was that "groovy" English fashion was appearing almost immediately, making *The Avengers* seem even more "current" and satisfying the insatiable demand for things new and different. Nowhere to be seen was the black-and-white drabness of bed sits, East end back rooms, and off-the-rack suits—not even the ill-fitting fetish gear that defined the show's shadowy early years.

The chaos that occurred at the end of series five may account for the strange sequencing of the season's final episodes. The show had six different directors in eight episodes, making focus and continuity even more haphazard and contributing to the sense that time was never very clear in *The Avengers*.[37] Rigg had announced that she too would leave the series, to appear shortly after with Bond on the big screen. When the series completed production in September 1967, ABC in the United States announced that 20-year-old Canadian Linda Thorson would replace Rigg. The production team was sacked, including Clemens and Albert Fennel, and John Bryce was called in to return the series to a more realistic format. After much difficulty, Clemens and Fennel were recalled, and wrote and produced the episode which now marks Emma Peel's departure, "The Forget-Me Knot" (6.01), shown in England on September 25, 1968.[38]

In the tag for Rigg's final appearance, Steed is glancing at a newspaper while talking to Mother, the head of "The Agency." The headline reads:

PETER PEEL alive
Air ace found in Amazonian jungle
WIFE EMMA WAITS

Emma is at Steed's flat to say her goodbyes. They share a friendly kiss, and she leaves after giving him some motherly advice. As she descends the stairs, Tara King is going up. Emma tells Tara that Steed likes his tea stirred "anti-clock wise" and then continues on her way. From his window, Steed watches Mrs. Peel get into a Rolls Royce Silver Shadow beside a man wearing a bowler and a Pierre Cardin suit—a very touching moment. Tara is dressed in elbow-length opera gloves and skin-tight thigh-high leather boots, a wide black patent leather belt, and a leopard-print fur-lined coat, very street chic—signaling the final retooling of *The Avengers*.

While Mrs. Peel and Steed were keeping the world safe from mad scientists, avaricious businessmen, ill-tempered millionaires, and "spooks" from the other side, the world outside the studio gates continued to redefine itself at the same breakneck pace as the series. If popular culture between 1963 and 1967 can be understood primarily by those things British, the late 1960s shifted focus to San Francisco and the hippie movement. It highlighted DIY fashions, complex rock music, and personal world views cobbled together from a patchwork of pre-existing, at times conflicting, philosophies. In the spring of 1967, American Top 40 radio was imploring young people to migrate to the Bay Area with flowers in their hair. The once adorable "mop-topped lads from Liverpool" had grown up and embraced social critique, drugs, yoga, and meditation, while openly rejecting Christianity. Marches to Ban the Bomb, allow free-speech, and end the war in South East Asia had replaced shopping, cellar clubs, and learning the latest dance craze.

In England, in 1967, *Last Exit to Brooklyn* was on trial for obscenity; it was like the *Lady Chatterley* case had never occurred. The Glimmer Twins, Jagger and Richards, bad boys of the rock aristocracy, were arrested for drug possession. On March 13, 1967, students at the London School of Economics staged an all-night sit-in. Pirate radio was shut down in the Summer of Love. While more conservative elements in society tried to slam on the brakes, now there were Love-Ins, Be-Ins, marches, protest, and greater defiance of authority.

Front and center in the many critiques of bourgeois adult culture were those related to sexuality. Ian MacDonald notes the proliferation of the "sex industry" in an increasingly more permissive Western culture.[39] Bernard Levin observes that in the maelstrom of 1960s modernism "nothing was sacred," especially sex and gender.[40] In youth culture across the decade, sex became decidedly more casual and experimental. Nudity was part of the popular arts and on the stage. In 1968, *Hair* appeared on Broadway and a year later *Oh! Calcutta!* attracted crowds to London's West End; both shows featured nudity and frank sexual discourse. In the "new morality" there was sex for fun, sex for self discovery, sex for experimentation, sex in place of war, sex for money, and sex as protest. It was all made possible by the post-war baby-boom assault on Victorianism, and easy access to safe and reliable birth control.

By *The Avengers'* final series there would be a relaxation of sexuality on the small screen, in the person of Tara King. At 20 years old and as an Agency trainee, Tara was more the ingénue than Gale or Peel. Sherrie Inness asserts that Tara was "only slightly more threatening than the Avon Lady,"[41] but possibly in the final series, this was the intent. In the introduction to the Steed and King series, Tara snakes out of the tall grass in a tight-fitting, low-cut evening dress and a string of pearls, menacing without martial arts or guns. Thorson herself understood the new series would be more overtly sexualized: "I win battles on the fact that I am a woman. The clothes are feminine—silks and chiffons. And we are bringing back the bosom."[42]

The story lines of the final series were often rehashes of previous shows, but this was never unusual for *The Avengers* and increasingly so after the Cathy Gale episodes. The 1968–69 episodes were still full of mad scientists, gun dealers, killer robots, evil butlers, spies and counter-spies, and a liberal dose of diabolical undertakers. Steed and King battled bad clowns, worldwide destruction from dry rot, and what appears to be an Emma Peel character named Diana. If the American ABC network had once attempted to return the series to a more realistic format, it was abandoned completely, certainly after Clemens and Fennell were reinstated. It would seem that the show now attempted to be even more consciously contemporary and playful. Steed spent time at home in cardigans and floral shirts. In a nod to *The Avengers'* new US competition, *Laugh-In* (1967–73), in "The Morning After" (6.18), Steed ends the episode with their catch phrase "Sock It to Me!" In "The Interrogators" (6.14), Steed gains access to Mother's hidden domain via a phone booth, à la *Get Smart*. And the final episode features Steed dancing, hopelessly, to "rock" music at a house party (6.33, "Bizarre"). The final series was not really much different than most US television fare, having lost what had truly made it both English and appealing up to 1967.

With the introduction of the young, sometimes clumsy, ingénue there was also the return to more overt fetishism in fashions—the look of the hyper-sexualized late 1960s. The producers took every chance they could to get Tara King into a miniskirt or dress, as well as culottes, obviously designed to emphasize her long legs. It seemed that the over-costuming of the female lead had become an aspect of the show's playfulness. Thorson was tall and voluptuous, with skin more regularly exposed than Cathy Gale or Mrs. Peel. Her sexuality was more overt, in keeping with the late 1960s trend toward relaxed sexualization. She was flirtatious and there seemed the possibility that she and Steed were more than pupil and mentor. The entire season highlighted Thorson's physicality, rather than giving her any of the academic, artistic, or cultural attributes or instincts of her predecessors.

While the Peel years featured surrealism, season six had become outright joke-focused comedy. Tara was encased in butter at a creamery (6.07, "False Witness"); Steed cooked a steak on a Rolls Royce engine (6.08, "All Done With Mirrors"). There was a baddy with a big round black bomb, with BOMB printed on the side (6.11, "Look—(Stop Me If You've Heard This One) But There Were These Two Fellers"). The sixth series also featured wheelchair-bound "Mother" (the head of The Agency) and his muscular mute minder Rhonda, to provide added "humor," but it was clear that *The Avengers* had little left to offer (Macnee called the Mother character "ridiculous").[43]

While popular in France and the United States, Linda Thorson's character never rivaled Cathy Gale or Emma Peel in the UK. Thorson, like *The Avengers* in its final season, was probably just too American and too immature for many UK viewers who had been raised on the series. US reviews of season six included "great fun" and "a sprightly little comedy"; Tara was dubbed "a sexy tease."[44] Tara was much less the ideal of modern feminism than the Blackman or Rigg characters. As Thorson

noted in the 1969 *TV Times* interview, the series was now about femininity, not feminism. While Peel and Gale worked with Steed as equals, Tara
was "the pupil." Season six seems to reflect a neo-conservative attitude
toward gender relationships in the heat of the sexual revolution.

Placing the floundering spy spoof in competition with *Laugh-In* may
not have been the only reason for the show's abrupt finale. It had simply
lost the ability to retool in a period of relentless modernism. Macnee had
grown too old for the part of Tara's potential love interest. Both stars of
the final series struggled with weight problems while filming, and were
forced to diet.[45] Even with a new female star, *The Avengers* seemed tired
and outdated in 1969.

During the BBC Radio 3 program *Night Waves*, featuring Clemens,
Sandbrook, Sarah Dunant, and Bea Campbell, the participants raised a
very intriguing idea as to why *The Avengers*—a series which had always
been so versatile—had so much trouble making similar remarkable transformations in the late 1960s. By the end of the decade, spies and counter-
espionage agents were not the nameless, shadowy figures who risked
their lives so that ordinary people could feel secure in 1961. They were
not the heroes they had been in the days of Keel, Gale, and even Peel.
They were now "the enemy" who represented conservative government
institutions that sent young people off to unpopular wars, and sup-
pressed freedom of speech. Spies and agents in the later years of the
decade were "tools of state oppression" used against progress and innovation, always *Avengers* hallmarks.[46]

Lez Cooke rightly notices that *The Avengers* was at once a reflection of
the rapid redefining of society in the 1960s, as well as contributing to
what made England "cool."[47] Clemens concedes that *The Avengers* was
whatever you wanted it to be, "a fetish dream, a romp, or a dark shadowy thing."[48] In autobiographical memories of the 1960s, the show has
become different things to different people because it kept pace with the
changes that define the decade. Almost seamlessly, *The Avengers* had
redefined itself, much in the same way the decade had done.

Mark Donnelly dismisses the series as being a "high-velocity, sexy,
espionage series" and mere "escapism";[49] others who grew up as part of
the Cathy Gale, or Emma Peel, or even the Tara King and David Keel
eras, perhaps can appreciate a different, deeper, personal meaning in the
series, but season six better reflects Donnelly's general assessment than
any other. It would seem that in the end, in spite of its remarkable ability
to change on the fly, almost anticipating or determining the direction of
postwar popular culture, *The Avengers* itself fell victim to an incessant
demand for "new and shiny things" that a weekly television series based
on comic-book storytelling could no longer provide.

Impressionistically, *The Avengers* worldwide—and especially in North
America—is understood as part of the era of Beatlemania from 1964
through 1967, featuring Emma Peel, Carnaby Street fashions and a

"quirky" England.[50] The Peel era is the period many people think of when "remembering" the show. Neither before, nor after, Diana Rigg's tenure did *The Avengers* speak so comprehensively and immediately to a generation within the baby boom who had been raised on The British Invasion and a forward-looking, positive, youth-focused culture based on those things assumed to be English. Steed and King's dismissal from the small screen coincided with the demise of the Fab Four, and the emergence of pop music trends toward rural, roots-style music, or industrial heavy blues-based rock, both very much anathema to the fast-paced urban modernism of mid-decade popular culture.

The Avengers, as a feature of the Anglophile 1960s, was able to survive as long as it did because like music, fashion, film, art, and literature, and social attitudes of the decade, it responded quickly and effectively to the insistence for fun and novelty. By 1969, the British had embraced new, dynamic approaches to television and humor. While America enjoyed *Laugh-In*, England was enamored with dark sketch-based comedy. *Monty Python's Flying Circus* (1969–74) aired for the first time in the UK the same week *The Avengers* finished in the United States (October, 1969). The age of playful apolitical youth culture and Carnaby Street fashion was surely gone.

FILMS AND TV SHOWS

The Avengers. ITV, 1961–69.

Batman. ABC, 1966–68.

Cleopatra. Directed by Joseph L. Mankiewicz. 1963. Twentieth Century Fox.

Coronation Street. ITV, 1960–.

Dr. Strangelove or: How I Learned to Stop Worrying and Love the Bomb. Directed by Stanley Kubrick. 1964. Columbia Pictures.

The Ed Sullivan Show. CBS, 1948–71.

A Fistful of Dollars. Directed by Sergio Leone. 1964. United Artists.

From Russia With Love. Directed by Terence Young. 1963. United Artists.

Get Smart. NBC, 1965–69. CBS, 1969–70.

Goldfinger. Directed by Guy Hamilton. 1964. United Artists.

A Hard Day's Night. Directed by Richard Lester. 1964. United Artists.

It's A Mad, Mad, Mad, Mad World. Directed by Stanley Kramer. 1963. United Artists.

Laugh–In. NBC, 1967–73.

The Loneliness of the Long Distance Runner. Directed by Tony Richardson. 1962. British Lion–Columbia Distributors.

The Man from U.N.C.L.E. NBC, 1964–68.

The Monkees. NBC, 1966–68.

Monty Python's Flying Circus. BBC, 1969–74.

My Fair Lady. Directed by George Cukor. 1964. Warner Bros.

The Pink Panther. Directed by Blake Edwards. 1963. MGM.

Police Surgeon. ITV, 1960.

Steptoe and Son. BBC, 1962–74.

This Sporting Life. Directed by Lindsay Anderson. 1963. J. Arthur Rank
    Film Distributors.

Top of the Pops. BBC, 1964–2012.

NOTES

1. *The Avengers Declassified,* accessed May 4, 2013, http://declassified.theavengers.
tv/keel_main.htm.

2. Jerome R. Sehulster, "In My Era: Evidence for the Perception of a Special Period
of the Past," *Memory* 4, no. 2 (1996): 147–148.

3. Patrick Macnee (with David Rogers), *The Avengers and Me* (London: Titan,
1997), 13.

4. Ibid., 22–23.

5. Mark Donnelly, *60s Britain* (London: Longman, 2005), 23.

6. Arthur Marwick, *Culture in Britain Since 1945* (London: Penguin, 1991), 54–55.

7. Arthur Marwick, *British Society Since 1945* (London: Penguin, 1996), 90–93, 111.

8. Peter Bailey, "Jazz at the Spirella," in *Moments of Modernity: Reconstructing
Britain 1945–1964,* ed. Becky Conekin, Frank Mort, and Chris Waters (London: Rivers
Oram, 1999), 22.

9. Marwick, *British Society.*

10. Richard Aldrich, *Espionage, Security and Intelligence in Britain 1945–1970* (Manchester: Manchester University Press, 1998), 121–138. See chronology.

11. John Seed, "Hegemony Postponed," in *Cultural Revolution? The Challenge of the
Arts in the 1960s,* ed. Bart Moore-Gilbert and John Seed (New York: Routledge, 1992),
16; David Buxton, *From The Avengers to Miami Vice: Form and Ideology in Television Series*
(Manchester: Manchester University Press, 1990), 24.

12. Macnee, *The Avengers and Me,* 32–33.

13. There are a number of *The Avengers* fan sites online that embrace the minutia of
the series and rightly take great pride in the comprehensiveness of their sites' attention
to detail. The issue of chronology is especially important to both The Avengers Forever (http://theavengers.tv/forever/) and The Avengers (http://www.dissolute.com.au/
avweb/episodes.html). Both sites offer their own understanding of episode production
dates and airing dates, but they differ at times. For a full explanation see both sites for
their (very good) reasons for the differences. Simply due to ease of access, this chapter
uses the http://www.dissolute.com.au/avweb/episodes.html episode guide throughout.

14. Macnee, 37–39; "The Avengers," *Night Waves,* BBC Radio 3 (April 27, 2011),
host: Matthew Sweet.

15. *Night Waves.*

16. Macnee, *The Avengers and Me,* 41.

17. Buxton, *From The Avengers to Miami Vice,* 97–98.

18. The Avengers Forever (http://theavengers.tv/forever/peel1–21.htm) rates this
episode #3. The Avengers Episodes (http://www.dissolute.com.au/the-avengers-tv-se-
ries/series-4/) rates it #1.

19. For a range of discussions on *The Avengers* and the emergence of 1960s feminism, suggested readings include Rosie White, *Violent Femmes: Women as Spies in Popular Culture* (London: Routledge, 2007), 59–66; Francis Early and Kathleen Kennedy,
Athena's Daughter (New York: University of Syracuse Press, 2003), 2; Lez Cooke, *British*

Television Drama, A History (London: BFI, 2003), 85; Sherrie Inness, *Tough Girls* (Philadelphia: University of Pennsylvania Press, 1999), 33–34; Ian MacDonald, *Revolution in the Head* (London: Pimlico, 1995), 33–35; *Night Waves*, BBC Radio 3 (April 27, 2011).

20. *Night Waves*; Macnee, *The Avengers and Me*, 50.
21. The rhythm and blues combo led by Ray Davies got its name, The Kinks, from the song. Thomas M. Kitts, *Ray Davies: Not like Everybody Else* (London: Routledge, 2008), 33.
22. *Night Waves*.
23. 1960s Britain as a confident and modernist culture can be best understood in Mark Donnelly's discourse on "the long decade."
24. H. Kandy Rohde, "The Top Fifty: 1963," *The Gold of Rock and Roll* (New York: Arbor House, 1970), 219; H. Kandy Rohde, "The Top Fifty: 1964," *The Gold of Rock and Roll* (New York: Arbor House, 1970), 243.
25. *Night Waves*.
26. Ibid.
27. Ibid.; Macnee, *The Avengers and Me*, 81.
28. *Night Waves*.
29. "Episode 99," The Avengers Forever, http://theavengers.tv/forever/peel1–21.htm.
30. Macnee, *The Avengers and Me*, 80–81.
31. Buxton, *From The Avengers to Miami Vice*, 77.
32. Macnee, *The Avengers and Me*, 84–85.
33. Inness, *Tough Girls*, 33.
34. "The Fear Merchants," The Avengers Forever, http://theavengers.tv/forever/peel2–2.htm.
35. Nigel Farndale, "Diana Rigg: her story," *The Telegraph*, July 6, 2008, accessed August 1, 2013, http://www.telegraph.co.uk/culture/film/3555923/Diana-Rigg-her-story.html.
36. For a schedule of production and airing as well as discussions of reasons for chronology, see The Avengers Forever (http://theavengers.tv/forever) and The Avengers Declassified (http://declassified.theavengers.tv).
37. Ibid.
38. Macnee, *The Avengers and Me*, 95–98.
39. MacDonald, *Revolution in the Head*, 32.
40. Bernard Levin, *The Pendulum Years* (London: 1970), 325.
41. Inness, *Tough Girls*, 34.
42. The Avengers Declassified (http://declassified.theavengers.tv/king_quotes.htm). Quoted in the March 1–7, 1969 issue of *TV Times*.
43. Macnee, *The Avengers and Me*, 101.
44. Ibid., 107 and 110.
45. Macnee, *The Avengers and Me*, 103.
46. *Night Waves*.
47. Cooke, *British Television Drama*, 86.
48. *Night Waves*.
49. Donnelly, *60s Britain*, 81.
50. White, *Violent Femmes*, 68.

SIX

Once Upon a Time in the 21st Century

Beauty and the Beast *as Post-9/11 Fairy Tale*

Carlen Lavigne

The story of "Beauty and the Beast" has known a number of incarnations. Originally an eighteenth-century French tale by Mme. Leprince de Beaumont, intended to instruct young women on the rewards of genteel behavior, it first appeared in English as a translation in *Young Misses Magazine* in 1761.[1] While there are variations on the theme, the gist of the traditional story is that a young woman must take residence in the castle of a hideous beast in order to ransom her father's life; in time, her love restores the cursed beast to a handsome prince, and they are married. The tale's best known film versions are Jean Cocteau's *La belle et la bête* (1946) and Disney's animated *Beauty and the Beast* (1991). On television, CBS's *Beauty and the Beast* (1987–90) starred Linda Hamilton and Ron Perlman as Catherine and Vincent (the "beauty" and her titular monster), while the newest version, the CW's *Beauty and the Beast* (2012–present) stars Kristin Kreuk and Jay Ryan. The CW series is most directly indebted to its CBS predecessor—it has retained the names "Catherine" and "Vincent" for the leads, and both series are set in New York City.[2] But every era creates the fairy tales it needs; while the CBS series was a reflection of American political realities of the 1980s, the CW has created a text symptomatic of post-9/11 culture.

Of course, "post-9/11" is itself difficult to quantify. The term most directly refers to the period after the September 11, 2001, terrorist attacks that downed four planes in the United States—two of those planes striking and destroying the twin towers of the World Trade Center in New

York City, resulting in 2,753 deaths.[3] Images of the towers falling were broadcast live on multiple stations both nationally and internationally. Twenty-six days later, the United States bombed Afghanistan.[4] Over the next decade and beyond, the United States and the world saw renewed terrorist attacks and wars in both Afghanistan and Iraq, along with boosts to domestic surveillance, border controls, and airport security programs (among, of course, many other developments). These events have been accompanied by a resurgence of military themes in popular American media, from television hits like *NCIS* (2003–present) and *Homeland* (2011–present) to the upcoming comedy *Enlisted* (2014–present) and films like *Black Hawk Down* (2002) or *The Hurt Locker* (2008). Even a rise in military-themed fashions[5] may demonstrate the same "renewed audience appetite for narratives of conflict" also seen in Hollywood after WWI.[6]

No single media text (or analysis) can capture the complexities of post-9/11 American culture, but a comparison of lead roles, settings, and narratives (from 1987 to 2012) reveals notable changes in the televised *Beauty and the Beast* mythos. The CBS *Beauty and the Beast* was primarily a class-based discourse and a reaction to the rise of neoliberalism in the years of Reagan conservatism; it was strongly inflected by second-wave feminism and civil rights concerns. The CW remake has been retooled as a crime procedural; it is postfeminist and postracial, and it trades class injustice for military conspiracy, surveillance, and the lingering shadow of a traumatic past.

A. VINCENT

The alterations made to the Beast are the most clearly linked to post-9/11 America. Ron Perlman's 1987 Beast is extensively made up to look leonine; he has fur, long features, a cleft palate, a feline nose, and sharp, pointed teeth. He wears a long cloak when forced to venture out in public, for his appearance would frighten city residents and cause a threat to his own safety. No explanation for Vincent's bestial appearance is offered in the CBS series canon; he was found as a baby and raised in loving safety by a community of outcasts living beneath the sewers. In many ways, his mysterious animal appearance lends him a fictional ethnicity that allows him to act as a stand-in for the series' treatment of racial issues; while the CBS *Beauty and the Beast* avoids dealing directly with issues of civil rights or racism, Vincent suffers the unfair judgment of the outside, privileged world.[7] Admittedly this is a fundamentally flawed comparison—Perlman is Caucasian, and having him wear "bestial" makeup as substitute for non-white racial difference is more than highly questionable—but the link is made explicit in the pilot episode, when Vincent's adoptive father Jacob (a doctor) laments his son's lack of educational opportunities: "When I started medicine they wouldn't admit minorities . . . I wonder what they would've done with you? Let's not even think about it" (1.01, "Once Upon A Time in the City of New York"). Vincent has a gift as a healer, but cannot pursue his calling or even safely go out in public due to systemic racial prejudices he cannot hope to combat.

The CBS Vincent is also not particularly masculine; while he can be violent in Catherine's cause, he can also recite classic poetry at will, and helps to educate small children in his spare time. He is also an empath; his psychic bond with Catherine allows him to read her emotions, knowing when she is in danger but also when she is happy or sad. With no agenda of his own, he waits peacefully in his underground world, surrounded by books and the flotsam of bygone years, seemingly ready at any moment that Catherine might require his aid. While he primarily plays the romantic role of knight-protector, in the pilot episode of the series, he in fact fails to save Catherine; when she is assaulted and thrown from a van, he is instead the nurturing companion who finds her, binds her wounds, and nurses her back to health (1.01, "Once Upon A Time in the City of New York").

In the CW remake, Jay Ryan's new Vincent is a former soldier who fought in Afghanistan, having enlisted after losing his two brothers when the World Trade Center towers fell (1.01, "Pilot"). He is the victim of military experiments that have altered his DNA and left him with an innate, Jekyll-and-Hyde type of beastliness. His connection to 9/11 is explicit;[8] in this, he joins other television characters like Mac, the lead of *CSI: New York* (2004–13), who lost his wife in the attacks. It is hardly surprising that a series taking place in New York City in 2012 might incorporate this monumental event into a character's history; further, such highly personalized depictions of terrorism and its consequences may in part be symptomatic of a cultural inability to process the wider scope of nationally devastating events—in effect, a reflection of our desire to put a human face on tragedy.[9]

Vincent/CW's status as the Beast who walks New York City streets is also worth noting; while Vincent/CBS's otherness was clearly marked by his feline appearance, the new Vincent's only "bestial" distinction is a scar marring one cheek. While some of this might be attributed to budget differences (CBS is a larger and richer network; doubtless Ron Perlman's makeup was expensive) or target demographics (the CW's programming is primarily teen dramas),[10] it seems significant that Vincent/CW goes abroad—prowls among the populace—wearing average street clothes and a ball cap pulled low over his eyes. In the twenty-first century, the Beast walking among us looks just like us, and the man in the baseball cap is the new Other; he joins a cultural resurgence of alien invaders, body snatchers, and zombies,[11] all of which may relate to fear of terrorist attack and betrayal from unmarked strangers.

Conversely, however, the new Vincent is also a man of privilege; he is no longer a stand-in for racial difference. He might worry about exposure, but he can also "pass" in a crowd, without the older Vincent's visible differences in face and form. The CW's Vincent is an educated white male—a qualified doctor who at one point had access to the same opportunities that CBS's Vincent lacked. His position as the lurking figure of suspicion is significantly ameliorated by his need to act as the romantic lead. He is, ultimately, a force for good in the text; he may be incognito, but he can be trusted. The same is not true of assistant district attorney Gabe Lowen (Sendhil Ramamurthy), whose role effectively negates any suggestion that Beast status in the CW series might allow any sympathetic commentary on the marginalization of racial minorities. In the original CBS series, when a suspicious-seeming new ADA arrives, he turns out to be Vincent's long-lost (adopted) brother Devin (Bruce Abbott)—an ally to the underground community (1.16, "Promises of Someday"). In the CW remake, Gabe Lowen is still a "brother" of sorts to Vincent, but no ally—as a child, he was subject to early versions of the same genetic experiments. His inner beast is less advanced than Vincent's, and subsequently uncontrollable; Gabe also walks among the general populace, but without medication, he might explode into violence and kill indiscriminately at any moment. Vincent may struggle to retain control of his inner beast, but Gabe is simply incapable: "I'm not aware when I'm like that" (1.21, "Date Night"). Ramamurthy is Indian-American;[12] it is difficult not to compare the monster-of-color Gabe with Ryan's distinctly white Vincent, and note that Gabe possesses far more animalistic tendencies. In the first season (all that has aired at the time of writing), Gabe is the dangerous character who betrays Vincent and is punished in the ensuing helicopter raid, shot down by the same military forces that created him (1.22, "Never Turn Back").[13] His Otherness cannot be safely contained. The CBS series deals indirectly with racial issues by segregating and disempowering Vincent due to his appearance, suggesting that such prejudice is morally wrong; the CW series remakes Vincent as a privileged white male while simultaneously suggesting that a non-white male with similar combat abilities cannot be trusted or controlled.

Finally, New Vincent cuts a much more definitively masculine figure than his predecessor—a variety of hypermasculinity that serves as "a rather traditional response to moments of national instability that are regressively equated to threats to masculinity."[14] This Vincent neither recites poetry nor teaches children; he secretly fights crime while staying on the run from shadowy forces known as "Muirfield," the conspiracy that created him, and while he has heightened animal senses (hearing, smell, etc.), he displays no empathic abilities. He does save Catherine on their first meeting, as he blocks bullets with his body and then rips apart the gunmen attacking her (1.01, "Pilot").

Mathias Nilges has traced a pattern of apocalypse in recent American television and film—a wish-fulfilling apocalypse that destroys the current social and cultural disruptions caused by global terrorism, feminism, and environmental decay, and instead (re)creates a hegemonically simpler time that in part works to preserve traditional gender roles. While the new *Beauty and the Beast* is not post-apocalyptic, it is marked by this same return to gender essentialisms; likewise, news coverage of 9/11 itself reinforced a gendered focus on male heroes and female victims. [15] Perlman's Vincent may have been a poet-empath, a "pre-Raphaelite" hero [16] starring in a series that highlighted postmodern "fragmentation and disconnectedness," [17] but Ryan's Vincent is harder and fiercer; his aggression is doubled, as it is both innate (in his animalistic Beast side) and learned (through his experience as a war veteran). Both Vincents protect their respective Catherines with violence; both play the role of the Beast who can only be tamed by true love. The new Vincent, however, lacks the old Vincent's feminized sensitivity; he fights a constant battle for control of his masculine violence, and indeed, early in the first season, suffers from hypermasculine rage blackouts (1.07, "Out of Control").

Both Vincents harbor desires for a life with Catherine; on the CBS series, this is made impossible both by Vincent's bestial appearance and by his desire for Catherine to have a fulfilling life and career in the public eye. The CW's Vincent, on the other hand, might be cured; he and his scientist friend J.T. (Austin Basis) spend much of the first season analyzing his DNA and working to end his "condition." This Vincent wants very much to be "normal"; he would knowingly poison himself to buy a few public years with Catherine (1.21, "First Date"). Despite his apparent desire for traditional American domesticity, however, when a cure is in fact discovered, he must reject it; his animal side is what allows him to effectively fight Muirfield (1.22, "Never Turn Back"). His hypermasculinity is his prime tool of survival, and without it, he cannot hope to survive in the new *Beauty and the Beast's* militarized, conspiracy-riddled world. Notably, it is Catherine who makes this choice, by jabbing a syringe into his neck. While the Catherine of the original series craved the empathic connection she and Vincent shared, the CW's Catherine reinforces the need for Vincent's continued aggressiveness.

B. CATHERINE

There are significant differences between the female series leads. In *Beauty and the Beast's* original television incarnation, Catherine rejects her domineering father and her patronizing fiancé. She abandons a promising career in her father's corporate law firm and chooses instead to work as an assistant district attorney—a position from which she can advocate for social justice (1.01, "Once Upon A Time in the City of New York").

The CW's Catherine is a NYPD homicide detective; in *Beauty and the Beast*'s re-envisioning as a crime procedural, she spends a portion of most early episodes tracking killers.[18] Both Catherines are involved in the legal profession, making the distinction subtle, but Catherine/CBS's quest to help the needy shifts to Catherine/CW's need to punish the guilty. According to Elayne Rapping, the focus of American prime-time television tends to shift according to the predominant political issues of the time; crime procedurals and related programs may be congruent with "tough on crime" politics, and their popularity may promote a sense of safety for audiences who want to see the bad guys captured at the end.[19] If so, it is telling that the crime procedural has remained prevalent in the last decade—particularly with military overtones, and with elements of vigilante justice.[20]

The original series presented a tension between public and domestic ambitions that is lacking in the CW version, which replaces this focus with psychological trauma and accompanying homicide mystery. Catherine/CBS lost her mother to cancer at an early age, and now—unmarried, childless—she is torn between her more traditional dreams (a husband, children, a big house) and her desire to achieve something new with Vincent.[21] Catherine/CW is instead consumed by the need to solve her mother's violent murder, which occurred—in the series' timeline—ten years in the past, placing it just after the turn of the millennium. This, again, relates to the CW series' positioning as a post-9/11 American text. Catherine's new connection to 9/11 is less explicit than Vincent's, but many recent crime series seem to spotlight similar protagonists—those haunted by the mystery of a past, violent trauma, particularly involving the death of a loved one. As Wheeler Dixon has written, "Commodified and repackaged, cheapened by commemorative plates or hastily assembled 'memorial' videos, the stark human tragedy of 9/11 obliterated all attempts to comprehend the scope of its impact."[22] Indeed, the only news footage provided of 9/11 both during and after the event was distant and mysterious, partly due to censors and partly because journalists and videographers could not get close enough to the scene.[23] Catherine/CW thus joins other recent American series leads investigating the murders in their own damaged histories in programs such as *Monk* (2002–09), *Castle* (2009–present), *The Mentalist* (2008–present), and *Unforgettable* (2011–present).[24] Certainly such narratives existed before the twenty-first century, but the psychologically damaged lead seems to be increasingly common.

Beauty's role is also to be the feminine half of the fairy-tale couple; in both versions of the television series (and, indeed, in the original story) her role is to tame the savage Beast. She is the one person he would never harm; hers is the voice that can calm his violent rages. Catherine/CBS is not wholly feminine; for example, she spends part of the CBS pilot episode training in self-defense. The 1980s fashion also means that she sports notable "power" shoulder pads, making her frame appear larger than it is. This is not to say that her appearance is masculine; she frequently wears expensive (though modest) lingerie, and the leonine Vincent looms over her. But her gendered behavior is somewhat androgynous, as is Vincent's; her legal crusader complements his romantic bard.[25] Much of the romantic tension in the series stems from her inability to rectify her traditional feminine role with her new, nonstandard aspirations. In the first season finale, she is unsure if Vincent's love is enough for her when he can never leave the sewers and provide her with a "normal" domestic life. She leaves the city and goes north to visit a married female friend. She plays with her friend's children, makes a tentative date with an old crush, and contemplates her possible future, only to ultimately go rushing back to NYC and Vincent's arms: "I could never doubt it. What we have is all that matters. It's worth everything" (1.22, "A Happy Life"). She rejects the domestic dreams of the past in order to embrace an unconventional lover who is wholly supportive of her work, even if their partnership can never fully be consummated. In this manner, Catherine/CBS's narrative is ultimately a quest for fulfillment—for a life that can allow her to craft a new ending to a fairy tale in which the Beast will never magically turn into a handsome prince, and in which Beauty has a successful career outside the home. She cannot wholly be with Vincent because choosing him would mean abandoning her ambitions and the work she accomplishes; the series is marked by this seemingly impassable stasis, though also by implicit hope.

In comparison, Catherine/CW also demonstrates feminine and masculine behaviors, but her gender contrasts sharply with Vincent/CW's hypermasculine Beast. By 2013, trend changes mean that Catherine/CW wears tight, fitted clothes and no shoulder pads; her hair is longer. She is also skilled in self-defense, though there's no explanation for this within the series (it is apparently part of her police training). In short, she occupies the role of post-9/11, twenty-first-century American hero: a "hypersexualized female, complete with firm, perky breasts, stiletto thin legs, a designer wardrobe, and black-belt karate skills."[26] This Catherine's career is divorced from feminist concerns, as is Catherine herself; during one of her first appearances in the pilot, she is using her police vehicle (sirens blaring) to dodge traffic in Times Square because she is late for a date (1.01, "Pilot"). She arrests criminals while chatting about romance with her partner; she even spends half an episode worrying that she might attend her father's wedding unaccompanied (1.09, "Bridesmaid Up!"). She exists in a postfeminist world where her gender poses no difficulty in the workplace; despite her performance of hyperfeminine tropes in a historically masculine profession, she is free to "choose" (and she chooses to abuse her authority to get to a date on time).

While Catherine/CBS spends a full episode debating whether a life with Vincent is worth sacrificing her traditionally feminine aspirations of home and children, Catherine/CW repeatedly dismisses the possibility of a domestic future:

> Catherine: Vincent, you and I can't even go to a restaurant together. Of course there is no baby.

> Vincent: No house? No marriage?

> Catherine: There are a lot of people in this country who can't get married either. And I'm not the kind of person who needs a white picket fence and a big rock on my finger to be happy. (1.21, "Date Night")

When the promise of a cure looms, Catherine and Vincent do happily discuss their potential "picket fence" aspirations (1.21, "Date Night"), but Catherine/CW also offers to give up her life and family (a father and sister) in a heartbeat, proposing to leave town and assume a new identity with Vincent using the fake IDs she has already obtained (1.22, "Never Turn Back"). Rather than devote much time to pondering her future, she has a military conspiracy to track down and her mother's murder to solve. Both Catherines have agency, but Catherine/CW's social position, career, and choices are taken for granted; the unlikely nature of her post-feminist positioning goes unacknowledged.

Remake Catherine also exists in a postracial world; while Catherine/CBS was very much the daughter of white privilege, Catherine/CW is portrayed by Kristin Kreuk, a Canadian actor of Chinese and Dutch heritage[27] whose onscreen mother is played (in flashback) by the Vietnamese-Canadian Khaira Ledeyo (1.01, "Pilot"; 1.08, "Trapped"; 1.19, "Playing With Fire").[28] Catherine's biracial ethnicity is implicitly acknowledged onscreen, but never explicitly raised in the CW narrative; she has apparently experienced no discrimination in her career, nor do others make reference to her ethnicity over the course of the series' first season. This may help gloss over the racial implications of Ramamurthy's highly animalistic Beast—Kreuk's Catherine, after all, lives in a world where racism does not exist, a world where she unproblematically played Rosa Parks in a second-grade play (1.20, "Anniversary").

Like Catherine/CBS, Catherine/CW must balance her romantic dreams against her desire for an unconventional and more emotionally fulfilling love. Both Beauties are also active agents in their own narratives—notably within limits, as each iteration of the series has Beauty being rescued repeatedly by her Beast. Catherine/CW, however, retains her predecessor's feminist political and social advances but takes them for granted, instead focusing on conspiracies and the past psychological damage she must understand and overcome before she can move forward with her life. She shares Catherine/CBS's blend of masculine/feminine behaviors, but she is more feminized in comparison to the hypermasculine new Vincent, allowing the CW series to skew back toward a simplified gender essentialism while still granting Beauty a badge, a gun, and the independence that might be expected of a twenty-first-century career woman.

C. DIFFERENT WORLDS

Supporting cast and setting also distinguish each series, and it is significant that New York City serves as a backdrop for both versions. In the 1980s, NYC was "regarded as a national 'panic center,' the scene of extreme race hatred, record-setting levels of homelessness, and AIDS phobia";[29] it was an ideal setting for *Beauty and the Beast*/CBS's engagement with issues of race, gender, and class. Now, NYC is the site of the 9/11 attacks, and thus remains an appropriate stage for the CW series' more militarized themes.

The CBS series bases much of its conflict on the tensions between Catherine's upper-class circles and Vincent's sewer community, establishing a primary division that ensures a consistent focus on class issues. As the opening monologue describes:

> Vincent: This is where the wealthy and the powerful rule. It is her world . . . a world apart from mine. Her name is Catherine. From the moment I saw her, she captured my heart with her beauty, her warmth, and her courage. I knew then, as I know now, she would change my life forever.

> Catherine: He comes from a secret place, far below the city streets, hiding his face from strangers, safe from hate and harm. He brought me there to save my life . . . and now, wherever I go, he is with me in spirit. For we have a bond stronger than friendship or love. And although we cannot be together, we will never, ever be apart.

The CBS series' focus is not on racial diversity so much as class difference—the cold luxury of Catherine's World Above vs. the warm and rather utopian[30] poverty of Vincent's World Below[31] —and it does not necessarily offer successful critique of race or gender issues: the outsider World Below is still led by the patriarch Jacob, a straight white man known as "Father."[32] Still, the World Above (where the "wealthy and the powerful rule") is privileged, rich, and pale—reflected, subtly, early in the first season, where Catherine attends an elegant art show amidst a crowd of upper-class white guests and African-American wait staff (1.03, "Siege"). Catherine herself is established as non-racist through her romance with Vincent and her friendships with two African-American characters—Issac (Delroy Lindo), the gym owner who teaches her to fight, and Edie (Renn Woods), a coworker. Both vanish after season one as the series shifts to focus more on white supporting characters: Catherine's boss Joe (Jay Acovone) and her best friend Jenny (Terry Hanauer).

However, while *Beauty and the Beast*/CBS's thematic engagements were not always as successful or provocative as they might have been, it did consistently focus on gender issues and capitalism. Catherine's legal cases (her work in fighting the injustices of the world above) involve not only thwarting or investigating assaults on women and children (1.01, "Once Upon A Time in the City of New York"; 1.02, "Terrible Savior"; 1.10, "A Children's Story"; 1.16, "Promises of Someday"; 1.17, "Down to a Sunless Sea"), but also protecting senior citizens from eviction (1.03, "Siege"), or stopping the construction of a luxury office tower that would destroy the sewer world (1.21, "Ozymandias"). In the CBS series, Vincent's main romantic rival is corporate head Elliot Burch, who offers Catherine wealth and (morally corrupt) opulence among the city elite. The binary oppositions between Catherine's world and Vincent's mean that anti-capitalist themes arise in nearly every episode, as the difficulties of Catherine's luxurious World Above are balanced with the supportive community of Vincent's World Below. Gender and class conflicts are major episode plot points.

These narrative threads are dropped in the 2012 remake, which emphasizes the crime procedural and romance elements of the narrative. The first season has two different voice-over introductions, the first for episodes 1.03 ("All In")–1.15 ("Any Means Possible"). It lays the basis for the investigative and military elements of the show:

> Catherine: Nine years ago, I witnessed my mother's murder. I would have been killed too, if it hadn't been for Vincent.

> Vincent: I was part of an experimental special forces group. Their goal was to create the perfect super-soldier. But something went wrong.

The second version of the voice-over opens the back end of season one (starting at 1.16, "Insatiable"), and concentrates wholly on the romantic plotline, while asserting a postfeminist power equality between the two leads, as—contrary to weekly events—Catherine is posited as having an equal role in "saving" Vincent:

> Catherine: From the moment we met . . .

> Vincent: We knew our lives would never be the same.

> Catherine: He saved my life.

> Vincent: And she saved mine.

> Catherine: We're destined.

Vincent: But we know it won't be easy.

Catherine: Even though we have every reason to stay apart.

Vincent: We'll risk it all to be together.

Notably, the introduction to the remake series makes no mention of class tensions. Moreover, while the CBS *Beauty and the Beast* may have restricted its racial themes to allegory, the CW *Beauty and the Beast* elides them entirely, presenting a simplified NYC culture and police force in which racism is simply not an issue onscreen. In addition to the series' acknowledgment of her own biracial heritage, the CW's Catherine reports to her boss Joe (Brian White), now an African-American man, and works with her Latina partner Tess (Nina Lisandrello). Feminist concerns are similarly obscured. While *Beauty and the Beast*/CBS repeatedly returned to issues of abused women, for example, *Beauty and the Beast*/CW's most direct engagement with women's issues might be distilled to a single exchange between Tess and Joe (who are secretly in a relationship) as Joe asserts that "going public" could be damaging to Tess's career: "Me?" she objects, to which he quickly amends, "Both of us" (1.20, "Anniversary"). This tertiary conversation is the only hint that power relations may not be 100 percent equitable in this twenty-first-century world. Moreover, while the original Catherine typically helped victims of capitalist patriarchy, the CW's more postfeminist Catherine has ceased fighting for victims of domestic violence or sexual abuse. Instead, her first case involves the murder of a successful female fashion editor who was competing with another woman over a promotion. As the CW's Catherine no longer fights the patriarchy, the perpetrator is the victim's husband's mistress, who killed because she was jealous over a man (1.01, "Pilot").

The CW's *Beauty and the Beast* shifts its focus from the anti-capitalist, anti-classist, anti-misogynist narratives of the CBS series; it does away with the World Below altogether, thus eliminating any inherent tensions between Catherine's circles and Vincent's. While Vincent/CW spends one episode volunteering at an illegal street clinic (1.11, "On Thin Ice"), thus implying some sympathy for the underclasses, his only companion in seclusion is another straight white male (the scientist J.T.). Instead of coming from different worlds, Catherine and Vincent share almost incestuously similar origins: Catherine's mother was the scientist whose experiments helped create Vincent's "beastly" side, and her biological father is (secretly) a soldier working for Muirfield (1.22, "Never Turn Back"). She and Vincent were effectively both birthed from the same military conspiracy. Their salvation—and the key to their romance—lies not in resolving the endless conflicts between their two communities, but rather in solving the mystery of their past traumas and eluding the secretive, unknowable forces that now shadow their existence and threaten them with violent attack.

D. CONCLUSION

The CBS *Beauty and the Beast* was cut short in the third season after Linda Hamilton quit the series (and, ironically, a subsequent homicide investigation storyline failed to resonate with fans). Its implied social commentary was severely flawed, inflected by white privilege and never able to directly address many of its own ideas. Nevertheless, its predominant themes reflected the rise of second-wave feminism, neoliberal capitalism, and the civil rights movement; it serves as an artifact of American culture in the 1980s.

The CW's *Beauty and the Beast* is hardly a runaway hit, though as of this writing, its ratings have been respectable enough to grant it a second-season pickup. It has not taken America by storm, and in fact it has significantly fewer viewers than its CBS predecessor—although much of this decline might also be related to the rise of cable television and online streaming, and the fragmentation of network audiences since the 1980s (perhaps no single television series can now occupy the cultural imagination as in times past).[33] However, if our fairy tales reflect the moral lessons of the day, certainly the series' thematic shifts seem significant in terms of suggesting changes in American culture; this is the show that producers and executives gambled on, and the tropes borrowed from crime procedurals and conspiracy serials effectively realign the focus of this television story. This is what CW producers expected would be popular: a hypermasculinized Beast, a feminized, sexualized Beauty, and a focus on military culture, crime, and conspiracy that simultaneously drops any major questions relating to feminist, race, or class concerns. It is understandable that the military, and military-industrial technologies, should have become more prominent in American popular culture since 9/11; it is distressing that a too-myopic concentration on such themes might exclude feminist, race, or class concerns from public narratives or the public consciousness. Traditional fairy tales may take place in a nebulous "once upon a time," but "Beauty and the Beast" is not timeless; it has morphed yet again to present us with a postfeminist, postracial moral in which only the privileged may live happily ever after.

FILMS AND TV SHOWS

Beauty and the Beast. CBS, 1987–90.
Beauty and the Beast. The CW, 2012–.
Beauty and the Beast. Directed by Gary Trousdale and Kirk Wise. 1991. Disney.

Black Hawk Down. Directed by Ridley Scott. 2002. Columbia Pictures.

Castle. ABC, 2009–.

CSI: New York. CBS, 2004–13.

Enlisted. Fox Network, 2013–.

Homeland. Showtime, 2011–.

The Hurt Locker. Directed by Kathryn Bigelow. 2008. Summit Entertainment.

La belle et la bête. Directed by Jean Cocteau. 1946. DisCina.

The Mentalist. CBS, 2008–.

Monk. USA Network, 2002–09.

NCIS. CBS, 2003–.

Unforgettable. CBS, 2011–.

NOTES

1. Jack Zipes, "The Dark Side of Beauty and the Beast: The Origins of the Literary Fairy Tale for Children," *Children's Literature Association Quarterly* (1981 Proceedings): 123.

2. The CW is a joint venture between CBS and Warner Bros., and the links between the CBS and CW *Beauty and the Beast*s are explicit. While the CW's adoption of a 25-year-old property might seem uncharacteristic of a network known for "teen" programming, the new *Beauty and the Beast* was part of a network rebranding attempt, and may also have been intended to trigger the nostalgia of older women who make up a surprising percentage of the network's demographics. Lacey Rose, "The CW Prepping Brand Refresh for Fall (Exclusive)," *The Hollywood Reporter*, June 20, 2012, http://www.hollywoodreporter.com/news/cw-brand-fall-339375; Yvonne Villareal, "CW network revamp aims to draw wider audience," *Los Angeles Times*, March 26, 2013, http://articles.latimes.com/2013/mar/26/business/la-et-fi-ct-the-cw-20130326.

3. "9/11 By the Numbers: Death, destruction, charity, salvation, war, money, real estate, spouses, babies, and other September 11 statistics," *New York Magazine*, accessed August 15, 2013, http://nymag.c.om/news/articles/wtc/1year/numbers.htm.

4. Ibid.

5. For example, see Marissa Brassfield, "25 War and Military-Inspired Fashions," *Trendhunter.com*, March 9, 2009, http://www.trendhunter.com/slideshow/military-fashion.

6. Wheeler Winston Dixon, "Introduction: Something Lost—Film After 9/11," in *Film and Television After 9/11*, ed. Wheeler Winston Dixon (Carbondale: Southern Illinois University Press, 2004), 1.

7. David L. Pike, "Urban Nightmares and Future Visions: Life Beneath New York," *Wide Angle* 20, no. 4 (1998): 32.

8. In the pilot episode of the CW series, Jay Ryan's Vincent watches actual archival news footage of the 9/11 attacks.

9. Ina Rae Hark, "Today is the Longest Day of My Life: *24* as Mirror Narrative of 9/11," in *Film and Television After 9/11*, ed. Wheeler Winston Dixon (Carbondale: Southern Illinois University Press, 2004),123.

10. Both observations via Erik Adams and Todd VanDerWerff, "*Beauty and the Beast* S1/E1," *The AV Club*, October 11, 2012, http://www.avclub.com/articles/pilot,86436/.

11. Mathias Nilges, "The Aesthetics of Destruction: Contemporary US Cinema and TV Culture," in *Reframing 9/11: Film, Popular Culture and the 'War on Terror,'* ed. Jeff Birkenstein, Anna Froula, and Karen Randell (London: Continuum International Publishing, 2010), 24; see also Proctor, this volume.

12. Ramamurthy was born in Chicago, according to his biography on IMDB: http://www.imdb.com/name/nm0707983/bio, accessed August 13, 2013.

13. Recent television spoilers have suggested that rumours of Gabe's death may have been greatly exaggerated, which so far does not change my reading of his character. "'Beauty and the Beast' season 2 spoilers: Sendhil Ramamurthy confirmed to return," July 18, 2013, http://cartermatt.com/73927/beauty-and-the-beast-season-2-spoilers-sendhil-ramamurthy-confirmed-to-return/.

14. Nilges, "The Aesthetics of Destruction," 31.

15. Lynn Spigel, "Entertainment Wars: Television Culture After 9/11," *American Quarterly* 56, no. 2 (2004): 246.

16. Joe Sanders, "Shoring Fragments: How CBS's *Beauty and the Beast* Adapts Consensus Reality to Shape Its Marginalized World," in *Functions of the Fantastic: Selected Essays from the Thirteenth International Conference on the Fantastic in the Arts,* ed. Joseph L. Sanders (Praeger, 1995), 42.

17. Ibid., 37.

18. The third season of the CBS series presents a strangely transitional phase here, as Hamilton left the series and her version of Catherine was killed off, giving way to a new female lead—Diana Bennett (Jo Anderson), the police officer investigating Catherine's murder. The third season only ran for 13 episodes and proved unpopular with fans, leading to the series' cancellation.

19. Elayne Rapping, "Cops, crime, and TV," *The Progressive* 58, no. 4 (1994): 36–38.

20. *24* (2001–10) is an excellent example; it began airing before 9/11 but an American cultural focus on fighting terrorism likely helped the series' longevity. Hark, "Today is the Longest Day of My Life."

21. C. Lee Harrington and Denise D. Bielby, "The Mythology of Modern Life: Representations of Romance in the 1980s," *Journal of Popular Culture* 24, no. 4 (1991): 139.

22. Dixon, "Introduction: Something Lost," 4.

23. Mikita Brottman, "The Fascination of the Abomination: The Censored Images of 9/11," in *Film and Television After 9/11,* ed. Wheeler Winston Dixon (Carbondale: Southern Illinois University Press, 2004), 164; Hark, "Today is the Longest Day of My Life."

24. My examples here relate specifically to characters investigating the murders of loved ones; elsewhere in this volume, Karen Hellekson has detailed other recent instances of traumatized American investigators.

25. See also Cynthia Erb, "Another World or the World of an Other? The Space of Romance in Recent Versions of 'Beauty and the Beast'," *Cinema Journal* 34, no. 4 (1995): 50–70.

26. Rebecca Bell-Metereau, "The How-to Manual, The Prequel, and the Sequel in Post-9/11 Cinema," in *Film and Television After 9/11,* ed. Wheeler Winston Dixon (Carbondale: Southern Illinois University Press, 2004), 146.

27. According to her biography on IMDB, accessed August 9, 2013: http://www.imdb.com/name/nm0471036/bio.

28. The casting department's seeming conflation of Vietnamese with Chinese feeds the assertion that the CW's *Beauty and the Beast* positions itself as a postracial text.

29. Erb, "Another World or the World of an Other?," 58.

30. Sanders, "Shoring Fragments," 42.

31. In NYC in the 1980s, news reports detailed communities of disenfranchised people who really were living in the sewers, making *Beauty and the Beast*/CBS quite timely. Pike, "Urban Nightmares and Future Visions," 20.

32. As Cynthia Erb has noted, "for all its attempts to depict the Tunnel World as a sort of 'rainbow coalition' that welcomes people of color, the aged, the poor, and others, the major repeating characters of the Tunnel World tend to maintain its visual profile as a white middle-class community in nontraditional garb." Erb, "Another World," 59.

33. Spigel, "Entertainment Wars," 256.

SEVEN

Clear Eyes, Full Hearts, Romney Lost

Politics, Football, and Friday Night Lights

Matthew Paproth

In the closing scenes of the pilot for *Friday Night Lights* (2006–2011), a TV series which aired for five seasons on NBC and then DirecTV, Eric Taylor, head coach of the Dillon Panthers, motivates his players by quietly saying "clear eyes," to which they respond "full hearts, can't lose." Throughout the series, "clear eyes, full hearts, can't lose" comes to represent the focus, determination, and self-confidence that undergird the approach to life advocated by Taylor both on and off the football field. The saying is not only regularly chanted in practices and games, but it is also written in capital letters above the locker room exit. Players repeat it in both public and private spaces as a mantra to push them to overcome the various challenges thrown in their paths, and Coach Taylor routinely touches the phrase on the wall as he leaves the locker room.

The series was the second adaption of Buzz Bissinger's *Friday Night Lights: A Town, A Team, and a Dream*, which chronicles the 1988 season of the Permian Panthers, a real-life West Texas high school football team.[1] Published in 1990, the book was adapted as a film by Peter Berg in 2004; he then went on to create the series. The phrase, which appears in neither Bissinger's book nor Berg's film, has taken on a life of its own beyond the five seasons it appeared on television. A Google Image search demonstrates that it is thriving as a saying on motivational posters, and it has spawned a number of memes and tumblr pages, including "Academic Coach Taylor," in which scenes from the show are matched with advice like "I Didn't Travel a Thousand Miles to Hear a Presentation You Wrote on a Plane" and "Clear Thesis. Strong Analysis. Can't Lose."[2]

Perhaps the most public and influential re-appropriation of the slogan occurred during the 2012 US Presidential campaign. At various points in 2012, both Barack Obama and Mitt Romney co-opted the saying, inciting comments by writers and actors from various iterations of *Friday Night Lights*. Romney's use of the phrase, in particular, drew the ire of producers and actors from the show and became a national news story throughout the last month of the campaign. The tensions between liberal and conservative values staged in this debate parallel in various ways the tensions explored in the film and series. The texts share an interest in demonstrating the complicated relationship between high school football culture and the rural, deeply conservative Texas towns in which they take place. While coaches Gary Gaines (the real-life coach of the Permian Panthers) and Taylor preach hard work, honesty, and selflessness, the surrounding communities and the scaffolding surrounding Texas high school football are antithetical to the culture created in the respective Panther locker rooms. Both Odessa (the real town, described in the book and shown in the film) and Dillon (a fictional town in which the majority of the series takes place) become staging grounds to explore the successes and failures of a group of people who believe wholeheartedly in the collective power of football. In ways that the film is simply not interested in or capable of exploring, the series presents the deepest, most complex iteration of the tension between conservative and liberal values at work in the locker room, on the field, and in the stands on those Friday nights in West Texas.

As a rallying cry, "clear eyes, full hearts, can't lose" inspires the Dillon Panthers to look within themselves and find the determination and resolve to persevere. Both Romney and Obama took advantage of its inspirational qualities, with Romney in particular positioning himself as Coach Taylor, inspiring his players to give it all they've got. As a challenger who was losing in the polls for most of the campaign, Romney adopted the phrase as a slogan that positioned him as underdog, and he structured much of the public face of his campaign around the saying in the four weeks before the election. Romney's gravitation toward this message and continued use of it despite protest from the show's cast and crew is symptomatic of contemporary American political and cultural discourse. In viewing "clear eyes, full hearts, can't lose" first through the lens of its existence in political rhetoric, we can better appreciate how effectively the series both distills the messages of the book and film into six words and expands upon them over the course of 76 episodes. Then, by looking at the remaking of an apolitical film into a deeply political TV series, we can appreciate how this act of revision foreshadows the problems Romney would have in refashioning the message to suit his own purposes. Ultimately, by reading the series' valorization of Coach Taylor's philosophy and Romney's misappropriation of that philosophy against one another, we can better understand both how the phrase functions as a bridge between film and series, and how it malfunctioned for Romney in the 2012 Presidential campaign.

A. "HEY MITT: YOU SIR, ARE NO COACH TAYLOR"[3]

In October 2012, with a little over a month remaining until the presidential election, Mitt Romney adopted "clear eyes, full hearts, can't lose" as a campaign slogan. At this point in the campaign, Romney had alienated large groups of voters through a series of public gaffes; in the most damaging example, he was secretly taped at a fundraiser describing 47 percent of the American public as "victims, who believe the government has a responsibility to care for them, who believe that they are entitled to health care, to food, to housing, to you-name-it," concluding that his job "is not to worry about those people. I'll never convince them they should take personal responsibility and care for their lives." The video leaked on MotherJones in late September 2012, at which point Romney was trailing badly in the polls.[4]

In the first week of October, Romney began mentioning *Friday Night Lights* in his stump speech:

> We're a people also with clear eyes. We understand the significance of the events around us. . . . And I recall a line in a fictional football team show. It was called 'Friday Night Lights,' you probably didn't see it. . . . They had this fictional football team and every time they'd leave the locker room, and they typically were facing long odds, there was a sign up there, it said 'Clear eyes, full hearts, can't lose.' And I'm convinced the people of Iowa have very clear eyes about what's at stake in this election. And I know you have full hearts. And I'm convinced America can't lose when you help me become the next president of the United States.[5]

In interviews when asked about his adoption of the phrase as his personal campaign slogan, Romney described himself and his wife Ann as "fans" of the series, and in the month before the election, his supporters began chanting it during rallies and waving signs bearing it during his speeches.[6]

On October 8, around the time that the phrase was becoming a visible presence in Romney's campaign, Bissinger published an editorial in *The Daily Beast* titled "Why I'm Voting for Mitt Romney." In the piece, Bissinger, a lifelong Democrat, reported that he had been so thoroughly disenfranchised by Obama's lackluster performance in the first presidential debate that he was driven to support Romney, realizing that Romney "wants to be president. He showed vigor, and enthusiasm, and excitement, a man who wants to lead," as opposed to Obama, who Bissinger described as "burnt out, tired of selling his message," concluding that "I have never seen a performance worse than Obama's."[7] The timing of this piece led to internet speculation that it was somehow connected to Romney's increasingly prominent use of "clear eyes, full hearts, can't lose," despite the fact that the phrase did not originate in Bissinger's book and he had little involvement in the series.[8]

A more relevant connection is in Bissinger's use of the term "performance." The three presidential debates were held on October 3, October 16, and October 22. Romney clearly defeated Obama in the first debate, with a CNN poll showing 67 percent of voters believing Romney won, and only 25 percent favoring Obama—the largest disparity in the history of that poll.[9] Before the first debate, Romney was trailing Obama by at least four to six percentage points in most polls; however, in the two weeks following the first debate, Romney closed the gap and was tied with Obama in most major polls.[10] This was the closest that the two candidates had been during the presidential election season. Those two weeks also marked the rise in prominence of Romney's *Friday Night Lights* campaign.[11]

On October 12, Peter Berg responded. As director of the film *Friday Night Lights* and creator of the series, Berg made his position clear in a letter written to Romney and leaked to *The Hollywood Reporter*:

> I was not thrilled when I saw that you have plagiarized this expression to support your campaign. . . . Your politics and campaign are clearly not aligned with the themes we portrayed in our series. The only relevant comparison that I see between your campaign and "Friday Night Lights" is in the character of Buddy Garrity—who turned his back on American car manufacturers selling cars from Japan. . . . We are grateful for your support of our beloved show. . . . But we are not in any way affiliated with you or your campaign. Please come up with your own campaign slogan.[12]

Playing out like a plotline from the series (Berg is also Bissinger's cousin!), on the same day that the letter appeared in *The Hollywood Reporter*, Bissinger responded: "I love Pete but he is being childish and petulant. He should be flattered that Romney is honoring his show. Obama tried to use the slogan as well but unsurprisingly was ineffective in getting the message across."[13] Here Bissinger refers to Obama's earlier use of the phrase when, in March 2012, he tweeted a photo of himself throwing a football at Soldier Field with the caption "Clear eyes, full hearts."[14]

The distinction between Obama's playful use of the phrase (withholding the "can't lose," presenting himself literally playing the role of a sports hero) contrasts with Romney's repeated attempts to cast himself as a metaphorical Coach Taylor, which continued despite Berg's protest. Romney's rhetorical positioning of the debates and the election as games contrasts with Berg's attempts to contradict Romney-as-Coach-Taylor with direct textual comparisons. Throughout these vitriolic exchanges and during the final weeks of the presidential campaign, the slogan appeared on Romney's Facebook page, emblazoned on a banner image of him standing in the rain with his back to the camera, and campaign photos appeared showing him touching a sign with the phrase written on it as he made his way out the door to a rally. After the phrase became a recurring part of his rallies and social media campaign, Romney sold sets of red, white, and blue bracelets bearing the phrase "Clear Eyes, Full Hearts, America Can't Lose" on his campaign website.[15]

After Berg's letter failed to stop Romney from using the phrase, actress Connie Britton weighed in.[16] Like Berg, Britton is tied to both the film and the TV series, in which she played the relatively silent Sharon Gaines and routinely outspoken Tami Taylor, respectively. On October 28, Britton and Sarah Aubrey, an associate producer on the film and an executive producer on the TV series, wrote an op-ed piece for *USA Today*, in which they asked the question "What would the women of Dillon think about this?"[17] Their fascinating letter repeatedly cites both real-world politics and plots from the series to support their contention that "it is President Obama who has shown his values to be more closely aligned with those represented by the phrase." Like Berg's, Britton and Aubrey's letter uses direct textual comparisons to refute Romney's right to use the phrase: they cite the *Lilly Ledbetter Fair Pay Act* and its potential impact on Tami Taylor's career; Obama's *Affordable Care Act* and its potential benefit for Matt Saracen's grandmother; and Planned Parenthood and its repeated presence in the series, encouraging women to "take 'Clear Eyes, Full Hearts' back and use it as it was always intended—as a motivator for progress, power, and greatness." They conclude the letter by echoing Romney: "Let's use our clear eyes and full hearts to tell every friend, family member and neighbor about what's at stake for women in this election. What's at stake for all of us. If we women make ourselves aware of the issues and make our voices heard, we most certainly cannot lose."

The presence of the *Friday Night Lights* slogan in the news cycle came to an end in the first days of November, as Hurricane Sandy bore down on the country's east coast.[18] For a series that only averaged 6.2 million viewers during its most highly rated season, *Friday Night Lights* is an odd text to become part of the political discourse during the final month of a presidential campaign. The impassioned response from the cast and crew suggests a major disconnect between their perception of the show they created and Romney's vision for America. Romney's appropriation of the phrase for his campaign is demonstrative of his failings as a political candidate, particularly in his repeated failed attempts to connect with middle- and lower-class voters, with women, and with the Latino population.[19] Romney refashioned himself as the clear-eyed underdog, though he recycled the phrase against the wishes of its creators and monetized it in the form of campaign bracelets. Britton and Berg's contention that Obama's values were "more closely aligned with those represented by the phrase" is an interesting one to consider in the face of a series in which the majority of its characters would identify as conservatives, including (arguably) its protagonist, Coach Eric Taylor. Ultimately, then, we must ask the question: would Coach Taylor vote for Mitt Romney?

B. THE POLITICS OF *FRIDAY NIGHT LIGHTS*

Because of Peter Berg's central role in creating both texts and in responding directly to Romney's campaign, the subtle but significant shifts in the treatment of politics from film to series are particularly relevant. The film's increased focus on the gameplay makes it more appropriate campaign fodder than the series, which refused to ignore the problematic aspects both of football culture and of the sort of policies and programs that were part of Romney's Vision for America.[20] As argued in Berg's and Britton's letters, Romney's alignment with "clear eyes, full hearts, can't lose" lies more in its championing of the underdog than in the political perspectives set forth in the TV series. The film has been criticized for focusing on the football field at the expense of the racism, sexism, and classism running rampant in Texas high school football culture; significantly, these were all charges leveled at Romney during the campaign.

In many ways, the remaking of the film *Friday Night Lights* as a TV series is a case study in how to recreate and further develop the tone, atmosphere, and content of a two-hour film across a twenty-two-episode television season. The film chronicles the Permian Panthers' 1988 football season, with the beginning and ending of that season functioning as its boundaries. The first season mirrors the film in both structure and timeframe, chronicling one season, from first game to last, of the Dillon Panthers. The opening scenes of the film and the pilot are nearly identical; although the film states "The following is based on a true story which took place in West Texas in 1988," the opening shots of the rural West Texas sky and fields are otherwise interchangeable. Explosions in the Sky, a post-rock indie band specializing in emotive instrumentals, scored both the film and the series, using the same mixture of bleary, soporific background music and inspiring, goosebump-inducing grandeur. Both film and series open with the voice of Slammin' Sammy Meade on the radio, discussing the upcoming high school football season. In addition to immediately establishing a strong sense of place, the scenes demonstrate the incredible pressure being imposed from without upon the coach and the team.

The scenes that follow clearly demarcate both the privileges and responsibilities that come with being part of West Texas high school football culture. The coach and players are revered, they work hard, and the community rewards them with special privileges—attention from women, free food from local establishments, and a blind eye from the police. Each text focuses on the coach and his family, as well as on six players, with a few additional players given names and occasional speaking parts. Some of the respective players align in interesting ways: Boobie Miles and Jason Street, the star players brought down by tragic injuries in the first game of the season; Mike Winchell and Matt Saracen, unprepared players thrust into starring roles, both of whom have ailing family members and are embarrassed of their home lives; and Don Billingsley and Tim Riggins, both dealing with difficult family situations but clinging to their Texas roots. Each coach has a supporting wife and daughter; each must deal with external pressure from boosters, racial problems that emerge in the locker room, and trials of various kinds put in between the team and the state championship (a goal mentioned in the opening scenes and never far from either of their minds).

As Paul Levinson points out, the clearest difference between the film and the series is one of depth: "The length of the television drama—thirteen to twenty-two hours per season in the case of *Friday Night Lights* in comparison to just a single two-hour showing for the movie—allowed [Berg] to endow the television drama with levels of realistic narrative rarely seen on either the motion picture or television screen."[21] However, the differences are not simply of depth; as a film, *Friday Night Lights* is politically ambivalent. While it presents elements of racism, incredible pressure on the players and coach from the town, problematic relationships between players and their parents, and economic divisions within and without the Permian football team, it largely functions within the genre of a sports film. The film sidesteps many of the cultural and political issues explained in the book and explored in the series, continually choosing to foreground the on-field successes of the Panthers at the cost of engagement with the problematic aspects of Texas high school football culture. Alternately, the increasingly prominent role that class, race, and gender issues play in the TV series is indicative of its desire to move beyond the football field and show Coach Taylor's philosophy helping the characters navigate the complexities of life off the football field and eventually outside of Dillon, a desire that is absent from the film. Kevin Smokler discusses the relationship between the film and the series, identifying especially the focus on class and economics throughout the series as a major point of differentiation.[22] He argues that "its sorrow and beauty come from economic and class desperation, something rarely seen on American television."[23] Scenes at Applebee's, Wal-Mart, and TasteeFreez (a barely disguised Dairy Queen) ground the series in that reality, and the series' increased focus on the characters' off-field lives separates it from the film in a significant way. As a series, *Friday Night Lights* continually reminds viewers that these games on Friday night occur within a specific context of poverty, refusing to let the moments of glory on the field overshadow the problematic aspects of the town in which they take place.

Jeremi Duru argues that the film problematically excises many of the racial elements of Bissinger's book, in favor of focusing on the successes of its players on the field. He compares the film's elimination of most of the racial problems Bissinger identifies in Odessa with its increasingly dramatic rendering of the Panthers' loss in the championship game[24] (in real life they lost in a low-scoring semi-final game), arguing that "While the film's de-racialization of the story may, like its hyperbolic rendering of the team's success, have served to increase the film's appeal, it did so at a tremendous cost. Namely, it buttressed the idyllic picture through projecting a false portrait of the racial dynamics attendant to Permian football in 1988 and lent big-screen credence to the misguided view that sport is a bastion of meritocracy."[25] Although the film does recreate a number of significant moments of race-related conflict, Duru ultimately argues that, in changing some events and eliminating others, the film shows Odessa and Permian in a more favorable light than Bissinger's book.[26]

While the film certainly casts the coach and members of the Permian Panthers in opposition to the town and many of the other participants in Texas football culture, most of its running time is spent reveling in the successes of its characters on the field. Indeed, the satisfaction that characters receive as a result of the Panthers' success makes it hard to read the film as anything other than an endorsement of that football culture. Coach Gaines articulates the symbiotic relationship the football team has with Odessa in a speech at the beginning of their season: "It's a good day to think about responsibility . . . the responsibility that you have to protect this team, and this school, and this town. And make no mistake about it gentlemen, we are in the business of protecting this town. We are in the business of winning. Expectations couldn't be any higher. We will win state."

In his book *Loose Ends: Closure and Crisis in the American Social Text*, Russell Reising analyzes the ends of various texts, demonstrating how the closure (or lack thereof) provided for characters within a text forces us to reconsider the events of the narrative. He uses Disney's *Dumbo* as an example of a film which seems to reach a positive ending despite Dumbo's inability to escape from the confines of the circus.[27] Reising concludes that "the locus of evil is, therefore, not merely unchastened and unvanquished, but consolidated and further empowered—its dominant ideology is reinforced and reconstituted; its disciplinary and economic apparatus strengthened—by the very subject that had suffered most under its tyrannical operations."[28] The film version of *Friday Night Lights* operates similarly. Throughout, we see the particular problems of Odessa, Texas, and the larger problems of Texas high school football culture. However, despite the serious concerns that the film and Coach Gaines appear to have with that culture, neither does very much to suggest a way out of it. Coach Gaines is very much a figure within a system; we come to admire his stoicism, his reserve, and his quietude, but he functions as part of the system of Texas football culture. When Billingsley's father is harassing and abusing him on the football field—at one point, Billingsley is repeatedly punched in the head by his father—Gaines keeps his distance and allows the abuse to continue. Similarly, when the head booster's wife advises Gaines to play his star player on both offense and defense, concluding "That big nigger ain't gonna break," he says nothing. While we are meant to look on in horror at the scene, Gaines remains within that system and teaches his players how to function within it.

The closing moments of the film valorize high school Texas football culture and reinscribe Gaines within it. In his halftime speech during the state championship game, Gaines encourages his players to "be perfect," asking them: "Can you live in that moment, as best you can with clear eyes and love in your heart? With joy in your heart? If you can do that, gentlemen, then you're perfect." Here we see the seeds of Coach Taylor's motivational phrase; significantly, although the Panthers fail to win the state championship in the season shown in the film, the epilogue informs us that they go on to win the state championship the following year. The final scenes show the focal players tossing the football around, telling each other to "be perfect" and reminiscing about their high school football careers. By presenting the conclusion in the most positive possible light—the epilogue informs us that Permian won the following year, that Billingsley remained close with his father, that Boobie went on to play football in junior college—the film endorses the culture in a way that the series would repeatedly resist.

In contrast to the film, then, the series repeatedly pokes holes in the idyllic portrait of life in Dillon that one would see simply by watching high school football games. The increased voice of women is a major point of differentiation between the film and the series. One major method by which the series' coach and players break free from the Texas high school football culture is through their interaction with the women in their lives. Unlike the series, the film has little to say about the women associated with the Panthers; simply put, the film does not make space for the women of Odessa. There is no Lyla Garrity, through whom the series explores teen Christianity, religious hypocrisy, and the challenges of dating a member of the football team; Coach Gaines's daughter only has one line in the film, in contrast to Julie Taylor's complicated relationship with her parents and the culture in which she is raised; and, while the epilogue text of the film gives us a sense of where Coach Gaines and the six players go beyond the 1988 season, there are no words devoted to the women we meet in the film. Maria, the girl who deflowers Mike Winchell and in the next scene is on Don Billingsley's couch, receives none of the interiority of Tyra Collette, who begins the series as a similarly stock character but who eventually, with the help of the Taylor family, gains control of her future and escapes Dillon.

The character whose absence from the film is most noticeable is the coach's wife. Although Connie Britton portrays both Sharon Gaines and Tami Taylor, the characters could not be further apart from each other. Sharon Gaines is literally silent for the vast majority of the film; her first line in the film is "God bless us," and she is simply repeating her husband. In a later scene, he comes home after a difficult loss, and she is sitting on the steps; they do not speak. When they attend dinner with the boosters, she makes no real contribution to the discussion and demonstrates no concern at anything she hears. Her next appearance is when he is leaving town for a coin-flip which will determine whether or not the Panthers will go to the playoffs; she stands on the other side of the fence, kisses the coach through it, and is left behind. As they are preparing for the state championship, their daughter asks them if they will move; simultaneously he answers "it's possible" and she answers "no." Finally, the only scene of dialogue she has consists of her, on the night before Coach Gaines leaves for the state championship, lightening the mood by suggesting that they should move to Alaska and build an igloo.[29]

Sarah Marian Seltzer discusses the various ways in which the series repeatedly tackles complex gender issues with sensitivity and thoughtfulness.[30] Seltzer argues that "Tami's status as feminist icon for viewers (New York's NARAL chapter made 'don't mess with Tami' T-shirts) doesn't come from an explicitly political or ideological stance she took. . . . Instead, Tami's status comes from her own earned understanding that, to help women, you cannot parrot degrading patriarchal language or assumptions."[31] In the same way that Coach Taylor molds the young men of Dillon, Tami Taylor molds its young women, providing thoughtful, grounded advice on premarital sex and teen pregnancy, while, in her role as guidance counselor, helping them navigate their way out of Dillon into college. Furthermore, Tami's relationship with Eric— messy, fraught, but grounded in deep love and respect—is drastically different from the Gaines's marriage as portrayed in the film. We see throughout the series the many ways that Coach Taylor's perspective is changed by Tami's influence, first in their home life and eventually when she begins working at Dillon High School as a guidance counselor.

Particularly in the beginning of the series, Coach Taylor is willing to participate in the apparatus of Texas high school football culture, although he resists in ways that Coach Gaines never does and suffers the consequences of that resistance. For example, he reluctantly joins the line of coaches waiting to court displaced Katrina victim Ray "Voodoo" Tatum; however, he immediately regrets his participation and Tatum leaves after Taylor stops playing him after one game. Furthermore, when Tatum returns in the season finale as the quarterback of the opposing team, we see the typical antagonistic relationship between Coach Taylor's and the other football teams in the state.[32] Unlike the film, which presents Gaines as someone dedicated to that system and culture and his team as a part of it, the series presents Coach Taylor and his team as anomalies occupying a liminal position.

In fact, Coach Taylor's position is so tenuous in Dillon that, despite winning the championship in his first season there, he takes the first opportunity to leave for a job as a quarterback coach at Texas Methodist University. Although he soon returns to be with his family and make two additional unsuccessful bids to win the state championship with the Dillon Panthers, he is eventually ousted and relocated in poverty-stricken, racially diverse East Dillon, where he coaches the East Dillon Lions and, in the final episode of the series, wins a state championship with them. Unlike the film, which goes further toward endorsing the system (even the most villainous character, Billingsley's abusive, alcoholic father, receives a moment of grace), the series rejects it, instead, particularly in its later seasons, showing that the real victories in life occur off the field. While Coach Taylor achieves success within that system, first at Dillon and then eventually at East Dillon, the series carefully demonstrates that while football may be an important part of the lives of these characters, it cannot be the only part of their lives.

It is interesting to consider whether coaches Gaines (as portrayed in the *Friday Night Lights* film) and Taylor would vote for Mitt Romney. The political affiliation of Gaines is impossible to discern from the film, as politics is not what Berg is interested in exploring there. Instead, he explores the passion and the glory of a team playing with complete focus and intensity. That focus carries them through the championship game, which, although they lose in a close contest against a heavily favored opponent, demonstrates their indomitable spirit. Alternately, Coach Taylor's experience over the five seasons demonstrates his increasing awareness of life beyond the football field. Britton and Aubrey's letter reminds us of the many significant political differences between Romney's and the series' philosophies and, particularly given Coach Taylor's actions in the series finale, makes it hard to imagine him casting a vote for Romney. The final episode finds Coach Taylor poised to sign a contract to coach a reunited Panthers team, with East Dillon and Dillon reuniting to form one "super team," reinscribing him within the high school football system and providing a superficially happy ending. Meanwhile, Tami has received a dream job offer at Braemore College in Philadelphia, which would force them to move far from West Texas, where they have grown relatively comfortable, despite its many problems. She tells him: "It's my turn, babe. I have loved you, and you have loved me. And we have compromised. Both of us . . . for *your* job. Now it's time to talk about doing that for my job. Because otherwise, what am I gonna tell my daughter?" Eric eventually responds, "It's your turn. I want to move to Philadelphia. Will you take me to Philadelphia?" His embrace of his wife's request is indicative of the series' treatment of gender and its ultimate rejection of Texas high school football culture, as it repeatedly demonstrates that Coach Taylor, his players, and his teams succeed despite that culture, ultimately abandoning it in favor of something new. While the series repeatedly skirts labels of liberal and conservative, it is hard to imagine the Coach Taylor of the final seasons of *Friday Night Lights* embracing Romney's Vision for America.

C. *FRIDAY NIGHT LIGHTS* FOREVER

Victoria E. Johnson uses *Friday Night Lights* as a case study in how networks adhere to problematic paradigms of geographic interest when advertising new series.[33] She argues that "it apparently seemed inconceivable that a rural, Texan, working-class setting, focusing on teen and family life through the lens of football, could be quality TV characterized by sophistication and realness."[34] Johnson ties these geographical myths—a passion for football and hunting, low-culture taste (Wal-Mart and Applebee's, both of which regularly appear on *Friday Night Lights*), and conservativism—specifically to politics, arguing that "broadly shared mythologies of a rural U.S. heartland . . . linked, in the industrial, critical, and broader popular imagination, football to red-state myths that were intuitively contrary to historic understandings of quality television, high cultural pursuits, and their accompanying urban, coastal, major-market, niche viewing audiences with a presumptively more liberal skew."[35]

Johnson's discussion of the dissonance between the perceived and the actual audience for *Friday Night Lights* is interesting to consider in light of this discussion of the politics of the series and the use of its inspirational phrase in the real-world presidential campaign. With a potentially conservative main character teaching boys how to be men deep in the heart of Texas, *Friday Night Lights* must have appeared to be the perfect text for Romney to use in his situation. He was trailing in the polls, his "players" desperately in need of motivation, and these six words encapsulated all that, providing an easily quotable message with compelling visual elements and the potential to convert that enthusiasm into both dollars (through souvenir bracelets) and votes.

In his letter to Mitt Romney, Peter Berg compares him to the character Buddy Garrity. Throughout the early seasons of the series, Garrity represents the worst parts of Dillon and Texas high school football culture. As the head booster, he repeatedly threatens Coach Taylor's job and causes him on- and off-field problems; as a used car salesman, he shills cars on the local TV station and puts his signs up at Panthers games; as a former football star, he brandishes his state championship ring like a weapon; and as a self-proclaimed family man, he cheats on his wife repeatedly and squanders his daughter's college fund on foolish investments. In

"Ch-ch-ch-ch-Changes" (1.19), we see an ad for Garrity's used car business playing in the background of a scene. In it, Garrity tells the audience: "We pride ourselves on three pillars of prosperity: honesty, loyalty, trust." He goes on to offer a discount at Applebee's and two Panthers playoff tickets as a contest prize, before concluding, "Just remember—deep in the heart of Texas, deep in my heart, I'm your buddy!"

What makes *Friday Night Lights* a politically significant show, and where it differentiates itself from the film, is in its complex relationship with both conservative and liberal perspectives and its refusal to marginalize either side. As malicious and wrongheaded as Garrity can be, for example, the show asks us to sympathize with him repeatedly, although this primarily occurs after he eventually joins Coach Taylor in East Dillon. In his essay "Come Home: West Texas Identities," Jacob Clifton considers the complicated politics of Dillon, Texas. Clifton, a native of West Texas, explains the "strange mix of conservatism and liberalism" that exists in West Texas, concluding that the show succeeds at showing "the sometimes ugly, behind-the-scenes parts of conservatism: gender biases, issues of race and religion, the profit motive, the usual demons of the Right" alongside "the positive aspects of that same order of philosophy—team play, leadership, military service, patriotism, even religious work—in a way that doesn't ping liberal sensibilities."[36] In arguing that Romney is closer in character to Garrity than Coach Taylor, Berg makes his own real-world political viewpoint known and makes clear where he imagines someone like Romney fitting in the world of Dillon. Similarly, Aubrey and Britton use specific textual evidence to refute Romney's right to present himself as a real-world Coach Taylor. While the series never overtly declares its liberality, in its rejection of Texas high school football culture and eventual removal of the Taylors and nearly all its major characters from Dillon, it presents a way out that is absent from the film. On November 6, 2012, Romney was presented with his own way out; despite his clear eyes and full heart, Romney lost.

FILMS AND TV SHOWS

Friday Night Lights. Directed by Peter Berg. 2004. Universal Pictures.
Friday Night Lights. NBC, 2006–11.

NOTES

1. H.G. Bissinger, *Friday Night Lights: A Town, A Team, And A Dream* (Cambridge, MA: Da Capo, 1990).
2. Academic Coach Taylor, February 12, 2012, http://academiccoachtaylor.tumblr.com/image/17490782532 and http://academiccoachtaylor.tumblr.com/image/44783090327.

3. Academic Coach Taylor responded to Romney's use of the "Clear Eyes, Full Hearts" phrase with memes showing Coach Taylor saying "Hey Mitt: You Sir, Are No Coach Taylor," and "Some Women Fill a Whole Binder," a response showing Tami Taylor and referring to Romney's debate blunder in which he said he had "a whole binder full of women," in response to a question about his attempts to find women to serve on his cabinet. October 11, 2012, http://academiccoachtaylor.tumblr.com/image/33401112125 and October 12, 2012, http://academiccoachtaylor.tumblr.com/image/33801486483.

4. David Corn, "Secret Video: Romney Tells Millionaire Donors What He Really Thinks of Obama Voters," *MotherJones.com*, September 12, 2012, http://www.motherjones.com/politics/2012/09/secret-video-romney-private-fundraiser.

5. James Hohmann, "Mitt plays off 'Friday Night Lights' in Iowa," *Politico*, October 29, 2012, http://www.politico.com/blogs/click/2012/10/mitt-plays-off-friday-night-lights-in-iowa-147638.html.

6. Rachel Streitfeld, "Romney's Softer Side in Florida," *CNN.com*, October 5, 2012, http://politicalticker.blogs.cnn.com/2012/10/05/romneys-softer-side-in-florida/.

7. Buzz Bissinger, "Why I'm Voting for Mitt Romney," *Daily Beast*, October 8, 2012, http://www.thedailybeast.com/articles/2012/10/08/buzz-bissinger-why-i-m-voting-for-mitt-romney.html.

8. Buzz Bissinger, "On Being Savaged by the Liberal Media after Backing Mitt Romney," *Daily Beast*, October 11, 2012, http://www.thedailybeast.com/articles/2012/10/11/buzz-bissinger-on-being-savaged-by-the-liberal-media-after-backing-mitt-romney.html.

9. Tom Cohen, "Romney Takes Debate to Obama," *CNN.com*, October 4, 2012, http://www.cnn.com/2012/10/03/politics/debate-main.

10. Jeffrey M. Jones, "Romney Narrows Vote Gap After Historic Debate Win," *Gallup*, October 8, 2012, http://www.gallup.com/poll/157907/romney-narrows-vote-gap-historic-debate-win.aspx.

11. The attempt to refashion debate season in the context of an athletic performance is symptomatic of contemporary political discourse, as news correspondents and pundits regularly use the tools and techniques of sportswriters to analyze speeches and debates, and opinion trackers at the bottom of the screen give second-by-second analysis of who is "winning" each debate.

12. Matthew Belloni, "'Friday Night Lights' Creator Accuses Mitt Romney of Plagiarism in Threatening Letter," *Hollywood Reporter*, October 12, 2012, http://www.hollywoodreporter.com/thr-esq/friday-night-lights-creator-accuses-378606.

13. Bissinger concluded that "I am frankly sick and tired of Berg and everyone else acting as if he was the creator of *Friday Night Lights*. Without the book there never would have been a television show. He should feel lucky that anyone cares about it." Matthew Belloni, "'Friday Night Lights' Author Slams Peter Berg's Letter to Mitt Romney: 'Uninformed and Offensive'," *Hollywood Reporter*, October 12, 2012, http://www.hollywoodreporter.com/thr-esq/friday-night-lights-bissinger-romney-berg-378729.

14. @BarackObama, Twitter, May 21, 2012, https://twitter.com/BarackObama/status/204655373905432578.

15. Kia Makarechi, "Clear Eyes, Full Hearts, Can't Lose: *Friday Night Lights* Star, Producer Decry Romney's Use Of Slogan," *Huffington Post*, October 28, 2012, http://www.huffingtonpost.com/2012/10/28/clear-eyes-full-hearts-cant-lose-friday-night-lights-romney_n_2036282.html.

16. In a hilarious interview with MTV News, Kyle Chandler sidesteps the controversy altogether. When asked about it, he responded: "I saw that. Pete sent me a letter, saying, 'What the hell is this? They're stealing my line.' There were a few letters written." Kevin P. Sullivan. "'Friday Night Lights' Movie? Kyle Chandler Weighs In," *MTV*, December 5, 2012, http://www.mtv.com/news/articles/1698404/kyle-chandler-friday-night-lightsmovie.jhtml.

17. Connie Britton and Sarah Aubrey, "Romney Wrong to Use 'Clear Eyes, Full Hearts'," *USAToday.com*, October 28, 2012, http://www.usatoday.com/story/opinion/2012/10/28/women-birth-control-friday-night-lights/1663895/.

18. The Romney campaign, however, continued to sell its bracelets and continued its use of the phrase in those final days: "You with full hearts and clear eyes can see what's happening across the country right now . . . And on the eastern coast of our nation a lot of people are enduring some very difficult times." Emily Friedman, "Romney Scrubs Campaign Schedule, Calls on Americans to Unite As Sandy Bears Down," *ABCnews.com*, October 29, 2012, http://abcnews.go.com/blogs/politics/2012/10/romney-scrubs-campaign-schedule-calls-on-americans-to-unite-as-sandy-bears-down/.

19. Alan Silverleib, "Analysis: Obama's new Democratic majority," *CNN.com*, November 7, 2012, http://www.cnn.com/2012/11/07/politics/exit-polls-analysis.

20. Mitt Romney, "Op-Ed: Mitt Romney Shares his Vision for America," *ABCnews.com*, November 5, 2012, http://abcnews.go.com/ABC_Univision/Politics/mitt-romney-op-ed-vision-america/story?id=17642336.

21. Paul Levinson, "Friday Night Lights, NBC, and DirecTV: How an Unlikely Partnership Saved a Great Show and Pointed the Way to the Future," in *A Friday Night Lights Companion : Love, Loss, and Football in Dillon, Texas*, ed. Leah Wilson (Dallas, TX: BenBella, 2011), 175–195; quotation at 176–177.

22. Kevin Smokler, "Class Not Dismissed: The Role of Economics and Money in the Story of Friday Night Lights," in *A Friday Night Lights Companion: Love, Loss, and Football in Dillon, Texas*, ed. Leah Wilson (Dallas, TX: BenBella, 2011), 27–41.

23. Ibid., 38.

24. Jeremi N. Duru, "Friday Night 'Lite': How De-Racializiation in the Motion Picture Friday Night Lights Disserves the Movement to Eradicate Racial Discrimination from American Sport," *Cardozo Arts & Entertainment Law Journal* 25, no. 2 (2007): 485–530.

25. Ibid., 489–490.

26. This is a major shift from Bissinger's book. The negative reaction in Odessa and much of West Texas to Bissinger's book caused him to cancel that leg of his book tour, as a result of multiple death threats. Despite the incredible acclaim that he received for the book, Bissinger did not return to Odessa for nearly twenty years. Jerome Solomon, "Bissinger can't escape the Friday Night Lights," *Chron.com*, February 12, 2011, http://www.chron.com/sports/solomon/article/Solomon-Bissinger-can-t-escape-the-Friday-Night-1597595.php.

27. The chapter "'The Easiest Room in Hell': The Political Work of *Dumbo*," argues that, in addition to being problematic as a children's film for a number of overt reasons (particularly its racism), *Dumbo* resists closure by denying Dumbo and his mother exit from a system characterized by "violence, exploitation, and humiliation," reinscribing them within that system in the final minutes. (Russell Reising, *Loose Ends: Closure and Crisis in the American Social Text* (Durham: Duke UP, 1996), 281). Throughout the film, Dumbo and his mother are punished and derided for Dumbo's large ears and their ability to allow him to fly. Although the circus is "portrayed throughout the film as an arena of pain, humiliation, thwarted desire, hierarchical elitism, incompetence, exploitation, and greed," it "emerges triumphant in the film's conclusion, and is significantly strengthened by Dumbo's ability to fly, which translates directly into his viability and profitability as an act." Ibid., 283.

28. Ibid., 283. Reising contrasts this ending with the endings of every other Disney film, in which the loci of evil are overcome, vanquished, or killed. Near the end of the film, Dumbo takes to the sky and attacks his enemies by shooting them with circus peanuts; however, rather than leading to his removal from the circus, it leads to "Dumbo and his mother reunited and enjoying what appear to be the plush amenities of a streamlined circus train car—their easiest room in this modernized and secular hell." By presenting this as a happy ending—Dumbo's ability to fly is now sung about by the other elephants, and they move to a nicer circus car—the film ignores the fact

that "the circus in *Dumbo* is an inescapable and hellish environment characterized by greed, profit, dehumanization, and exploitation." 282–83.

29. Connie Britton discusses the difficulty she had in trying to decide whether she should take on the role of Tami Taylor, following the frustrating experience of portraying Sharon Gaines in the film: "When Pete got in touch with me and said, 'We're going to make a *Friday Night Lights* TV show. Why don't you come play that part?' I was like, 'No way!' The only thing worse than playing a nothing part in a movie is [playing it] for years and years on TV." Robert Mays, "Clear Eyes, Full Hearts, Couldn't Lose: An oral history of *Friday Night Lights*," Grantland.com, July 13, 2011, http://www.grantland.com/story/_/id/6766070/clear-eyes-full-hearts-lose.

30. Sarah Marian Seltzer, "It's Different for Girls," in *A Friday Night Lights Companion: Love, Loss, and Football in Dillon, Texas,* ed. Leah Wilson (Dallas, TX: BenBella, 2011), 195–220.

31. Ibid., 196.

32. For the most part, the film presents other teams in a more favorable light than the series does. In the film's state championship game, for example, we repeatedly crosscut between the locker rooms of the Permian Panthers and their opponents, where the coach is pushing a message similar to what Coach Gaines is pushing and where the players possess the same sort of urgency and drive to succeed.

33. Victoria E. Johnson, "The Persistence of Geographic Myth in a Convergent Media Era," *Journal of Popular Film & Television* 38, no. 2 (2010): 58–65.

34. Ibid., 62.

35. Ibid., 61.

36. Jacob Clifton, "Come Home: West Texas Identities," in *A Friday Night Lights Companion: Love, Loss, and Football in Dillon, Texas,* ed. Leah Wilson (Dallas, TX: BenBella, 2011), 241–255; quotation at 249.

EIGHT

"These Aren't Your Mother's Angels"

Feminism, Jiggle Television, and Charlie's Angels

Cristina Lucia Stasia

On September 22, 1976, ABC's *Charlie's Angels* (1976–81) set a first-season premiere record when it debuted in the number five spot on the Nielsen ratings. By the end of the first season, *Charlie's Angels* had 59 percent of viewers in its time slot and was the first television show to demand more than $100,000 per minute for advertising.[1] On September 22, 2011, the 35th anniversary of the record-setting premiere, the ABC reboot[2] of *Charlie's Angels* debuted—and was cancelled after only four episodes.[3] Despite a heavy marketing campaign and name recognition, its premiere garnered only 8.76 million viewers, leaving it third in its timeslot; it lost 1.5 million viewers the following episode and by week three, only 5.9 million viewers were tuning in. While the premiere scored a 2.1 rating in the 18-to-49-year-old demographic coveted by advertisers, by the third episode it had dropped to 1.3. The reviews of the premiere certainly did nothing to increase viewership—*Chicago Sun Times'* Lori Racki wrote: "Charlie's Angels is proof that angels exist in hell, because that's where it felt like I was during most of this hour-long drivel."[4] *TV Guide's* Matt Roush agreed: "It's not just a lazy idea, it's atrociously executed, pathetically acted and cynically conceived."[5] While the original series was a cultural sensation, inspiring a new term for shows that objectified women ("jiggle TV"[6]) and drawing criticism from feminists for objectifying women, the reboot failed to capture either popular or critical attention.

Farah Fawcett, who played original Angel Jill Munroe, joked about the success of the original series: "When the show was number three, I figured it was our acting. When it got to be number one, I decided it could only be because none of us wears a bra."[7] Fawcett's comment is particularly interesting in light of the failure of the reboot. Despite the reboot's increased focus on the sex appeal of the stars, both in the promotion of the series and in the series itself, the reboot still failed to find an audience. By analyzing each series within its respective cultural moment, I argue that the reboot failed not because it repeated the gender politics of the original series but, rather, because it rejected them. The reviews of both the original series and the rebooted series index not only the very different cultural climates in which each series was received, but also each series' different relationship with feminism. While the critical reception of the original *Charlie's Angels* largely repudiates the series for objectifying women and having the Angels work for an unseen patriarch, the critical reception of the new series instead critiques the scripts and acting. There are no reviews of the rebooted series that mention feminism, objectification, or sexism. While the original series was received by a population enlightened, if not radicalized, by second-wave feminism, the reboot debuted to a population anesthetized by postfeminism.

Action television reduces subtle and burgeoning cultural tensions into their most concentrated form; this is why action television originated in, and continues to peak during, times of gender and racial upheaval. The original series debuted during Women's Liberation and was inflected by second-wave feminism. The reboot failed because the show's producers, like Fawcett, attributed the success of the original series to the "jiggle," obfuscating the ways that the original series not only offered a feminist critique of male power, but also introduced an active femininity that was a sharp contrast to previous television femininities. The original series was both a product of, and response to, the gains in women's rights during second-wave feminism. In 1963, Betty Friedan's *The Feminine Mystique* sparked a national dialogue about sexism and women's limited opportunities. The Women's Liberation movement raised the consciousness of hundreds of thousands of women, and not a few men, through multiple means—including dramatic protests, most notably the 1968 Miss America protest and the formation of feminist advocacy groups including the National Organization for Women (1966) and the National Abortion Rights Action League (1969). Second-wavers were also successful at passing equal rights legislation including the *Equal Pay Act* (1963), *Title VII* and the *Civil Rights Act* (1964), *Title IX* (1972), and *Roe v. Wade* (1973). In 1972, the first issue of *Ms. Magazine* featured Wonder Woman on the cover and "claimed 500,000 subscribers and an estimated readership of 3 million,"[8] underlining the popularity of feminism. It was in this tumultuous time of successful challenges to traditional gender roles and conventional femininity that the original *Charlie's Angels* debuted. The series featured three female police officers offered a more exciting career path— the opportunity to be private investigators known as "Angels"—by a never-seen billionaire named Charlie. The first season featured Kate Jackson (Sabrina), from the television program *The Rookies* (1972–76), and two newcomers, Farrah Fawcett (Jill) and Jaclyn Smith (Kelly).[9] A *TV Guide* survey showed *Charlie's Angels* was one of the top five programs preferred by both teenagers and women under 50[10] and producers carefully selected the time slot of 9 p.m. because that is when "women become the dominant force in program selection and the largest segment of the audience—60 percent."[11] Newly sensitive to sexist portrayals in popular culture, critics were quick to critique the Angels' objectification and sexualization. *Time* magazine's cover story on the series summarized the infamous "Angels in Chains"[12] episode (1.04) and asked: "What is this? A report on the latest skin flick? A case study on the fantasy life of a troubled adolescent? Nope. Just a plot summary of an episode from the hottest new television show of the season. Television? That's right, television."[13] The article clearly connects the show to second-wave feminism: "Once the feminists started gaining attention, how could a producer fail to concoct something like *Charlie's Angels*?" *Time* reached out to feminist journalist Judith Coburn for her take on *Charlie's Angels* and she responded: "*Charlie's Angels* is one of the most misogynist shows the networks have produced recently. Supposedly about 'strong' women, it perpetuates the myth most damaging to women's struggle to gain professional equality: that women always use sex to get what they want, even on the job." She called the program "a version of the pimp and his girls. Charlie dispatches his streetwise girls to use their sexual wiles on the world while he reaps the profits."[14] Despite this negative reception, it is positive that critics were taking feminism seriously and engaging in feminist analysis; even a harsh feminist critique of a television program is a feminist act, and draws attention to the gender politics of the program. The lack of critique regarding the sexism, objectification, and gender politics of the reboot indexes not only the postfeminist moment but the way the reboot was complicit with it.

Postfeminism dismisses the second-wave critique of institutionalized sexism in favor of a "lifestyle, attitudinal feminism."[15] Postfeminism can be traced to the early 1990s, when the "daughters" of second-wave feminism began rejecting the feminism they grew up with in favor of neoliberal individualism. In her 1994 *New York Times* notable book and national bestseller, *Fire with Fire: The New Female Power and How to Use It*, Naomi Wolf declared: "in the First World, and certainly in the United States, political equality—indeed, political primacy—is within women's grasp, if they choose to seize it."[16] Shifting the cause of women's oppression from structural inequality to a personal problem, Wolf, along with Katie Roiphe, Christina Hoff Sommers, and the emerging men's movement, attributes inequality to failure to "choose" equality. Postfeminism was more easily reconcilable with not only neo-liberal individualism but capitalism. Sarah Projansky advocates thinking about postfeminism discursively, as a *"cultural response to feminism,* one that seeks to rework—to *steal* rather than to supersede—feminism."[17] Postfeminism was mainstreamed and marketed via Girl Power, which maintained that all a girl or woman had to do to achieve equality was exercise her Girl Power—which presumed that all girls were born equal and with access to the same tools. Girl Power was iconicized by the Spice Girls and the increase in the number of, and popularity of, female action heroes. In film, the *Lara Croft: Tomb Raider* (2001; 2003), *Charlie's Angels* (2000; 2003), and *Resident Evil* (2002; 2004; 2007; 2010; 2012) franchises, *Mr. and Mrs. Smith* (2005), *Colombiana* (2011) and *Haywire* (2011) (among others) featured white (or, in *Colombiana,* whitened), heterosexual, conventionally feminine, sexualized female heroes who navigated worlds free of sexism, racism, or classism, refracting the postfeminist tenet that in an equal world all a girl had to do to save the day was look hot and stare fiercely (which the reboot Angels did exceptionally well).

Unlike the reviews of the original series, which drew attention to, if not outright lambasted, objectification and sexism, the reviews of the reboot ignored the objectification and sexism completely. Further, reflecting on why *Charlie's Angels* failed to find an audience and was cancelled, television critics cited not only the "atrocious writing"[18] and "truly and genuinely terrible acting,"[19] but also identified that, unlike in 1976, the Angels were no longer a novel concept. *Variety's* Brian Lowry noted that today, "women aren't hurting for butt-kicking surrogates who don't take marching orders from masculine voices"[20] and Michael Landweber at *PopMatters* agreed: "It has been a long time since anyone is surprised to see pretty girls kick ass on TV, after *Alias, Dark Angel,* and *Buffy, the Vampire Slayer."*[21] If the reboot were to be successful, it had to acknowledge the changes in televisual active femininity since 1976 and/or the changes in women's lived femininity. It did neither. Instead, it tried to secure a female audience while denying their lived reality.

Despite accusations that the original series was nothing more than "jiggle TV," it directly engaged with both feminism and women's lived realities in the 1970s. This is confirmed by the fact that viewership for the original *Charlie's Angels* was 68 percent female.[22] The original *Charlie's Angels* was such an immediate cultural sensation that just two months after the series' debut, the Angels appeared on the cover of *Time* magazine with the headline "TV's Superwomen."[23] Jeffrey Brown argues, "for many viewers it was difficult to believe these women were truly liberated when their images were so massively circulated as bikini-class pinups."[24] But Brown is perpetuating one of the dominant myths about the original series: that it was pure objectification. The Angels were not circulated as "bikini-class pinups." The promotion of the original *Charlie's Angels* was, contrary to the way it has been mythologized by both popular and academic critics,[25] fairly unproblematic. The first licensed poster[26] featured the Angels in 1970s working women's clothing: Jill in a white suit with a plaid blouse underneath, Sabrina in a striped shirt with a vest, and Kelly in a casual sweater. In the first season, Smith was the only Angel to wear a bikini. Jackson was never seen in a bathing suit and Fawcett never in a two-piece.[27] As the show's popularity soared, the number of promotional products increased dramatically, but the images on the puzzles, tumblers, t-shirts, kids' luggage, and other products almost without exception featured the Angels in the functional, practical clothing they wore most often in the series.

While the promotion of the original series did not rely on, nor exploit, the sexuality of the stars, the promotion of the reboot offered nothing else. The reboot Angels included "sexiest woman alive"[28] Minka Kelly (Eve French), Rachel Taylor (Abby Sampson), and Annie Ilonzeh (Kate Prince). There was a fourth angel, Nadine Velazquez (Gloria), but she was killed minutes into the pilot and not featured in any of the promotional materials. The main promotional image for the reboot featured the three Angels in short, clingy, white cocktail dresses and nude stilettos. Instead of posing with their guns, the Angels were pictured laughing as they strutted down a sunny street. The pilot was sponsored by Covergirl cosmetics.[29]

While the Covergirl sponsorship suggests producers were targeting a female audience, other promotion shows they were also targeting a male audience. To promote the series, Angels Kelly and Ilonzeh posed seductively on the carpet of the sexist Spike TV's *Guys' Choice Awards* and presented an award together. Another popular promo was "leaked" photos of Kelly and Taylor kissing on set, supposedly part of an upcoming episode. These photos were "leaked" after the disappointing numbers for the third episode. The story that garnered the most attention for the new series, however, was about a crew member sexually harassing Kelly. The crew member slapped her butt while holding a hundred dollar bill. Kelly responded with: "Don't you ever disrespect me or another woman again." The next day, when he tried to apologize, she slapped him and he was fired.[30] The incident happened on August 23, but the story broke September 21: the eve of the premiere of the reboot. The positioning of Kelly as a real-life Angel, defending not only herself but also other women (". . . or another woman!"), was clearly timed to boost the show's profile.[31] Unlike the original series, which clearly targeted a female audience and trusted women to both identify with and support the series, the reboot's marketing indicates that producers were not clear on whom they expected or wanted their audience to be. This is one reason that the reboot failed: it wanted women to see the Angels as heroes yet also pandered to straight men, sexualizing the Angels.

While the original series and the reboot had very different promotional strategies, they shared similar opening sequences, inflected by the feminisms of their cultural moments. The original series began with a voice-over by Charlie explaining the show's premise. The viewer was told that there were "three little girls who went to the police academy," and that they were undervalued and underused. Charlie intones that the Angels were assigned to "very hazardous duties." The credits showed the Angels performing their assigned "very hazardous duties," including writing tickets, connecting phone calls, and directing traffic. The ironic comment about their "hazardous duties" is particularly important as it both directly addresses the way qualified women were discriminated against in the workplace and recognizes that the viewer is aware of sexism in the workplace—an awareness facilitated by second-wave feminism. Charlie ends his voiceover with "But I took them away from all that and now they work for me. It's Charlie, Angels. Time to go to work." The opening sequence is most often critiqued as the Angels swapping working in patriarchy to working for a patriarch.[32] Jeffrey Brown argues, "The fairy-tale-like opening of *Charlie's Angels* ('Once upon a time there were three little girls') may seem comical in retrospect but it is a reminder that these women, like many of the heroines they preceded, are rescued, trained and now work for men."[33] But, as Whitney Womack also notes, the visuals contest such a straightforward reading.[34] If we read this opening in its cultural moment, we see a refraction of second-wave critiques of workplace discrimination. Because the opening credits highlight the sexism that women experienced in their workplace, and the limited avenues for promotion or adventure, Charlie's offer to be an "Angel" is a chance for three highly skilled female police officers to perform the duties that male officers are allowed to perform: shooting, car chasing, interrogating, and saving the day.

The rebooted Angels are all also in male-dominated fields: military, police, and burglary. Charlie's voiceover is "Once upon a time there were three young women who got into very big trouble. Now they work for me. My name is Charlie." However, Charlie does not offer the women a chance to be Angels because he recognizes the glass ceiling and wants to offer them a way out. The Angels in the reboot are rescued from "very big trouble": they are criminals. Latina soldier Gloria is court-martialed, African-American Kate is a dirty police officer who gets caught, and WASP Abby is a "Park Avenue Princess" who is also a cat burglar. Latina Eve,[35] who replaces Gloria, is a car thief. These are not active women oppressed by a sexist system; these are women who prove women cannot hack it in male-dominated occupations. Charlie is not offering them a reprieve but, instead, rescuing them after they fail to succeed in these male fields. The positioning of Charlie as an invisible, omnipotent, benevolent patriarch is consistent with the original series, but now he is also a *forgiving* father, offering them redemption via a "second chance": a chance to prove themselves as worthy and capable as men. The message of the original series was clear: "even if you have excellent training and job skills, you still won't be given the opportunity to advance to senior management positions . . . this representation of the 'glass ceiling' struck a chord with women in the late 1970s." [36] The message of the new series is equally clear: even if you have excellent training and job skills, you will fail at your job—not because of sexism or racism, but because you are a woman.

Although Womack claims "[i]t is fair to say that [the original] *Charlie's Angels* did not set out to raise America's feminist consciousness," [37] it actually did. The show was conscious of navigating feminism from the outset. Jackson was brought in for brainstorming *Charlie's Angels* as her star vehicle; it was originally called *The Alley Cats* and based on "three leather dressed ladies fighting crime" and she hated it. [38] It was Jackson who helped reconceptualize the series. Producer Leonard Goldberg was also keen to showcase positive female role models: "having just welcomed a baby girl into our family, I thought it would be important to have a series on television that would offer female heroes to the audience. And to make the point that women are equally as capable in the action-adventure arena which had heretofore been reserved [39] for men." [40] Echoing Jackson's concerns, test audiences wanted producers to make the Angels "more intelligent and capable, rather than . . . three dumb models who get themselves into trouble." [41] This desire was largely met.

The original series repeatedly acknowledged feminist leaders, events, and terms, including repeated references to the "male chauvinist pigs" who dismissed and objectified them. In "The Mexican Connection" (1.02), when the Angels are briefed on their assignment, Charlie informs them that the police are too scared to pursue the head of a drug smuggling ring because he is rich and influential. Sabrina pointedly asks, "And that's where we come in, Charlie? Where police*men* fear to tread?" While the Angels were undervalued and underused by the LAPD, they now need their help. In "Target: Angels" (1.05), Jill coaches an all-girls basketball team, one perhaps made possible by Title IX. While watching the game, Kelly's date says, "Hey, they're really good, you know," and Kelly responds, "You mean, for girls?"; he admits, sheepishly, that he does mean that. The original Angels also used feminist terms and referenced feminist leaders and other active women. In "Target: Angels," Jill says of the assassin: "he's a male chauvinist who wants us out of the private eye business!" In "To Kill An Angel" (1.07), a man asks the Angels to pose nude for his pornography magazine in exchange for the information they need. In a moment that refracted the flurry of anti-pornography activism by second-wave feminists, the Angels appear to consider his offer but then discuss "charging him with a 602" and busting him for porn propositioning. In "Lady Killer" (1.08), the Angels go undercover in a men's club to stop a killer, and they worry, without any irony: "You know, I just had this horrible image of Gloria Steinem drumming us out of the corps for not solving this case!" They could be confident that their viewer would understand the reference. The final episode of season one, "The Blue Angels" (1.22), was particularly feminist, returning the Angels to the sexist police chief who did not believe female officers capable of active duty—except now he is hiring them to investigate corruption on the vice squad. At the end of the episode, Charlie announces that perhaps their work on the case can end the LAPD's "bastion of sexism."

The critique of sexism extended to the way that crimes against women were seen as not just the fault of individual men, but crimes supported and encouraged by patriarchy. I disagree with Douglas, who argues that the original *Charlie's Angels* "tried to pretend that there was no such thing as patriarchy . . . instead, there were just a few bad men, isolated deviates, and if only these guys were exterminated or locked up, women would have nothing to fear."[42] The original series repeatedly referenced patriarchy and the "individual men" were repeatedly situated within a patriarchal context. In "To Kill an Angel," a mother tells the Angels that her husband forced her to abandon her autistic child; dependent on her husband's income, she could not afford professional help for the boy and was forced to send him to the orphanage. The Angels reunite mother and son. This episode acknowledges that beyond "individual men," patriarchy maintains its power by encouraging women to abandon education and careers, rendering them financially dependent on, and thus submissive to, "individual men." As independent career women, the Angels would never find themselves in the same situation as the mother in this episode. Further, as Gough-Yates explains, "the Angels also often found themselves solving crimes in the sphere of the workplace—invariably in fields renowned for their sexism, exploitation and/or objectification of women and that were targets of campaigning women's groups during the 1970s."[43] In "Night of the Strangler" (1.03), a model working for clothing manufacturer Kevin St. Clair (Richard Mulligan) is murdered and Jill and Kelly go undercover as models while Sabrina poses as a photo stylist. St. Clair's wife is found strangled, and it is revealed that St. Clair determined that, because of her life insurance policy, his wife is more valuable dead than alive. His associates—and fellow stranglers— Jesse Woodman (Dean Santoro) and Alec Witt (William Beckley) are equally misogynist: Jesse commits violent acts of sexual assault and Alec has been convicted of two counts of statutory rape. This episode is explicit about critiquing the sexism and misogyny in the fashion industry, and represents workplace sexual harassment and sexual violence. Further, it explicitly refuses to "blame the victim," specifically by placing the intelligent, resourceful Sabrina as going willingly to Witt's apartment (she is on an undercover mission). We see her actively resisting Alec's advances and his increasing aggression as he attempts to sexually assault her. When she leaves, she winces in pain and declares that he has bruised her ribs—underlining sexual assault as an assault, and not a crime of "passion." Not only is Sabrina not blamed, but Alec also admits to his "predilection for pornography" and we see him shooting a porn film. The refusal to blame the victim and the connection of pornography consumption with increased sexual violence against women directly takes up second-wave feminist critiques of rape culture, specifically Susan Brownmiller's *Against Our Will: Women, Men and Rape* (1975).

The Angels' articulation of a new, active, independent femininity also included their lifestyles. Gough-Yates identifies their independence as masquerade: "The potential threat of three gun-wielding, kick-flipping career women is neutralized through the knowledge that independence is, like femininity itself, only a masquerade."[44] But the original Angels were independent: they were not dependent on any man—except Charlie, obviously, but they chose him as their employer and he paid generously. Their independence was such an integral part of the Angels brand that no Angel was ever shown in bed with a man. The extremely rare romantic storylines were part of undercover work, emphasizing sexuality and romance as performance. Conversations were about work, not boyfriends. More importantly, the Angels had the rarest thing for working women: leisure time. The Angels are shown at their respective homes, which are large and well-appointed. Each Angel owns a car and travels on vacations. In the opening credits for the pilot, the Angels are shown riding horses (Sabrina), playing tennis (Jill), and enjoying time in the pool (Kelly; notably, it's her pool).[45] Most importantly, they are engaging in these leisure activates contentedly alone. For the original Angels, action was not their life; it was their occupation and they balanced it with leisure time. They sometimes fought for survival, but mostly they fought for a paycheck. The reboot features no such independence.

Like the original Angels, the reboot Angels are all single; unlike the original Angels, they are completely defined by the men in their past and present. In the reboot series, the Angels depend on men to direct and protect them. Although still problematic as the unseen patriarch, at least the original Charlie acknowledges sexism; in the reboot, Charlie eschews critiquing sexism in favor of choosing to "forgive" the Angels for not succeeding in a male-dominated field. He also ensures that they do not mess up again, by providing them with 24/7 male supervision and assistance: Bosley (Ramon Rodriguez) functions as a fourth Angel. Bosley is transformed from bumbling comic relief into a sensitive, emotionally connected, Krav Maga expert with killer abs. Bosley underscores the need for male intervention. "In the guidelines given to the series writers [of the original series], the producers insisted that Bosley be given only a supporting role; the Angels, the producers wrote, were 'capable of doing practically everything a man can do (and *more*)'—a sharp contrast to the assumptions that the LAPD makes about women's crime-fighting abilities."[46] Unfortunately, in the reboot, Bosley is a critical part of every mission, not just as guide, but as tech genius and, most importantly, physical fighter. Of course, in postfeminism, this is not an issue: if there is no more sexism, there is nothing sexist about being supervised, lectured at, and rescued by a man.

In the reboot's arithmetic, one man equals three women. "Angels in Chains" (1.04), a remake of the popular "Angels in Chains" episode from the original series, is one example of this. In this episode, the Angels go undercover in a women's prison and discover that the women are being forced into prostitution. While the Angels are beaten, threatened with sexual violence, and risk their lives to save the women, it is Bosley who saves the day by taking charge of the mission, directing the Angels and even directing a CIA agent, Samantha Masters (Erica Durance)—who just happens to be his ex-girlfriend. Bosley reprimands Agent Masters: "Six American women have been falsely imprisoned under your nose and I've got people on the inside trying to remedy the situation!" A highly trained CIA agent is, like the Angels, incapable of protecting women. Later, Bosley orders the Angels to put their guns down: "As an old friend used to say, 'never do with a gun what you can do with a phone'." Clearly, the old friend is Charlie. Men do not need guns, because they have intelligence and resourcefulness—again, this underscores the opening where the reboot Angels have all failed at their jobs in traditionally male occupations. It is men who are logical and capable; they do not need guns to save the day. When Eve asks Bosley how he could excuse the warden after her criminal actions, Bosley responds: "Believe me, it wasn't an easy call. Fact is, I'd do anything to protect you guys. All of you. No matter what the cost." Four exceptionally well-trained women, a former police officer, soldier, thief, and CIA agent, are protected by a . . . former computer hacker.

Most tellingly, the best action sequence of the series, and the only one to be shown twice, at both the beginning and near the end of the episode "Black Hat Angels" (1.06), belongs to Bosley. The episode opens with Bosley running across rooftops, pursued by police on foot and in a helicopter. This is the *only* action sequence to feature long takes, which emphasize that Rodriguez is performing the action himself; the action sequences featuring the Angels are always rapidly cut. The action sequence also features pulse-pounding rock music instead of the pop music that accompanies the Angels' action sequences. At the end of the episode, Bosley figures out the villain's trap and literally saves all three Angels' lives.

Equally problematic, in addition to Bosley being stronger and smarter, he is also the most compassionate. In "Angel with a Broken Wing" (1.01), Bosley interrupts Kate's poor efforts to comfort a girl rescued from sex trafficking and sagely comforts her himself. In "Runway Angels" (1.02), after the Angels fail to convince a model forced to run a sex trafficking ring to turn her male bosses in, it is Bosley who pats her hand and helps her see that she has had the strength to stand up for herself inside her all along. Repeatedly, Bosley is not only the better fighter and strategist, but the better nurturer. The reboot Angels are postfeminist career women after all, and postfeminist career women cannot have careers and emotional aptitude; as ambitious, independent women, the Angels need to learn how to balance their ambition with compassion, and they learn this from a man.

Bosley is also there to stop the cat fighting. While the original Angels always spoke kindly and supportively to each other, even when meeting a new Angel for the first time, the reboot Angels greet Eve with barely concealed disdain. The tension in "Angel with a Broken Wing" gets so bad that Bosley intervenes: "Ding ding ladies! Get back to your corners." The original Angels were friends who worked together at the LAPD and struggled to break the glass ceiling together. They were chosen as a trio, not put together by a patriarch like crime-fighting Spice Girls. The reboot Angels, however, were chosen individually and forced to work together by Charlie. This is not sisterhood; this is product differentiation.[47] In the reboot, the Angels do not bond over shared experiences of workplace discrimination and commit to fighting it together; rather, they are individually redeemed by Charlie and then forced to find a way to work together.

Perhaps the reboot Angels struggle to work together because they do not associate with other women, nor do they support them. If there is a woman in power, she is revealed to be the villain. In "Black Hat Angels," the female villain's motivation for kidnapping, besides seeking revenge on her former hacking partner Bosley, is money. Like a Vaudevillian villain, she laughs, "You can't stop me! I've printed enough money for a lifetime!"[48] In "Royal Angels" (1.07), the sharpshooter who assassinates the King is a woman, ex-army—like the deceased, disgraced army lieutenant Gloria. Women with (unsupervised) power are deadly. Even when not actual villains, women are demonized and mocked. In the pilot, Abby runs into the Wentworth Sisters, who are stereotypically vapid, bitchy, and blonde. The sisters mock her for working (undercover) as a cocktail waitress. Abby responds by offering them bellinis spiked with a laxative. In "Runway Angels," the (very thin) Angels take issue with the models— not out of concern for their well-being, but out of catty jealousy. Eve even suggests shoving ice cream down a model's throat until she talks. In "Angels in Chains," Eve smirks that the female warden got "exactly what she deserves" by having to serve time in her own prison, ignoring that the warden is a woman of different class, nationality, and political circumstances. This is repeated in "Royal Angels" when the poor, Latina girlfriend of a prince defends leaking information about his whereabouts by explaining that she desperately needed the money for school: "I didn't have a choice." Bosley yells at her, "You always have a choice!" Unlike the Angels, however, the choice for these women is not as simple as mojito or martini.

This brings the sisterhood of the original series into sharper relief. Sharon Ross writes: "In the past, and in the realm of action adventure in particular, strong female heroes have been represented as isolated from other women socially."[49] Ross is right about the isolation of the female hero, but the original Angels provided one of the few models for action sisterhood. The original Angels not only treated each other like sisters, but extended sisterhood to all the women they met: "The Angels were always extremely sympathetic and helpful to these girls, suggesting a female bond across class barriers that many feminists were trying to achieve in real life."[50] They were advocates and protectors of women who did not have the privilege or advantages they had. They also chastised women who did not do the same. In "Angels Go Truckin" (4.2), the Angels discover that the owner of a trucking company that employs only women is stealing her own cargo. Angel Kris (Cheryl Ladd) is furious with her: "You could have proved once and for all that women can do anything men can do!"

While the original Angels could do anything a man could do, in both narrative and spectacle, the reboot Angels are denied full entry into the spectacle. As private detectives, the original Angels were active lookers, and each episode featured them actively looking for evidence and/or a suspect. This complicates the reading of them as only looked-at "jiggle." The reboot Angels, although still private detectives, do not look. Bosley is the "eyes," augmenting his own looking with technology to analyze scenes and then provide the Angels with that information. The action the Angels are allowed to engage in is not only limited, but bloodless—literally. Action heroes have to suffer in order to prove their indestructibility and underline their sacrifice; in the original, the Angels sustain injuries and complain about pain.[51] In the reboot, only Bosley is allowed to suffer. In the pilot, after Eve is strung up, punched in the face, choked and tasered, she has only a trickle of blood on her mouth and a small cut on her nose.[52] When Bosley's cover is blown in "Bon Voyage Angels" (1.03), he is hit three times (backhand, slap, punch) and falls to his knees, spitting copious amounts of blood. The scene cuts to Eve being slammed down repeatedly and continuously punched in the face. She suffers more violence than Bosley, but she barely bleeds—blood trickles across her lips, so subtle that it could be lipstick. The violence against women is also sexualized. In "Runway Angels," model Gabriella is found naked, wrapped in a clear shower curtain in the bathtub. In "Angels in Chains," after freeing the sex-trafficking victims via a Jeep from a cocktail party where they were dressed in evening gowns, the women inexplicably arrive sweaty, dirty, and with their dresses falling off.

While the Angels are denied full participation in action spectacle, they are costumed like they are always undercover. In the original series, the Angels were costumed and shot differently in the narrative versus the spectacle (where they were most often undercover). The narrative and spectacle also served different functions. In the reboot, the difference between spectacle and narrative is collapsed. Missions are interrupted to talk about men or troubled pasts. More critically, the reboot Angels are costumed provocatively and sexualized equally in the spectacle and the narrative. They always look like they just left a *Vogue* cover shoot: smoky eyes, glossy lips, excessive accessories and sky-high stilettos. In the original series, the Angels were most often clothed in functional clothing: pants, turtlenecks, athletic wear. They sometimes wore skimpier garments for their undercover work, and these are the outfits that led to the accusation of "jiggle TV," but these outfits were exceptions. While they did go undercover as roller derby queens, models, call girls, and servers in a gentlemen's club, they entered these jobs to expose the sexual harassment and violence inherent in these all-female workspaces; they also went undercover as truck drivers, stunt performers, WACs in basic training, prison inmates, race car drivers, and football players. The original Angels dressed in comfortable clothing that facilitated physical activity. In the reboot, the Angels not only dress like they are going clubbing instead of crime fighting, but they receive makeovers when they become Angels. In the original series, the only physical difference the Angels experienced was that they ditched their police uniforms for civilian clothing. In the reboot, the Angels ditch their tank tops and minimal makeup for tight white dresses and glamorous styling.

While the reboot lasted only seven episodes, these episodes underline that what this series was selling was not sisterhood and active femininity but, rather, postfeminist lifestyle feminism. Susan Douglas attributes the success of the original *Charlie's Angels* to the way it "exploited, perfectly, the tensions between antifeminism and feminism."[53] The work of the original series was to show that feminism and femininity were not—and never had been—diametrically opposed. The *Charlie's Angels* merchandise targeting children affirmed this idea, offering *Charlie's Angels* action figures, a communications center, AM wrist radio, walkie-talkies, and a target shooting set as well as a cosmetic beauty kit and cosmetic beauty hair-care set and school notebooks.[54] Children could mix and match these items to articulate their own inflection of active "femininity"; at a time when gender roles were quickly changing, the program and the merchandise provided ways to reconcile old and new inflections of femininity. The original series created enough anxiety that a psychologist with the Aggression Research Group at the University of Michigan's Institute for Social Research executed a study of girls who grew up watching *Charlie's Angels*, *The Bionic Woman* (1976–78), and *Wonder Woman* (1975–79). The study concluded that girls who watched "aggressive[55] heroines on television" grew up to be more aggressive adults and "got involved in more confrontations, shoving matches, chokings and knives than women who as girls watched few or none of these shows."[56] The fact that there was enough concern about the effect of these "aggressive heroines" on girls underscores that the Angels and their colleagues were more than just "jiggle TV."

While the original series deliberately referenced the political climate in the United States, the reboot existed in a political and cultural vacuum. The reboot series did not find a female audience not only because of its muddled marketing, where it sexualized and reified the heroes it expected women to look up to, but also because it created a trio of apolitical, cat-fighting Angels who functioned in a world free of not only sexism and racism, but also of autonomous women. Action television is supposed to be escapist, but it is not supposed to be fantasy. The original series succeeded because it directly targeted and appealed to women, offering Angels who refracted feminism and validated women's experiences with sexism. The reboot series is partially redeemed only because it brings the feminist politics of the original series into sharper relief. In a plot twist worthy of an Angels episode, it is the original Angels, so long villainized as betrayers of feminism, who emerge as the good guys. Putting the two series in dialogue exposes that the memorialization of the original series is revisionist and obfuscates the way the series directly responded to second-wave feminism. Critics have judged the original Angels on their appearances instead of their job performance. Unlike the original Angels, the reboot Angels may still work for Charlie, but they no longer work for feminism.

FILMS AND TV SHOWS

Alias. ABC. 2001–06.
Angeles. Telemundo. 1999–2001.
The Avengers. ABC. 1966–69.
Buffy the Vampire Slayer. The WB, 1997–2001. UPN, 2001–03.
Charlie's Angels. ABC, 1976–81.
Charlie's Angels. ABC, 2011.
Charlie's Angels. Directed by McG. 2000. Sony Pictures.
Charlie's Angels: Full Throttle. Directed by McG. 2003. Sony Pictures.
Cleopatra Jones. Directed by Jack Starrett. 1973. Warner Bros.
Coffy. Directed by Jack Hill. 1973. American International Pictures.
Colombiana. Directed by Olivier Megaton. 2011. Sony Pictures.
Dark Angel. Fox. 2000–02.
Get Christie Love! Directed by William A. Graham. ABC, 1974.
Get Christie Love! ABC, 1974–75.
Honey West. ABC, 1965–66.
Haywire. Directed by Steven Soderbergh. 2012. Relativity Media.
Lara Croft: Tomb Raider. Directed by Simon West. 2001. Paramount Pictures.
Lara Croft Tomb Raider: The Cradle of Life. Directed by Jan de Bont. 2003. Paramount Pictures.

Mr. & Mrs. Smith. Directed by Doug Liman. 2005. Twentieth Century–Fox Film Corporation.

Police Woman. NBC, 1974–78.

Resident Evil. Directed by Paul W. S. Anderson. 2002. Sony Pictures.

Resident Evil: Apocalypse. Directed by Alexander Witt. 2004. Sony Pictures.

Resident Evil: Extinction. Directed by Russell Mulcahy. 2007. Sony Pictures.

Resident Evil: Afterlife. Directed by Paul W. S. Anderson. 2010. Sony Pictures.

Resident Evil: Retribution. Directed by Paul W. S. Anderson. 2012. Sony Pictures.

The Rookies. ABC, 1972–76.

NOTES

The title quote "These Aren't Your Mother's Angels" is a marketing tagline from the reboot series. See "Charlie's Angels Reboots for a New Generation," *ETonline*, September 21, 2013, accessed March 24, 2013, http://www.etonline.com/tv/114474_Charlie_s_Angels_Reboots_For_a_New_Generation/.

1. "TV's Superwomen," *Time*, November 22, 1976, http://www.time.com/time/magazine/article/0,9171,914689,00.html.

2. This was the first literal reboot of the *Charlie's Angels* series. In 1988, there was an attempted reboot, *Angels '88*, which was to feature four Angels instead of three. However, production was halted before the pilot was shot due to a Writer's Guild strike and script issues. A Spanish version of *Charlie's Angels* called *Angeles* played on Telemundo in 1999; it was cancelled after 13 episodes. The two *Charlie's Angels* movies (2000; 2003) were box office successes. In 2003, a *Charlie's Angels* animated adventure series appeared online as a "prequel" to *Charlie's Angels: Full Throttle*. The Angels, however, do not speak in the series and are costumed like cartoon pornography.

3. Eight episodes were shot; seven aired. The eighth episode is available on the DVD release.

4. "Forget 'Charlie's Angels,' 'Prime Suspect' is the remake to watch," *Chicago Sun-Times.com*, September 21, 2011, http://www.suntimes.com/entertainment/television/7786645–421/forget-charlies-angels-prime-suspect-is-the-remake-to-watch.html.

5. "Matt's Guide to Thursday Night TV: New and Returning Shows," *TV Guide*, September 22, 2011, http://www.tvguide.com/News/Matts-Guide-Thursday-1037919.aspx.

6. The term "jiggle TV" was coined by NBC executive Paul Klein to critique ABC's strategies and programming under Fred Silverman. Klein defined "jiggle TV" as "when you have a young, attractive television personality running at top speed wearing a limited amount of underwear." Qtd. in Sally Bedell, *Up the Tube: Prime-Time TV and the Silverman Years* (New York: Viking Adult), 204.

7. Ronald Bergan, "Farrah Fawcett: All-American actor best known for her role in the classic 70s TV series Charlie's Angels," *The Guardian*, June 25, 2009, http://www.guardian.co.uk/culture/2009/jun/25/farrah-fawcett-obituary.

8. Amy Erdman Farrell, *Yours in Sisterhood: Ms. Magazine and the Promise of Popular Feminism* (Chapel Hill: UNC Press Books, 1998), 1.

9. Because the reboot was cancelled after seven episodes, I will limit my detailed analysis to the first seven episodes of the first season, while briefly referencing other episodes from other seasons.

10. Sumiko Higashi, "'Charlie's Angels': Gumshoes in Drag," *Film Criticism* 2, no. 2/3 (January 1978): 55.

11. "TV's Superwomen."

12. When a female inmate goes missing, the Angels get themselves into a sadistic prison and end up masquerading as prostitutes.

13. "TV's Superwomen."

14. Ibid.

15. Bonnie Dow, *Prime-time Feminism: Television, Media Culture, and the Women's Movement Since 1970* (Philadelphia: University of Pennsylvania Press, 1996), 214.

16. Naomi Wolf, *Fire with Fire: The New Female Power and How to Use It* (Toronto: Vintage, 1994), xv.

17. Sarah Projansky, *Watching Rape: Film and Television in Postfeminist Culture* (New York: NYU Press, 2001), 88.

18. Tim Goodman, "*Charlie's Angels*: TV Review," *The Hollywood Reporter*, September 22, 2011, http://www.hollywoodreporter.com/review/charlies-angels-tv-review-238843.

19. Linda Holmes, "The New 'Charlie's Angels': The Depressing Spectacle of a Project No One Loves," *NPR*, September 22, 2011, http://www.npr.org/blogs/monkey-see/2011/09/22/140700388/the-new-charlies-angels-the-depressing-spectacle-of-a-project-no-one-loves.

20. "Review: *Charlie's Angels*," *Variety*, September 16, 2011, http://variety.com/2011/tv/reviews/charlie-s-angels-1117946126/.

21. "Hollywood Continues to Resurrect the Familiar with *Charlie's Angels*," *PopMatters*, September 22, 2011, http://www.popmatters.com/pm/review/148933-charlies-angels/.

22. Jack Condon and David Hofstede, *The Charlie's Angels Casebook* (Beverly Hills: Pomegranate Press, 2000), 47.

23. "TV's Superwomen."

24. Jeffrey Brown, *Dangerous Curves: Action Heroines, Gender, Fetishism, and Popular Culture* (Jackson: University Press of Mississippi, 2011), 144.

25. Sherrie Inness also contributes to this myth: ". . . this was an era of *Charlie's Angels* fame, with the trio slinking around in skimpy outfits and getting kidnapped by bad guys every time they wandered to the local 7–11 for a six-pack of Tab." Introduction, "'Strange Feverish Years': The 1970s and Women's Changing Roles," in *Disco Divas: Women and Popular Culture in the 1970s*, ed. Sherrie Inness (Philadelphia: University of Pennsylvania Press, 2003), 2.

26. Created by Bi-Rite in 1976.

27. Fawcett shot the infamous red swimsuit poster before *Charlie's Angels* even started filming. She also retained the rights to it.

28. Kelly was voted "Sexiest Woman Alive" by *Esquire* magazine. "Minka Kelly is *Esquire*'s Sexiest Woman Alive 2010," *Esquire.com*, October 11, 2010, http://www.esquire.com/women/the-sexiest-woman-alive/sexy-minka-kelly-pics-1110.

29. And OnStar, which promised to "add safety to your car"—makeup and constantly monitored protection, exactly what women need.

30. Accounts differ, with some repudiating the slap—albeit days after the story first circulated. Kelly reportedly felt "awful" about the firing. Kelly and her management refused to comment. ABC refused to release the name of the crew member. Rhenna Murray, "Minka Kelly slapped on 'Charlie's Angels' Set; ABC fires crew member for sexual harassment," *NY Daily News*, September 21, 2011, http://www.nydailynews.com/entertainment/gossip/minka-kelly-slapped-charlie-angels-set-abc-fires-crew-member-sexual-harassment-article-1.956552#ixzz2Z2Z62GjW.

31. I am not denying the incident, but rather pointing to the convenient timing of this story that is so at odds with Kelly's previous star text.

32. Elana Levine, *Wallowing in Sex: The New Sexual Culture of 1970s American Television* (Durham: Duke University Press, 2007), 147; Cathy Schwichtenberg, "A Patriarchal Voice in Heaven," *Jump Cut: A Review of Contemporary Media* 24/25 (March 1981):

http://www.ejumpcut.org/archive/onlinessays/JC24–25folder/CharliesAngels.html; L. Gamman, "Watching the Detectives: The Enigma of the Female Gaze," in *The Female Gaze: Women As Viewers Of Popular Culture*, ed. L. Gamman & M. Marshment (Seattle: Real Comet Press, 1989), 104.

33. Brown, *Dangerous Curves*, 82.

34. Whitney Womack, "Reevaluating 'Jiggle TV:' Charlie's Angels At Twenty-Five," in *Disco Divas: Women and Popular Culture in the 1970s*, ed. Sherrie Inness (University of Pennsylvania Press, 2003), 155.

35. Eve is very vaguely Latina. Not only is her last name "French," but she is played by Kelly, who is white. Eve's parents were killed while they were aid workers in El Salvador, and Eve spent a year in an orphanage with Latina Gloria. This apparently makes her "ethnic." The series asserts a postracial, as well as a postfeminist, politic.

36. Womack, "Reevaluating 'Jiggle TV'," 155.

37. Ibid., 154.

38. Mike Pingle, *Channel Surfing: Charlie's Angels* (Angelic Heaven Publishing: 2012), 17.

39. It is not true that the "action-adventure arena" was reserved for men. The first female action heroes appeared in Blaxploitation cinema. Notably, in 1973, *Coffy* was twentieth on *Variety*'s list of top grossing films and *Cleopatra Jones* was twenty-third ("50 Top-Grossing Films," *Variety*, April 4, 1973). *Get Christie Love* was a 1974 made-for-television film that became a series about a black female police detective with the catch line: "You're under arrest, Sugah!" *The Avengers* (1961–69) and *Honey West* (1965–66) and *Police Woman* (1975–76) also predated the Angels.

40. Pingle, *Channel*, 23.

41. Condon and Hofstede, *The Charlie's Angels Casebook*, 35.

42. Susan Douglas, *Where the Girls Are: Growing up Female with the Mass Media* (New York: Random House of Canada, 1995), 216.

43. Anna Gough-Yates, "Angels in Chains? Feminism, Femininity and Consumer Culture in Charlie's Angels, in *Action TV: Tough Guys, Smooth Operators and Foxy Chicks*, eds. Bill Osgerby and Anna Gough-Yates (London: Routledge), 89.

44. Ibid., 96.

45. After the pilot, the credits presented a split-screen montage that featured images from these scenes juxtaposed with glamour shots.

46. Womack, "Reevaluating 'Jiggle TV'," 156.

47. The original Angels had different personas too, of course, but first and foremost they were sisters who chose each other.

48. This demonization of powerful women who work for themselves is consistent with *Charlie's Angels: Full Throttle* (2003), which Drew Barrymore also produced. In the film, Angel Madison (Demi Moore) is power- and money-hungry, a result of her decision not to "take orders from a speaker box anymore." For more on this, see my article "'My Guns are in the Fendi!:' The Postfeminist Female Action Hero," in *Third Wave Feminism: A Critical Exploration*, 2nd ed., ed. Stacy Gillis, Gillian Howie, and Rebecca Munford (New York: Palgrave Macmillan, 2007), 237–249.

49. Sharon Ross, "Tough Enough: Female Friendship and Heroism in Xena and Buffy," in *Action Chicks: New Images of Tough Women in Popular Culture*, ed. Sherrie A. Inness (New York: Palgrave Macmillan, 2004), 235.

50. Douglas, *Where the Girls Are*, 214.

51. The female hero of *Prime Suspect* (2011–12), a show that debuted the same night as the reboot, allowed the female hero full entry into the action spectacle and showed the effects of this entry. When Detective Jane Timoney (Maria Bello) is beaten, she not only bleeds and suffers, but her face remains swollen and bruised for (at minimum) the entire episode.

52. This scene mirrors the infamous scene in *Lethal Weapon* (1987) where Mel Gibson is tortured in a similar manner—except his body is excessively marked by the torture.

53. Douglas, *Where the Girls Are,* 213.

54. Critics, including Gough-Yates, who mention the merchandise focus on the beauty products and ignore the items that do not reconcile with conventional femininity.

55. Their active femininity and aggression are not limited to the action sequences; in "Target: Angels," Jill gets so frustrated with a ref's call against the all-girls basketball team she is coaching that she yells at him and kicks over a bucket.

56. Jessica F. Moise and L. Rowell Huesmann, "Television Violence Viewing and Aggression in Females," *Annals of the New York Academy of Sciences* 794, no. 1 (September 1996): 380–383.

NINE

Forbrydelsen, The Killing, Duty, and Ethics

Karen Hellekson

Forbrydelsen, the original twenty-episode version of the long-form murder mystery TV series, first aired in Denmark in 2007, then was subtitled
in English and aired on the BBC in the UK in 2011, thus garnering it a
much larger audience.[1] The program was redone for an American audience as *The Killing,* with the original atmospheric Copenhagen setting
moved to drizzly Seattle. *The Killing* aired what began as the same plot in
twenty-six episodes over two seasons in 2011–12, although the series
quickly deviated from the Danish version and has a different ending,
with a different killer. The US version of the show is notable for its failure
to close the case in its first season, antagonizing fans and resulting in a 33-
percent drop in viewership from its two-hour pilot.[2]

The *New York Times* called *Forbrydelsen* (The Crime) "a shrewd mix of
police procedural, political thriller and domestic drama,"[3] highlighting
the three prongs of the story: the police investigation, the machinations of
a politician running for office, and the parents coping with the tragedy of
their daughter's death. The focus, however, is on the primary detective
on the scene and her slide into obsession as the case proves tough to
solve. Thus, both texts are primarily in the justice genre, "narrative texts
that depict ideological discourses, institutions, and practices of justice—
of crime, law, and social order," the goal of which is to "constantly define
and redefine what justice or injustice might mean in ever-changing cultural and mediated circumstances."[4] Both texts examine the personal costs
of a murder investigation—not only for the family members left mourning the death of a loved one but also for suspects and for the investigating

detectives. Both texts examine what it means to perform a duty and to seek justice in a fraught environment where motives and choices are unclear.

The US remake fundamentally alters the nature of the main character, Nordic-sweater-wearing police investigator Sarah Lund (Danish version: Sofie Gråbøl)/Sarah Linden (US version: Mireille Enos). Both Lund and Linden are depicted as driven, perhaps even obsessed, with discovering the identity of the killer; both take ridiculous risks, defy authority, neglect their sons, and lead their partners into danger. However, the fundamental driving force behind them differs. In the Danish version, Lund seeks the truth because it is morally right. She will follow the clues to the killer, regardless of the path, because it is the right thing to do. She expresses Kantian good will: what she does is good in itself. In the US version, Linden seeks the truth because of her own personal foibles, as we discover when she is locked up in a mental ward and placed under watch. We learn that she seeks the truth because the cases remind her of a childhood trauma.

I analyze these motivations in Kantian terms to indicate that Lund, but not Linden, has moral worth: what she does conforms with duty and is done from duty. Of the two, she is the morally righteous one. The different Sarahs provide two different sets of character motivation that may be related to cultural norms related to the justice genre: American protagonists are often provided with a personal motivation, making the duty they perform less moral.

A. KANT'S METAPHYSICS OF MORALS

Immanuel Kant's (1724–1804) concept of good will is laid out in his *Fundamental Principles of the Metaphysics of Morals* (also known as the *Groundwork of the Metaphysics of Morals*), which appeared in 1785 and which outlined ideas that Kant later expanded on in *The Metaphysics of Morals* (1797). In the *Fundamental Principles,* Kant outlines a rational, Enlightenment-informed metaphysics of action and morality that relies on notions of duty and goodness. Kant attempts to lay out a "metaphysic of morals [that] . . . examine[s] the idea and the principles of a possible pure will, and not the acts and conditions of human volition generally, which for the most part are drawn from psychology."[5] The concept of good will is central to Kant's argument:

> A good will is good not because of what it performs or effects, not by its aptness for the attainment of some proposed end, but simply by virtue of the volition; that is, it is good in itself, and considered by itself is to be esteemed much higher than all that can be brought about by it in favour of any inclination, nay even of the sum total of all inclinations. Even if it should happen that, owing to special disfavour of for-

tune, or the niggardly provision of a step-motherly nature, this will should wholly lack power to accomplish its purpose, if with its greatest efforts it should yet achieve nothing, and there should remain only the good will . . . then, like a jewel, it would still shine by its own light, as a thing which has its whole value in itself.

The person exhibiting good will may therefore not be able, by circumstance or nature, to bring about a purpose or effect a desired action, but if action is motivated by good will, then to Kant, it is worthy. The result of this is that "reason commands us to abide by principles rather than consequences"[6] —that is, universal principles must be followed, regardless of what might happen, no matter the outcome.

In terms of impetus to action, Kant notes the existence of two sorts of imperative, categorical and hypothetical, that may cause the agent to act. The categorical imperative is "that which represented an action as necessary of itself without reference to another end, i.e., as objectively necessary"—that is, a moral principle that is universally true. The hypothetical imperative, on the other hand, is "the practical necessity of a possible action as means to something else that is willed," or action out of expediency, desire, or inclination. Of the categorical imperative, the worthier of the two, Kant remarks, "It concerns not the matter of the action, or its intended result, but its form and the principle of which it is itself a result; and what is essentially good in it consists in the mental disposition, let the consequence be what it may. This imperative may be called that of morality."

Morality is thus linked to action, with every action having the possibility of being executed from a categorical or hypothetical imperative. Categorical imperatives are moral because, by definition, they are universally true. Kant ends the *Fundamental Principles* by weaving together good will with the impetus to action:

Since the validity of the will as a universal law for possible actions is analogous to the universal connexion of the existence of things by general laws, which is the formal notion of nature in general, the categorical imperative can also be expressed thus: Act on maxims which can at the same time have for their object themselves as universal laws of nature. Such then is the formula of an absolutely good will.

This means that the reason for an action will affect whether it is an act of good will: the same action could be performed in two different sets of circumstances, and according to the categorical imperative, in one circumstance it may be right and in another wrong.[7] It depends on the agent, the action, and the circumstances. However, central to the shining light of good will is the motivation of the agent and the action executed within those circumstances. Kant urges action that may be expressive of the "universal laws of nature."

A major aspect of performing an action is doing one's duty. Although a mismatch between an agent's desires and an agent's duty may occur, "the requirements of the law may dovetail with one's own happiness by and large. Indeed, they probably do, as Kant himself thinks."[8] Kant links moral worth to doing one's duty: an action is morally worthy if the impetus to action is driven by duty and if the action is performed out of the categorical imperative.[9] Further, sometimes an action may be performed out of more than one motive, a state known as overdetermination of action; however, although a nonmoral reason may be the initial cause of consideration of taking an action, this nonmoral reason may cause the agent to consider the motive of duty.[10]

Thus, according to Kantian tenets, a moral agent acting in good willing—that is, "good of itself, without regard to any further end"[11] —acts primarily out of a sense of duty, to which is attached the universality of the action performed selflessly, according to universal laws. This action may or may not be in conflict with the motives and desires of the agent, but the moral worth of the action may be judged by these criteria. Further, the same action may performed for different motives and may be judged differently, so "consequently the goodness of everything must depend on its context."[12]

B. SARAH LUND AND SARAH LINDEN

Forbrydelsen and its remake, *The Killing,* share the bare bones of plot: evidence is discovered implying that someone is dead. Police detective Sarah Lund/Sarah Linden grudgingly responds to the case; it is her last day at work before she and her son move to a new town, where she is to marry her fiancé. The case quickly escalates into a full-on murder investigation when the dead body of a young woman is found bound in the trunk of a submerged car. Lund/Linden's exit is endlessly delayed. Her replacement becomes her partner, and they work together as the investigation takes them to an up-and-coming politician's campaign for office. Powerful people associated with the campaign seem interested in covering something up. The dead girl's shattered parents try to cope with her death even as they learn that their daughter had dark secrets. Lund/Linden becomes obsessed with the case. She neglects her son, who ends up being cared for by his (absent) father, and her long-suffering fiancé withdraws, leaving her alone as the twists of the case, with its red herrings and dead leads, draw her in deeper. Yet time after time, solid police work combined with intuition indicate that she is the only one who can crack the case.

I've described both series in such a way as to highlight the commonalities of the two plots. They differ in a number of respects, not only related to the different settings—Copenhagen and Seattle—and the different structures and methods of two different sets of police rules and procedures, but also the identity and motive of the killer. In terms of Sarah herself, importantly, Lund has a mother. Linden, on the other hand, was a ward of the state and was in foster care, although someone from that system, Regi Darnell (Annie Corley), who lives in a houseboat, remains an important part of her life. Lund's fiancé comes to her aid and helps her with the case; Linden's fiancé gets her out of the mental ward but then disappears, refusing to further engage with her. Lund's relationships and history hint at permanence and stability, Linden's of transience and flux.

Both Sarahs start out laughing and happy, then decline throughout the series, although Lund's nature seems to be the less dour of the two; her descent into obsession is the more striking because of this, although Mireille Enos (Linden)'s tightly wound performance and expressive silences speak volumes. Both take up smoking again after having quit. Both make ridiculous demands of their colleagues, with requests to perform extensive searches that are overruled by their bosses. Both ignore loved ones—fiancé, son—in favor of the case. Lund becomes passionate, manic, and frenzied, pacing and shouting orders; Linden becomes quietly, determinedly obdurate, refusing to obey direct requests and forgetting to eat and sleep, until she is finally institutionalized.

Linden's time in the mental ward provides explanations for her behavior—explanations not present in Lund's case. In addition to Linden's peripatetic childhood and lack of a permanent mother figure, a previous case haunts her. In "71 Hours" (2.10), Linden, suspended from the force, awakens in a mental ward after being struck in the head while illegally searching a site she believes is connected to the crime she's investigating. However, the story that was told when she was admitted, unconscious, was that she had tried to kill herself, which is why she was brought to the mental ward. She is placed in seventy-two-hour lockdown and suicide watch.

During Linden's conversations with the psychiatrist assigned to her case, Ann Kerry (Janet Kidder), we learn that this is not the first time she's been in this institution. When she was there last time, she had been carrying around the same child's drawing of trees, which her psychiatrist at the time thought had significance for Linden and the case she was then working. Kerry, armed with a photocopy of the drawing from Linden's file—a drawing that watchers will find familiar, as Linden has been contemplating it and has mentioned the case to a colleague—thus wants to analyze Linden's past.

The story Linden tells Kerry seems familiar: "It was nonstop working a murder," Linden says with a tight smile—which could describe the case she's working on now. Kerry elicits the past case's tragic story. Linden describes a six-year-old boy, Adrian, whose father was convicted of killing the boy's mother. Adrian drew the same picture over and over as he sat for days in a room with his mother's rotting corpse. Linden had previously told a colleague that child protective services took the orphaned boy, which undoubtedly reminded her of her own time in care.

Kerry tries to tie together the two cases, past and present. She repeatedly directly queries Linden about the connection between the two cases, and she asks Linden what they have in common. Linden provides a rationale: "They'll bury this case—they'll make it go away." Further, Linden was unconvinced that the father did it; she may have been involved in a miscarriage of justice (2013's season three of *The Killing* returns to and explicates this case).

Kerry: Sarah, maybe what they went through is something you relate to. Have you thought about that?

Linden: What? I told you why it matters.

Kerry: Let's talk about your mother, about when she abandoned you. . . . She left you in the apartment, alone. You were five years old. Do you remember that?

Linden: No.

Kerry: Surely you must have some memories.

Linden: The lights had been turned off. She hadn't paid the bill. That's all I remember.

Kerry: CPS [Child Protective Services] found you the next morning, after she left. So you spent the night in that place alone.

Linden: [Unconvincingly] It was a long time ago. I'm fine now. [A tear runs down her cheek]

Kerry: Your son is gone. You were supposed to be married a few days ago. You've lost your job. Really?

Linden: Whatever you want me to say, I'll say it. Just please let me go.

Kerry: You spent the night alone in the dark?

Just as Linden is about to respond—just as she is ready to drop her guard and reveal the event and her feelings—a knock comes at the door. She's been released. The moment is gone, and Linden does not have to directly confront her past. However, we know now that an event in her childhood has traumatized her: she stayed in a dark room, the dead girl died in the dark trunk of a car, and Adrian was in a small, dark closet. We can make the final leap, even if Linden can't: by solving the case, she can redeem her failure to obtain justice for Adrian, and she can save herself.

C. LUND AND LINDEN AS MORAL AGENTS

To revisit notions of duty in Kantian terms, a moral agent who acts in good will acts for the categorical imperative, or performs an action that adheres to a moral principle that is universally true. Action performed from the hypothetical imperative, or action out of inclination, is not moral because of its lack of universality: it is specific to a person, not general to humanity. In *Forbrydelsen* and *The Killing,* as justice dramas, action is also performed as a duty related to justice: they have a duty to find the truth and solve the case. Both Lund and Linden, at great personal cost, discover the identity of the killer. Certainly the ultimate outcome is the same, regardless of motive: the killer is revealed. Yet Kantian thought attaches morality to motive, not to action.

In the absence of any other evidence, we conclude that Lund's motivation is justice. Lund acts out of the categorical imperative: her duty is to seek justice, and her actions are performed to that end. Thus she performs actions that defy her superiors: she continues to work on the case even after she has been suspended. For example, when she discovers that the murdered girl's luggage is being held in a baggage claim area, she misrepresents herself as an active-duty officer and walks off with the luggage when the clerk is distracted. In another instance, she lies to obtain the help of a lip reader to translate silent CCTV footage. She performs unethical actions out of a motivation of greater good; they are presented not as immoral but as necessary to bring about a moral end based on the principle of justice. By acting out of the categorical imperative, she is acting in good will. Her motive is the transcendent and universal notion of justice.

Linden, on the other hand, acts out of the hypothetical imperative. Linden performs similar acts of misrepresentation; she also continues to work on the case despite her suspension, as when she illicitly enters a Native American casino linked to the murdered girl to search a room under construction. Yet her primary motivation is revealed to be the result of personal trauma; she acts out of individualistic reactions to that trauma and her subsequent guilt. Her motive is personal, not universal.

The key to judging actions as moral or not moral lies in what Kant calls mental disposition. We must judge the individual's impetus to action, not the results of the action themselves, which in both Lund and Linden's cases are ultimately the same. The outcome is a good one—for society, for the questioning bereaved family, for the police officers involved in the case whose duty is justice. Yet despite this outcome, we must judge Lund as the worthier of the two because she acts out of good will. Barbara Herman notes that "an action has moral worth if it is required by duty and has as its primary motive the motive of duty. The motive of duty need not reflect the only interest the agent has in the action (or its effect); it must, however, be the interest that determines the agent's acting as he did."[13] Thus Linden could be acting from more than one motive, duty, and interest; *The Killing* demonstrates, through her mental and physical decline and especially through her telling stint in the mental institution, that interest comes before duty and that she is not acting from love or compassion.[14] She does not act out of moral worth.

D. TRANSLATING THE JUSTICE GENRE ACROSS CULTURES

The personal-stake motivation that drives Linden is present in other American justice dramas; indeed, the justice drama has long been a dominant genre in American TV, from westerns to cop shows. Other American texts in this genre that rely on the hypothetical imperative include *Fringe* (2008–13), whose lead character, FBI agent Olivia Dunham (Anna Torv), studies bizarre happenings somehow related to her own childhood experiences in a drug trial; *Law & Order: Special Victims Unit* (1999–present), in which detective Olivia Benson (Mariska Hargitay), the product of rape, seeks to bring justice to the victims of sexually based crimes; *In Plain Sight* (2010–12), where federal marshal Mary Shannon (Mary McCormick), whose fugitive father abandoned her as a child, works with people in witness protection; and *Bones* (2005–present), in which forensic anthropologist Temperance Brennan (Emily Deschanel), the brilliant child of a criminal father who abandoned her to the foster system when she was a teen, works with bones to solve crimes—and this is just a brief listing of TV justice programs with the arbitrary criterion of women as lead characters. Suffice it to say that in American television, the protagonist is often presented as having a personal stake in the task at hand, and it is no surprise that to target the American audience, Lund, in her transformation into Linden, was provided with a personal stake as well. Giving her a personally traumatic backstory provides an individualistic context that the story can be read against rather than a universal, communal one. This change remains consistent throughout the texts aired to date: the stunning ending of the *Forbrydelsen* series with its season three finale in 2012 and the whodunit season three ender of *The Killing* in 2013. Both Sarahs take justice into their own hands, further emphasizing the gulf between primary motivations. Lund acts because if she does not, justice will be thwarted; Linden acts because she was betrayed.

Although it's not possible to make sweeping generalizations about the nature of Danish versus American TV from this case study, the protagonist's change hints at culture-specific notions of what would be acceptable to an audience and what motivations might resonate with them. We might assess the changes made, as Jason Mittell invites us to, by locating the genre "within the complex interrelations among texts, industries, audiences, and historical contexts"[15]; equally valid would be to use the justice genre to explore "individuality vis-à-vis intention,"[16] as the change from Lund to Linden makes clear. We might then contrast America's rugged individualism with Denmark's socialism, for example. Certainly many American justice dramas rely on "characters welded to their notions of right judgment, characters who will not deviate from their code of honor, regardless of consequences," as one critic remarks of the classic western, and which is evident in these texts as well.[17] Character motivation has been deliberately changed to focus on the individual over the collective.

The move in Lund/Linden's character motivation from *Forbrydelsen* to *The Killing* illustrates intercultural notions of morality and ethics. The Danish version of the text motivates Lund by referring to universal truths of justice. *The Killing* relies on a personal motive. Lund's and Linden's motivations for action cause the texts to be read differently: Lund's acting out of the categorical imperative means that *Forbrydelsen* is a tale of the personal cost of seeking a moral ideal of justice. *The Killing* stops at personal cost; the story does not resonate further. In *The Killing*, the solving of the crime shines less brightly because the moral imperative is not universal or communal but individualistic and ultimately selfish. By insisting on a personal context, *The Killing* undermines the larger point of *Forbrydelsen*: that it is possible to act out of duty, with good will, for universal principles that hint at a better humanity.

FILMS AND TV SHOWS

Bones. Fox Network, 2005–.
Forbrydelsen. Danmarks Radio, 2007–12.
Fringe. Fox Network, 2008–13.
In Plain Sight. USA Network. 2008–12.
The Killing. AMC, 2011–.
Law and Order: Special Victims Unit. NBC, 1999–.

NOTES

1. Jace Lacob, "'The Killing': How AMC's Adaptation of 'Forbrydelsen' Went Wrong," *Daily Beast*, May 14, 2012, http://www.thedailybeast.com/articles/2012/05/14/the-killing-how-amc-s-adaptation-of-forbrydelsen-went-wrong.html.
2. James Hibbard, "'The Killing' Ratings Drop for Season 2 Premiere," *EW.com*, April 2, 2012, http://insidetv.ew.com/2012/04/02/the-killing-ratings-2/.
3. Mike Hale, "The Danes Do Murder Differently: Comparing 'The Killing' to the Show 'Forbrydelsen'," *New York Times*, March 28, 2012, http://www.nytimes.com/2012/04/01/arts/television/comparing-the-killing-to-the-show-forbrydelsen.html.
4. E. Deidre Pribram, *Emotions, Genre, Justice in Film and Television: Detecting Feeling* (Abingdon: Routledge, 2011), 3, 4.
5. Immanuel Kant, *Fundamental Principles of the Metaphysics of Morals*, trans. Thomas Kingsmill Abbott, 1785, http://www.gutenberg.org/cache/epub/5682/pg5682.html. All references to Kant are to this online, unpaginated edition.

6. Daw-Nay Evans, "The Duty of Reason: Kantian Ethics in *High Noon*," in *The Philosophy of the Western*, ed. Jennifer L. McMahon and B. Steve Csaki (Lexington: University Press of Kentucky, 2010), 173.

7. Marcus G. Singer, "The Categorical Imperative," *Philosophical Review* 63, no. 4 (1954): 577–591.

8. Daniel Guevara, "The Impossibility of Supererogation in Kant's Moral Theory," *Philosophy and Phenomenological Research* 59, no. 3 (1999): 621.

9. Barbara Herman, "On the Value of Acting from the Motive of Duty," *Philosophical Review* 90, no. 3 (1981): 359–382.

10. Ibid.

11. Ibid., 375.

12. H. J. Paton, *The Categorical Imperative* (Chicago: University of Chicago Press, 1948), 39.

13. Herman, "On the Value of Acting from the Motive of Duty," 375.

14. Henning Jensen, "Kant and Moral Integrity," *Philosophical Studies* 57, no. 2 (1989): 203.

15. Jason Mittell, "A Cultural Approach to Television Genre Theory," *Cinema Journal* 40, no. 3 (2001): 7.

16. Margaret Mullett, "The Madness of Genre," *Dumbarton Oaks Papers* 46 (1992): 234.

17. Ken Hada, "The Cost of the Code: Ethical Consequences in *High Noon* and *The Ox-Bow Incident*," in *The Philosophy of the Western*, ed. Jennifer L. McMahon and B. Steve Csaki (Lexington: University Press of Kentucky, 2010), 187.

TEN

"I Was Hoping It Would Pass You By"

Dis/ability and Difference in Teen Wolf

Kimberley McMahon-Coleman

The 1980s *Teen Wolf* movies and the current MTV remake (2011–present) provide an interesting case study of the "rebooting" or re-imagining phenomenon. Both the filmic and television versions of the story follow ordinary high school-aged boys who suddenly discover that they are werewolves. In each case, this leads to popularity, sporting prowess, romance, and a number of other consequences, all of which the boys must manage while facing the usual trials and tribulations of adolescence. The updated version has altered the names and back stories of some of the main characters, included a more passionate teen romance and, being in series format, has allowed for greater character development over the three seasons to date. In addition to significant improvements in the quality of special effects, the tone has changed markedly, with the series being noticeably darker.

Both the earlier and later versions of the narrative focus considerably on notions of the abilities and disabilities inherent in becoming a shapeshifter. Perhaps the biggest change in the television series, however, has been to include the horror aspects which are traditionally associated with werewolf tales but which were noticeably absent from the comedic movies. In order to reintroduce the fear factor, show runner Jeff Davis returned to the notion of lycanthropy being transmissible by biting. This fundamentally changed the narrative about the "condition" faced by the eponymous teen wolf and his pack and opens it up to critique using the twin lenses of adolescence and disability.

A. *TEEN WOLF* (1985) AND *TEEN WOLF TOO* (1987): HEREDITY AND WOLF BUDDIES

The 1985 movie *Teen Wolf* and its 1987 sequel *Teen Wolf Too* focus on two members of the Howard family, Scott (played by Michael J. Fox) in the original and Todd (Jason Bateman) in the sequel. Both discover during adolescence that there is a family history of lycanthropy, and both are initially resistant to the news, reacting with denial. In each movie, becoming a werewolf brings athletic ability and social status. Those closest to the two leads express disappointment at the concomitant increase in arrogance and shift in priorities, and ultimately the Howard boys see the shallowness reflected in the popular people around them and eschew their werewolf alter egos in order to embrace the ordinariness of their human identities.

Teen Wolf's Scott Howard is an average high schooler being raised by his widower father in small-town middle America. He plays basketball for the school team—who play so badly as to be a local joke—and works after school in his father's hardware store. His best friends are the obnoxious Stiles (Jerry Levine) and childhood buddy, Boof (Susan Ursitti). Where Stiles is flamboyant and likes to surf on the roof of his van, the more conservative Scott is the driver, archly noting, "You'd never get me up there." Scott harbors a crush on popular girl Pamela (Lorie Griffin), about which he complains to Boof at length, evidently oblivious to Boof's own unrequited feelings for Scott. Scott feels stifled by the smallness of the town and his life, and laments to Boof that he is "sick of being so average . . . I'd just like my life to change." This predictable teenage plot takes a detour, however, when Scott undergoes some unexpected changes at a party on the night of the full moon. He returns to the safety of his home and locks himself in the bathroom in time to undergo his first transformation into a werewolf, accompanied by his father hammering on the bathroom door and demanding to be let in. When Scott faces his father, Harold (James Hampton), he learns that they share the condition of lycanthropy.

The revelation of Scott's inherited difference is presented as though it were a more conventional diagnosis, with the character demanding to know why his father did not warn him that it may develop. Harold admits that he had hoped Scott would not be similarly afflicted before offering some consolation which focuses on ability, rather than disability: "You're going to be able to do a lot of things the other guys aren't." Scott rejects this assertion out of hand, rehearsing a number of stereotypes about canines generally and werewolves specifically to which he assumes he will now be bound—biting the mailman, chasing cars, stealing babies, and dodging silver bullets. He complains: "I got a bad outside hook shot. I'm allergic to eggs. I got a six-dollar haircut. I mean, I have problems. I don't need this one."

Scott's "condition," however, is celebrated by his schoolmates when his animal strength, agility, and instincts turn him into the star of the school basketball team. With his new celebrity come confidence and popularity, and it is made clear to the viewer that Scott has changed when, in wolf form, he tells Stiles that the next lot of van-surfing "waves" belongs to him. The ever-pragmatic Stiles sees abundant business opportunities in being the self-appointed "Wolf Buddy" and assures Scott: "with the right angles, we're gonna turn this into something monstrous." For a time, this prediction seems to have come true: the basketball team starts to do well; Scott is cast in the school play without even trying out; Pamela not only notices him, but uses the play as both means and opportunity to seduce Scott (as the wolf) after a rehearsal; at the school dance, Scott is fêted by his peers who perform a "wolf dance" in his honor. Scott struts the halls assuring the Vice Principal that he is "just like everybody else," even when it is clear that he is attracting a great deal more attention than his peers.

Others respond to Scott's new physical differences by focusing on the monstrous. Scott's friend Lewis (Matt Adler) refuses to spend time with Scott and Stiles anymore, because Scott being a werewolf scares him. Scott is summarily fired from the school play when he refuses to play the part of a Civil War soldier in wolf form, being told, "Nobody wants to see *you.*" Pamela's boyfriend Mick (Mark Arnold) tells Scott that he's a freak and that "underneath all the hair, you're still a dork." When Scott retaliates and lunges at Mick, Pamela screams that Scott is "just some kind of animal." Those who know him best—his lifelong friend, Boof, and his father—view Scott's enjoyment of his notoriety as obnoxious and irresponsible. Boof declares that she misses "Scott Howard," and will only go as Scott's date to the dance if it is the human version of Scott, not the wolf, a condition with which he says he cannot comply. All of this ultimately leads to Scott once again rejecting his "condition" and opting to play in the basketball final as "himself"—that is, his human self—despite the disapproval of the crowd. Ultimately the ability to transgress boundaries and bodily limitations is rejected in favor of conformity and normalcy.

In the sequel, *Teen Wolf Too* (1987), Scott's cousin Todd Howard improbably wins a full athletic scholarship to college despite having shown no signs of sporting aptitude or even interest; indeed, the viewer is told that the only time Todd has been on a football field is whilst playing clarinet in the high school marching band. He is offered the scholarship based purely on Scott's earlier exploits, which are known to one of the college coaches, even though Todd has never shown any signs of lycanthropy himself. Todd is more interested in science, where he has been something of a prodigy. Todd's roommate is revealed to be Scott's best friend from high school, Stiles (Stuart Fratkin), who has changed all of Todd's classes to less academic courses which will provide him with a good time. Like the coach, Stiles believes from the outset that Todd will be able to transform and that being the "Wolf Buddy" once more will again bring business and social opportunities: "That boy's got werewolf written all over him. If everything goes as planned, he and I are going to take this school by storm."

Evidently Todd is a late bloomer, because he lives up to these expectations, sequentially becoming a werewolf, the star of the college boxing team and, by his own admission, a "jerk" over the course of the movie. Like Scott, Todd initially sees the family trait as a "problem," telling his Uncle Harold, "I'm here at a new school. It's the first time I've lived away from home. I've got to try and make new friends. I've got to try to fit in, without this hanging over me." Todd's first transformation is much more public than Scott's was—at a reception for scholarship recipients and donors—and as a result, he is teased by his classmates, who call him a "dog," ply him with fleas, and paste canine pictures over his assignments. He finds support from his biology professor (Kim Darby) and from another gifted biology student, Nicki (Estee Chandler). Todd's fortunes change when he transforms in the school boxing ring, bringing the team unexpected success. The sequel continues to follow the formula of the successful first movie, with the popular girls suddenly deciding to spend time with the new sporting star, and Todd behaving arrogantly as a result. Nicki tries to warn Todd that the attention is superficial, saying that the popular crowd do not like Todd, "only the wolf."

Todd's foray into popularity and superficiality is, of course, short lived. Because of his status on the boxing team, he does not need to study for finals as his teachers give him passing grades irrespective of his efforts or results. His decision not to include Stiles in dating opportunities leads even Stiles to declare Todd to be a "jerk" and reject him. At the end of semester, Todd finds himself alone and ill prepared for both the boxing final and the biology examination, which he has decided he should take seriously. He turns to his Uncle Harold, who offers life and boxing advice. Like Scott before him, Todd chooses to face a sporting final as his human self, not as the wolf.

Although the films are formulaic comedy and contain homilies about difference and acceptance, these are flawed representations which are ultimately undercut by the films' finales. Scott and Todd are both in turn encouraged by their romantic partners to eschew their differences and just be "themselves." In other words, their normalized selves are privileged over the condition which marks them as different, even though this is inherited and therefore very much a part of their identities. Nicki blithely tells Todd, "You can't face life as a wolf and expect it to solve all your problems," yet the narrative clearly insinuates that facing life as an average human *will* solve all of his problems. These messages are more pronounced in the sequel, with the introduction of Todd's biology professor, who offers him praise and encouragement in his studies, and warns him when he is distracted by boxing and popularity that he is "a bright young man" who will "find a way to deal with [his] other problems." This phrasing has much in common with narratives about "overcoming" disability, and is particularly troubling when the professor is revealed late in the film to be a werewolf herself, suggesting that she has succeeded in "passing" as "normal" by sublimating her own condition. Of similar concern is Nicki's earnest summation that Todd's transformation is "[b]iologically speaking . . . absolutely fascinating," which correlates with the practice of positioning people with disabilities as objects to be studied, rather than as individuals. The films thus unwittingly seem to deliver a message about "overcoming" conditions with which one is born, suggesting that individuals can overcome their differences by rejecting them and trying to be the same as their adolescent peers.

B. *TEEN WOLF* (2011–): HORROR AND WOLF HUNTERS

In the 2011 MTV reboot, the teen comedy genre is eschewed for fantasy/horror. The main character's surname is changed, removing him from the heredity of the Howard family's condition. Scott McCall (Tyler Posey) leaves his home late one night to go exploring with his friend Stiles (Dylan O'Brien), who has been listening in on the work calls of his father, the town sheriff, and has learned that there is a body in the woods (1.01, "Wolf Moon"). The two boys go exploring, Stiles in the lead with a half-formed plan (the first clue to his Attention Deficit Hyperactive Disorder diagnosis) and the asthmatic Scott trailing behind, dependent on his Ventolin puffer. The pair becomes separated and Scott is bitten by a creature, leaving him with a wound on his stomach which mysteriously heals overnight. Along with rapid healing, Scott's senses such as hearing are immediately enhanced. As the episode progresses and the full moon nears, Scott's behavior becomes increasingly more aggressive and erratic, leading Stiles to diagnose lycanthropy and tell Scott, "You're cursed."

A significant amount of airtime is given to the complex relationships between the main characters and their peers, especially within the high school setting. Drama is created through the romances between Allison (Crystal Reed) and Scott (which is problematic because she comes from a long line of werewolf hunters, and he is a werewolf); queen bee Lydia Martin (Holland Roden) and jock Jackson Whittemore (Colton Haynes); and the unrequited but clearly deep feelings of Stiles for Lydia. Social dynamics at Beacon Hills High are another major concern: Scott and another new wolf, Erica (Gage Golightly), find that their post-turn heightened abilities and attractiveness raise their social standing at school; Jackson seeks to bolster his popularity by asking to be turned; Allison is treated as a social pariah after her werewolf-hunter Aunt Kate (Jill Wagner) is killed in the line of duty and a cover story circulated that she is a serial killer; and Lydia's social standing also plummets after she is bitten by Alpha Peter Hale (Ian Bohen) and begins to experience hallucinations, culminating in her wandering naked about the woods in a fugue state for two days. Thus the everyday concerns of adolescence are always coupled with the supernatural concern of lycanthropy. Indeed, there is conjecture within the series that teens are turned because they are more resilient and therefore more likely to survive the process.

The possibility of not surviving the bite, or, in Jackson's case, of becoming a *kanima* (an alternative, vengeful shapeshifter which has its origins in South American mythology), are just two of the risks the teens face as werewolves. Perhaps the most obvious disadvantage of their condition is that it attracts the attention of Alison's werewolf-hunting family, the Argents, and their peers. It also increases risk to the werewolf's loved ones, as we see in early episodes when the newly-turned Scott struggles to control his animalistic urges and is a significant threat to the lives of both Stiles and Allison. Scott, Jackson, Boyd (Sinqua Walls), and Isaac (Daniel Sharman) embrace their increased abilities on the lacrosse field, but must also manage an increased risk of "wolfing out" and hurting someone because of their heightened aggression when on the field. Finally, Scott's worst fears about the responses of others to his lycanthropy are realized when he reveals his wolf form while rescuing his mother (Melissa Ponzio) from his psychotic schoolmate Matt (Stephen Lunsford) and the kanima over which Matt is master (2.10, "Fury"). Scott's mother recoils in horror, and in later episodes is shown to be avoiding Scott altogether (2.11, "Battlefield"). When they finally have their first conversation post-revelation, she is seen to be unable to look him in the eye. The relationship between only son and single parent, then, is markedly different in the series, where Scott's lycanthropy is introduced through an external agent, than it had been in the movies where the condition was inherited.

Homages to the earlier *Teen Wolf* films are peppered throughout the series. In the original *Teen Wolf*, Scott takes Pamela on a bowling alley date, much to the annoyance of her steady boyfriend, Mick, who is also present. In the new series, the first date between Scott and new girl Allison becomes a double date with high school power couple Lydia and Jackson at a bowling alley (1.03, "Pack Mentality"). There are parallel awkward locker room conversations with the respective versions of Coach Finstock trying to counsel the two Scotts about the "changes" they are facing (*Teen Wolf;* 1.02, "Second Chance at First Line"). Each coach erroneously assumes that the boys' awkwardness is caused by the more usual teenage flashpoints of sexuality or drugs. Even the notion of lycanthropy being hereditary is present in the form of the Hale family: Laura (Haley Roe Murphy), Derek (Tyler Hoechlin), and their Uncle Peter have all been Alphas during the first two seasons, and Derek warns the teens he turns that he is unsure how well he can train or teach them to control their condition, given that they have been bitten, rather than born (1.06, "Heart Monitor"; 2.04, "Abomination"). Perhaps the most telling echo of the earlier movies, however, is a reworking of Todd's assertion in *Teen Wolf Too* that the wolf is "a gift" into a line of dialogue spoken by were-wolf Derek Hale in the MTV series, namely, that "the bite is a gift." This has become an unofficial tagline of the series, adopted and adapted by fans who often post on social networking sites such as Tumblr and Face-book that show runner "Jeff Davis is a gift."[1] Certainly the bite concept has been a gift to Davis' storytelling, since it reanimates the Gothic within the *Teen Wolf* narrative; with the bite comes the threat that anyone could be transformed at any time.

Developing ideas from the earlier movies, lycanthropy is constructed throughout the series as simultaneously a "cure" or superpower through the ability to accelerate healing and enhance the senses, and a "condi-tion" to be managed and controlled, particularly at the full moon. Scott's asthma is cured by the bite (1.02, "Second Chance at First Line"), and teenager Erica is recruited by Derek from the Emergency Room at the hospital (2.03, "Ice Pick"). Derek wheels her into the morgue and prefaces their conversation with an examination of her epilepsy medication, not-ing that side effects "may include anxiety, weight gain, acne, ulcerative colitis." She is convinced by Derek that all her side effects and symptoms "could go away" and that "everything else"—that is, her social standing at school—can also get better. Indeed, Derek's bite does cure her epilepsy and she morphs from being rather unkempt and wearing baggy jumpers to appearing in the school lunchroom in high heels, a miniskirt and leath-er jacket, with curled hair and perfect make-up. The transformation is such that Lydia does not recognize her, asking, "What the holy hell was that?"—a comment which also signifies Erica's new, non-human status (2.03, "Ice Pick"). The bite is even offered to Scott's friend Stiles, who suffers from Attention Deficit Hyperactive Disorder (ADHD) and asth-ma, as indicated by his on-screen usage of medications Adderall and Ventolin (1.08, "Lunatic"; 2.04, "Abomination"). Alpha male and show villain Peter Hale offers to turn Stiles in return for assistance Stiles has given him (albeit under duress), telling him he could be as powerful and as popular as Scott (1.12, "Code Breaker"). Stiles rejects the offer, but Peter reads his hesitation as temptation.[2]

The most extreme case of medical conditions being cured by lycan-thropy is reserved for Alpha werewolf and Hale family patriarch Peter himself, who recovers from a decade-long comatose state and, once am-bulant, also managed to heal his face of scars incurred as a result of third-degree burns (1.9, "Wolf's Bane"). In season two, he reanimates his corpse through a curious combination of magic, the so-called worm moon (or last full moon in March), and the assistance of Lydia, who, according to series mythology, is the first known case of a human with immunity to a werewolf bite (2.03, "Ice Pick"; 2.09, "Party Guessed").

C. THE BODY AT WAR WITH ITSELF: ADOLESCENCE, DISABILITY, AND SHAPESHIFTING

The parallel between adolescence and shapeshifting is, of course, not new, having been explored as early as 1957 when Michael Landon starred in *I Was A Teenage Werewolf*, through 1980s cult films such as *Teen Wolf* and *The Lost Boys* (1987), and the *Buffy the Vampire Slayer* (1997–2003) era—which Davis cites as an inspiration for the current *Teen Wolf* series[3] —as well as dominating more recent texts featuring teenage werewolves, such as *Twilight* (2008, 2009, 2010, 2011, 2012) and *The Vampire Diaries* (2009–present). As Chappell notes, adolescence is often viewed as a time of metamorphosis because it is a period of radical physical, cognitive, and social changes.[4] As I have argued elsewhere, the supernatural genre generally and shapeshifting texts specifically "allow for distinctions between self and other, and life and death, to be framed against distinctions between childhood and adult responsibilities."[5]

Disability is defined as

> a state of decreased functioning associated with disease, disorder, injury, or other health conditions, which in the context of one's environment is experienced as an impairment, activity limitation, or participation restriction. Understanding both the health and the environmental aspects of disability allows for the examination of health interventions that improve functioning as well as interventions to change the environment to improve participation of people with disabilities.[6]

In the context of *Teen Wolf*, the lead characters face decreased functioning—in that they have safety concerns around the full moon—and social impairment because of societal fear about their abilities. Although in practice they find that they have increased physical function, there are issues around social participation and these are, at times, mismanaged. In the films, this leads to Scott and Todd eschewing their differences and embracing only the normalcy of the human selves. In the longer narrative arc of the MTV series, it remains to be seen how well Scott will handle his different abilities, but there have been incidents in both seasons where the ability to effectively manage the condition of lycanthropy so that it is not an impairment has been called into question.

Linking disability and monstrosity also has a long history. Even the scientific study of birth defects and developmental disorders is known as teratology, or literally, the study of monsters.[7] Aristotle had viewed disability as a "defective departure" from a valued standard of the body.[8] Ruth Bienstock Anolik has noted that the "impulse of Western culture to define the human norm by the physical ideal and to construe the non-normative as dangerously close to the non-human actually predates the Enlightenment by millennia."[9] As Yang Costello notes, prior to the adoption of a medical model to examine differently formed bodies in the early twentieth century, the births of non-normative children were viewed as evidence of either the glory or wrath of God.[10] She argues that when seeking to institutionalize as a profession, early obstetricians presented themselves as stoic when faced with "monsters," and that despite their focus on rationalism, terms from mythology were thus often used to describe malformed infants: conjoined legs were figured as a "mermaid fetus"; conjoined twins with one body and two heads were reported in the *Journal of Obstetrics and Gynaecology of the British Empire* as "a Janus monster," and an infant born with conjoined eyes was deemed a Cyclops baby.[11]

Non-physical disabilities have also been viewed with suspicion throughout history: it is well known that Victorian society problematized mental illness as "madness" and grounds for institutionalization, effectively removing the individual from society; Darwin's theory of evolution was mobilized by eugenicists as an argument for eliminating "defectives"—including the "feebleminded," deaf and blind,[12] and Lennard J. Davis points out that the English scientific magazine *Nature* endorsed the Nazis' proposal to sterilize patients with bipolar disorder, schizophrenia, epilepsy, blindness, deafness, alcoholism, and body malformation.[13] Gothic theorist David Punter has argued that "the history of dealings with the disabled body runs through the history of the Gothic . . . of the enemy within, of bodies torn and tortured, or else rendered miraculously, or sometimes catastrophically, whole,"[14] a description which certainly applies to werewolf lore. A number of contemporary werewolf stories— notably, both the UK and US versions of *Being Human* (UK 2008–13; US 2010–present) and *The Vampire Diaries*—have visually represented the transformation as painful, focusing on the biological difficulty inherent in breaking apart the human body in order to take on the werewolf whole.[15]

Despite all this, I acknowledge that disability may seem an unusual lens for a show which is, after all, light entertainment—aimed at a teenage audience and featuring equal parts romance and gore. Further, show runner Jeff Davis has insisted (arguably somewhat disingenuously, when embroiled in an online controversy about depictions of race in the series) that this is not "an issues show."[16] Davis has argued that all casting breakdowns explicitly welcome "all ethnicities," before claiming that he "skirt(s) the issues of race and sexual politics . . . I don't feel like I'm going to be very good at tackling those issues within a show about teenage werewolves."[17] Yet gender politics are still present, as when Erica is singled out as being better able to handle pain, because she is used to menstruation (2.09, "Party Guessed"). Racial politics have also been both evident and contentious, with the social media response above being prompted by criticism leveled at the program because the supporting teenage werewolf of color, Boyd, has significantly less well-developed storylines than the white supporting teenage werewolves, Isaac and Erica.

As Heidi Lewis has argued in response to Davis's comments, "pesky li'l issues about race, gender and sexuality . . . tend to converge from time to time,"[18] even if that is not the intention of the *auteur*. In this context, and bearing in mind that people with disabilities are the largest reported minority group in the United States,[19] it is possible to read *Teen Wolf*, with its narrative obsession on curing difference, as an ableist discourse. Scott's pre-existing physical impairment—chronic asthma, which prevents him from achieving at the highest levels in his preferred sport, lacrosse—is cured at the same time as his high school unpopularity (1.01, "Wolf Moon"; 1.02, "Second Chance at First Line"); that is, after he is bitten by a werewolf and becomes one himself, a fate which could befall any of the human characters at any time. He is therefore linked to the medical model of disability, which presumes that an individual's diagnosis is a personal medical condition that requires an individualized medical solution.[20] Within the television series, the first proposed solution for managing his asthma is the judicious use of an inhaler, which has had limited results but for which Scott is held personally responsible. The second and more effective solution is supernatural: a bite that turns him into a werewolf and cures him of human frailties. The medical model is the prevailing paradigm within the United States, but it seems to contrast with how other forms of discrimination are typically viewed. For example, discrimination against racial minorities, LGBTI individuals, and women is typically viewed as being more of a problem with the ways in which society accepts—or does not accept—difference. An alternative framework, the social model of disability, is more in line with this world view, defining disability as a social construct.[21] This also posits any barriers related to disability as social constructs; in other words, any perceived problems are not for the individual to solve by medical means, but for society to solve by adjusting the social context. In Scott, we see a medical model—wherein his asthma and even (at times) his lycanthropy are established as physical ailments which he must attempt to control. The biggest threat to Scott's health and well-being throughout the series thus far, however, has been social: the responses of the Argent family of werewolf hunters. Family members have been trained since adolescence to see lycanthropy as a threat to society and one which they are morally obligated to eradicate, echoing eugenicist arguments about eliminating difference.

All werewolf texts at some point deal implicitly or explicitly with the concept of "passing" or hiding one's difference; the werewolf, after all, is only a monster under certain circumstances (typically at the time of the full moon, although in the *Teen Wolf* franchise the lycanthropes can also change at will), and is human most of the time. This parallels histories in racial studies and disability studies of attempting to mask difference and blend in with the hegemony, and is therefore a trope which can be mobilized in a variety of ways within popular culture. In MTV's *Teen Wolf*, the characters who are to be turned into werewolves are often targeted because they have physical weaknesses and can therefore be convinced to embrace supernatural werewolf abilities which will cure these weaknesses, yet the bodily "defects"—asthma, ADHD, epilepsy—depicted within the show are all ones which are only apparent under certain circumstances. The message within these texts is that with medication, good management, and trigger controls, the individual can limit the affliction and therefore "pass" as "normal." Indeed, when Erica is admitted to the hospital for an epileptic fit suffered at school, she is chided by Scott's mother, the admitting nurse, about how she had been doing so well and they had not seen her for a while (2.03, "Ice Pick"). Erica, for her part, sees the episode as somehow shameful, suggesting hopefully that perhaps her mother does not need to be informed. It is also interesting to note that the trio of supporting characters turned by Derek are all also socially vulnerable: Erica has been harassed and mocked at school after having a very public fit in class, footage of which was later broadcast online (2.03, "Ice Pick"); Boyd is a social outcast who sits alone at lunch (2.03, "Ice Pick"); and Isaac's father beats him mercilessly (2.02, "Shape Shifted").

Finally, by reintegrating the horror element of the bite into the storyline, the new version of *Teen Wolf* also reflects the notion of the Temporarily Able Bodied, or TABs.[22] A term often used by people with disabilities to refer to the able bodied, it reflects that the majority of people with disabilities were not born with them, but have developed them as a result of illness or accident, and that there is a risk that, over a lifetime, any individual may become temporarily or permanently disabled. The characters who are bitten are temporarily super-able bodied, and in Lydia's immunity there is the suggestion that a cure may be possible, which will render the teen wolves once again wholly human and thus vulnerable to human frailty and illness. The abilities and physical strength of any particular character within the series are thus fluid, as they could increase (with the bite) or decrease (if the transformation is unsuccessful, or if a future cure is found).

Any werewolf-themed text will explore deviations from the idealized standard of the so-called normalized body. The figure of the shapeshifter offers possibilities to rethink boundaries around identity.[23] This is not to suggest that equating disability and monstrosity is unproblematic[24]; certainly it is as troubling as, for example, the oft-critiqued notion in the *Twilight* series that the ability to shift shape into an animal is raced.[25] When the ability to shift one's bodily shape is codified as both a physical vulnerability and conversely, a source of strength,[26] however, this kind of reading does provide opportunities to critique messages about physical and psychological difference which are being portrayed to a mass audience through popular culture.

In the *Teen Wolf* films of the 1980s, the narratives first position lycan-thropy as an inherited liability to be shunned and feared, then as a source of strength and popularity, before coming to the conclusion that it is better to eschew difference and conform. In the MTV remake, lycanthro-py is constructed as something which can either be inherited or transmit-ted, which is "sold" to potential werewolves as a cure for their physical ailments, but which then subjects them to social constructs around their difference. Both inadvertently send some troubling and at times contra-dictory messages about difference and disability, but strongly suggest to their adolescent viewers the importance of focusing more on ability than disability.

FILMS AND TV SHOWS

Being Human. BBC, 2008–13.
Being Human. Syfy, 2011–.
Buffy the Vampire Slayer. The WB, 1997–2001; UPN, 2001–03.
I Was A Teenage Werewolf. Directed by Gene Fowler, Jr. 1957. American International Pictures.
The Lost Boys. Directed by Joel Schumacher. 1987. Warner Bros.
Teen Wolf. Directed by Rod Daniel. 1985. Atlantic.
Teen Wolf. MTV, 2011–.
Teen Wolf Too. Directed by Christopher Leitch. 1987. Atlantic.
Twilight. Directed by Catherine Hardwicke. 2008. Summit.
The Twilight Saga: Breaking Dawn – Part 1. Directed by Bill Condon. 2011. Summit.
The Twilight Saga: Breaking Dawn – Part 2. Directed by Bill Condon. 2012. Summit.
The Twilight Saga: Eclipse. Directed by David Slade. 2010. Summit.
The Twilight Saga: New Moon. Directed by Chris Weitz. 2009. Summit.
The Vampire Diaries. The CW, 2009–.

NOTES

1. "Jeff Davis is a Gift," n.d., www.tumblr.com/tagged/jeff-davis-is-a-gift; Austin Joseph Anderson, "Jeff Davis is a Gift," n.d., jeffdavisisamaster.tumblr.com.
2. Kimberley McMahon-Coleman and Roslyn Weaver, *Werewolves and Other Shap-eshifters in Popular Culture: A Thematic Analysis of Recent Depictions* (Jefferson: McFar-land, 2012), 118.
3. Alex Pappademas, "We Are All Teenage Werewolves," *The New York Times Magazine*, May 2011.
4. Shelley Chappell, *Werewolves, Wings and Other Weird Transformations: Fantastic Metamorphosis in Children's and Young Adult Fantasy Literature.* (PhD dis., Sydney: Mac-quarie University 2007), 122.
5. McMahon-Coleman and Weaver, *Werewolves,* 17.

6. Matilde Leonardi et al., "The Definition of Disability: What's in a Name?," *The Lancet* (2006): 1219.

7. The Teratology Society, *The Teratology Society Fact Sheet*, n.d.; McMahon-Coleman and Weaver, *Werewolves*; Carrie Yang Costello, "Teratology: 'Monsters' and the Professionalization of Obstetrics," *Journal of Historical Sociology* 19, no. 1 (2006): 1.

8. Rosemarie Garland-Thomson, "Integrating Disability, Transforming Feminist Theory," *NWSA Journal* 14, no. 3 (2002): 1–32.

9. Ruth Bienstock Anolik, *Demons of the Body and Mind: Essays on Disability in Gothic Literature* (Jefferson, NC: McFarland, 2010), 4.

10. Yang Costello, "Teratology," 2.

11. Ibid., 25–26.

12. Lennard J. Davis, "Constructing Normalcy: The Bell Curve, the Novel, and the Invention of the Disabled Body in the Nineteenth Century," in *The Disability Studies Reader*, ed. Lennard J. Davis (London & New York: Routledge, 2006), 7.

13. Ibid., 10.

14. David Punter, "'A foot is what fits the shoe': Disability, the Gothic and Prostheis," *Gothic Studies* 2, no. 1 (2000): 40.

15. McMahon-Coleman and Weaver, *Werewolves*, 120–122.

16. "Jeff Davis comments about race and racism on Teen Wolf," *Oh No They Didn't!*, July 30, 2012, accessed February 18, 2013, http://ohnotheydidnt.livejournal.com/70761097.html; Rich Juzwiak, "Teen Wolf Creator Responds to Allegations of Racism, Deletes Post," *Gawker*, July 31, 2012, accessed February 21, 2013, http://gawker.com/5930518/racism-debate-ravages-teen-wolfs-online-community.

17. "Jeff Davis comments."

18. Heidi R. Lewis, "Jeff Davis, Teen Wolf and the Invisibility of Whiteness," *So You Think You Can Blog*, August 21, 2012, accessed February 19, 2013, http://community/feministing.com/2012/08/21/jeff-davis-teen-wolf-and-the-invisibility-of-whiteness/.

19. Barrier Free Choices, "Who's Disabled in America?," accessed May 31, 2013, http://www.barrierfreechoices.com/whodis/who_4.html; Karen Mcveigh, "Disabled 'World's Largest Minority'," *Sydney Morning Herald*, June 11, 2011, accessed May 31, 2013, http://www.smh.com.au/world/disabled-worlds-largest-minority-20110610_1fx19.html; Disability Funders Network, "Disability Stats and Facts," 2012, accessed May 31, 2013, http://www.disabilityfunders.org/disability_stats_and_facts.

20. Bradley A. Areheart, "When Disability Isn't 'Just Right': The Entrenchment of the Medical Model of Disability and the Goldilocks Dilemma," *Indiana Law Journal* 83 (2008): 181–232.

21. Ibid., 188.

22. Beverly Chapman, "Let the Wall of Misunderstanding Come Tumbling Down for Everyone," *Orlando Sentinel*, December 12, 1991; Bill Hughes, "Being Disabled: Towards a Critical Social Ontology for Disability Studies," *Disability and Society* 22, no. 7 (2007): 1–32.

23. McMahon-Coleman and Weaver, *Werewolves*, 117.

24. Roslyn Weaver, "Metaphors of Monstrosity: The werewolf as disability and illness in *Harry Potter* and *Jatta*," *Papers* 40, no. 2 (2010): 69; McMahon-Coleman and Weaver, *Werewolves*, 117.

25. McMahon-Coleman and Weaver, *Werewolves*, 98–102; Chappell, "Contemporary Werewolf Schemata: Shifting Representations of Racial and Ethnic Difference," *International Research in Children's Literature* 2, no.1 (2009): 21–35; Kristian Jensen, "Noble Werewolves or Native Shape-Shifters?," in *The Twilight Mystique*, ed. Amy M. Clarke and Marijane Osborn (Jefferson, NC: McFarland, 2010), 92–106; Natalie Wilson, "It's A Wolf Thing: The Quileute Werewolf/Shape-Shifter Hybrid as Noble Savage," in *Theorizing Twilight: Critical Essays on What's At Stake in a Post-Vampire World*, ed. Maggie Parker and Natalie Wilson (Jefferson, NC: McFarland, 2011): 194–208.

26. McMahon-Coleman and Weaver, *Werewolves*, 120.

ELEVEN

That Haunting, Eerie Return

Narrative, Genre, and Iconography in Dark Shadows *and* Dark Shadows: The Revival

Lorna Piatti-Farnell

In recent years, the vampire has returned to the television scene as an unavoidable presence. While contemporary incarnations owe a lot to a distinctly twenty-first-century brand of Gothic imagination, vampires populated the storylines of the small screen long before *True Blood* (2008–present) and *The Vampire Diaries* (2009–present) found their popularity with audiences. One such example was *Dark Shadows* (1966–71). Often defined as a "Gothic soap opera," *Dark Shadows* was characterized by melodramatic performances, atmospheric settings, and supernatural creatures, including the famous vampire Barnabas Collins.[1] Continuing to be produced and broadcasted for five more seasons, and maintaining a hold on the popular imagination even after its cancellation, *Dark Shadows* was then resurrected in 1991 under the name *Dark Shadows: The Revival Series*. In this version of the story, the attention shifted its focus from the dramatic uncanny to a decidedly more vampiric and love-centered interpretation of the plot. The re-elaboration of the supernatural motif, and its impact on narrative, genre definition, and characterization, opens the way for discussions of a cultural nature, exposing the Gothic's ability to engage with contextual anxieties, fears, and desires.

Using this contention as a starting point, this chapter analyzes the shifting representation of Barnabas Collins as a generationally—and contextually—delineated figure in the fictional world of *Dark Shadows*. My discussion begins by interrogating the complications involved in the re-

155

making process when Gothic elements are involved, concentrating particularly on issues of narrative and genre. This approach follows John Frow's suggestion that genre comprises a list of emblematic interactions that "create effects of reality, truth [and] plausibility within a given storytelling context."[2] In these terms, I analyze the series' versatile manipulation of culturally prescribed iconography—such as clothing and fangs—that has shaped the audience's understanding and appreciation of the vampire motif over time, and the relationship between predator and prey within a sexualized framework. My discussion focuses particularly on the enhancement of the romantic element in the 1991 remake and the effect this had on the Gothic nature of the storytelling. While hinting at symbolic connections that glamorize the paranormal romance, the generational vampires of *Dark Shadows* re-elaborate the Gothic genre within a television context, and pluralize the manners in which shifting political, aesthetic, and cultural paradigms colonize the supernatural.

A. THE "GOTHIC SOAP OPERA"

Dark Shadows originally aired on the US network ABC on June 27, 1966. The soap opera narrative began with the arrival of Victoria Winters (Alexandra Isles), a governess, at Collinwood, an ancestral mansion still housing the members of the Collins family. At the beginning, the series was established as a "classic female Gothic narrative," and, recalling many aspects of inceptional Gothic, it did not hinge on any supernatural concepts.[3] The supernatural element grew in response to low followings as an attempt to increase audience ratings. In the first season, the unexpected appearance of a ghost spiked the audience's interest. The inclusion of the supernatural proved so successful that, in season two, it progressed to the inclusion of Barnabas Collins (Jonathan Frid), a 200-year-old vampire who proved instantly popular with the viewers. Barnabas is said to have really caught the imagination of the audience,[4] so much of the plot was made to revolve around him as the principal character.

The cultural impact of the vampire here should not come as a surprise. As a character belonging to both the Gothic and the popular imaginations, the vampire has become, in Milly Williamson's words, a figure "of emulation," one in which we "find a version of . . . ourselves."[5] The vampire's ability to embody both commonality and difference proves an effective tool in capturing contextual dilemmas and desires. It is therefore not difficult to imagine how its presence would have transformed *Dark Shadows* into a saga that was "close to home" for the audience; through "otherness" comes identification, and the popularity of the original Barnabas within the domestic setting of the late 1960s testifies to the supernatural Gothic's ability to condense, as Fred Botting puts it, the "perceived threats," "imaginative excesses and delusions" which are particular to any given era.[6]

The 1966 debut date is particularly significant in terms of narrative context and genre identification. June 1966 was only a few months after two other famous monster-centered series, *The Addams Family* (1964–66) and *The Munsters* (1964–66), were cancelled. *Dark Shadows* followed in an established path of mixing Gothic elements and uncanny locations with everyday characters and situations, but, unlike *The Addams Family* and *The Munsters*, its tone, presentation, and subject matter took a different path. While its predecessors had merged the light-heartedness of the family sitcom with the gloomy outlook of Gothic horror, *Dark Shadows* dispensed with humor in favor of a conceptual fusion between the family feuds proper to the soap opera genre and the narrative characteristics of the Gothic storyline. The mixture of family narrative and horror elements was contextually significant, as it uncovered the shifts in the generic understanding of television programs within the wider cultural scope. Vivian Sobchank contends that "from the 1960s onward, family life and social life have continued to converge," and within this chronology, horror "has been transformed into a generic form that includes elements of the family melodrama."[7] In this context, the original *Dark Shadows* emerges as a Gothic family saga where horror and the supernatural converge to create an "opposing realism."[8] The series' heritage within the boundaries of the supernatural Gothic was clear from the very beginning in not only its use of particular stock characters and situations—from the meek but curious governess to the troubled lady of the house, and shady family friends with less-than-honorable, financially driven intentions—but also in its use of appropriate locations. Location is an important part of the Gothic mode, as it aids a construction of appropriate atmospheres that, as Botting reminds us, have been known to signal "the return of pasts upon presents."[9] As it entertained the return of Barnabas Collins, and his supernatural ability to bridge the gap between past and present, *Dark Shadows* made a virtue of its visual relationship to haunted mansions, shadowy rooms, and fittingly gloomy graveyards. While similar locations had previously appeared, at least in aesthetic terms, as the background scenery in horror-inspired comedy series such as *The Addams Family*, *Dark Shadows* transformed them into atmospheric settings that aided the construction of a Gothic world which was pivotally centered on feelings of uncertainty, hesitation, and even fear.

The categorization of *Dark Shadows* as a "Gothic soap opera" combined two aspects of narrative uncertainty in a number of ways. Richard Davenport-Hines identifies the very existence and stance of the soap opera as a television genre that is conceptually connected to the presentation of the Gothic as a mode of ambiguity and disbelief: "Improbable coincidences, melodrama, sudden death . . . television soap opera provides the twentieth century equivalent of gothic novels."[10] The success of

Dark Shadows as a "Gothic soap opera," however, rests not simply in its conceptual relationship to both narrative structures, and its knack for combining them, but in its distinct ability to transform the terror and gloom of the Gothic mode into an ordinary situation, one that does not trivialize death and deceit, but uncovers them as agents of the everyday. In the series, the secrets of the Gothic are the cogs of everyday family life, and it is precisely this synthesis of approaches that allowed the development of marvelous narratives, filled as they were with fantastic hauntings and supernatural creatures, to be accepted, as Helen Wheatley puts it, as "commonplace," and "absorbed into the everyday goings-on of the soap narrative." [11]

The original series was categorized as a soap opera and placed within the daytime period of programming. Considering the Gothic nature of the series, the decision to consign it to the afternoon slot was revolutionary and risky at the same time. Wheatley points out that in merging Gothic horror with the soap opera format the program broke "day time rules." [12] This split was connected to the subject matter, which made no attempt to include humor and sitcom situations in the Gothic framework. In spite of its Gothic influences and later supernatural deceits, however, the show was always conceived of as a soap opera, as Mark Dawidziak and Jay Stevenson remind us: "The storytelling always revolved around various love affairs and domestic disputes," leaving no doubt as to the genre categorization of the series and where it belonged in the programming schedule. [13] The time of broadcasting is perhaps the primary difference through which the remake of 1991 needs to be evaluated. *The Revival* did not follow in the original's footsteps and was conceived instead as a family drama; this conceptualization was mirrored in its primetime broadcast spot. At the time of release, creator Dan Curtis, who had also developed the original series, stated that the change in broadcasting time meant that "the essential characters and relationships" were the same, but the changed target audience required that the "things" they did were "different." Curtis also made it clear that the changes in *The Revival*'s narrative structure meant that "all the incidents" were different, and that the characters arrived "at similar points through a much different route." [14]

This shift in structural understanding inevitably had an impact on the genre and narrative categorization of the remake series; distancing itself from the domestic pitfalls of the soap opera, *The Revival* presented itself as a more "adult" series, one that promised to deal with adult and potentially sexual themes—a promise that it undoubtedly fulfilled. The narrative structure of the original *Dark Shadows*, set out as a soap opera, was also ideally suited to the generation of ambiguous situations and contested knowledge; as a genre, the soap opera relies on long and drawn-out evaluations of situations and characters, and most importantly, on shocking end-of-episode revelations that define the storyline as one of domestic doubt and suspense. Helen Wheatley argues that, in terms of narrative structures, *Dark Shadows'* greatest achievement was its ability to play with the soap opera's definitive feature of the cliffhanger and mold it into an agent of terror, providing "a threatening sense of suspense between episodes."[15] A famous instance of this common storytelling tool within the series can be found at the time of Barnabas Collins's first appearance in the show. At the end of episode 210—aired in April 1967— a mysterious hand emerges from a hidden coffin to grab the throat of greedy caretaker Willy Loomis. The narrative ends without explaining the situation and leaves the audience reveling in an overarching sense of atmospheric threat that is carried into the next episode. The existence of Barnabas Collins is not revealed until later episodes and, even then, the series makes no clear connection between "the hand in the coffin" and the suave English gentleman visiting Collinwood. The seemingly unresolved inclusion of a mysterious character becomes validated by the domestic setting of the family saga, even when the enigmatic presence of potentially supernatural tropes remains unanswered for a long period of time.

The development of the narrative in the original *Dark Shadows* is, in true soap opera style, carried out at a slow pace. Long dialogues and drawn-out expressions are the order of the day. The slow nature of both characterization and narrative in the series is made particularly eloquent by the presentation of Barnabas Collins himself, whose meditative moments find him staring into a fictional distance that overspills into oceans of time. Although they contribute greatly in slowing down the pace of the storytelling—especially in his early appearances in season two—Barnabas's pensive moments are a definitive characteristic of how the narrative develops a textual relationship with audience that is based on suspense, questioning, and unintelligibility. The real identity and history of Barnabas are uncovered over a long period of time, over a large number of episodes. When Barnabas presents himself as a long-lost family relative from England, the Collinses readily accept this strange coincidence without question and welcome him into the fold. The acceptance is inspired by the current Barnabas's resemblance to the old portrait of his "ancestor," the "original" eighteenth-century Barnabas Collins, that still hangs in the foyer of Collinwood. This seemingly unbelievable development is in keeping with the soap opera's unrealistic approach to narrative structures, where, as Lara Parker reminds us, "the absurdity of a ludicrous situation" is unquestioned and accepted as "normal."[16]

The narrative hints at the fact that Barnabas is a mysterious individual, and even gestures towards his connection to horrible and life-changing events, but his status as a vampire is not revealed until much later in the series. His vampiric activities are merely implied, but never actually entertained on the screen. The slow-paced narrative of *Dark Shadows* feeds into the feelings of hesitation that surround characters and situations, especially when the supernatural is involved. The aura of uncertainty is also strengthened by Barnabas's unbelievable knowledge of Collins family history—which he claims to have learned from diaries, journals, and chronicles—and his sardonic suggestions and references to the life of the original Barnabas (himself), that leaves the audience unsure about his real identity. As Barnabas's position as resident vampire is gradually revealed, the occurrence is no longer news; the narrative hints at this fact for so long, and for so many episodes, that when the supernatural element is in fact revealed, it is hardly a surprise. The series' characters—and, to some extent, the audience—accept what he is as a matter of fact, and his vampire identity is absorbed into a "sub-category of fantasy" to which the soap opera clearly belongs.[17] As the narrative develops, the drawn-out discovery of Barnabas's vampiric status, one could argue, appears to be reminiscent of the program's relationship with the wider scope of Gothic literature, and its connection to a heritage of horror and terror that relies on the slow explanation of mysteries as the basis for the uncanny.

The Revival, however, takes a different approach to the narrative structure, especially when Barnabas Collins—now played by Ben Cross—is concerned. The first element to notice is the conspicuous absence of the narrative arc centered on Victoria Winters (Joanna Going)'s arrival and encounters with Collinwood. Her uncanny relationship to the dark secrets of the mansion is readily discarded in the remake. While her arrival at the Collins family home is still placed at the beginning of the series, it coincides with the appearance of Barnabas himself within the narrative. It is made clear that the two events animate the plot of the series, and that a connection between the two characters—the obvious romance—is the center of the narrative structure. Dispensing with a decidedly uncanny part of the original series is not the only point on which the narrative of the remake deviates from the original. Barnabas's status as a centuries-old vampire is revealed quickly and without ceremony in the very first episode. While the pretense that he is a long-lost relative is maintained within the character-relationship part of the exegesis, Barnabas's vampiric nature is revealed to the audience as he attacks two patrons at the local bar. Barnabas's characterization loses the sense of mystery that made him so uncannily appealing in the original series. The newly conceived narrative of the vampire in the 1991 remake is undoubtedly "fantastic," but its relationship to the Gothic mode is challenged. According to Tzvetan Todorov, the delineation of "fantastic narratives" hinges on the play between the normal and the supernatural. Storylines can be viewed as being in this class if they begin with the presentation of something extraordinary, but "end with an acceptance of the supernatural."[18] The limits of the fantastic, as delineated by Todorov, still exist in the remake, but they lose their distinctive uncanny allure as the storyline abandons the understanding of the vampire as a Gothic presence of furtivity in favor of a romanticized vision of the creature as simply supernatural. If the remade vampire Barnabas's presentation remains Gothic, it does so by virtue of its maintained relationship to boundaries of life and death, and the feelings of fear that derive from it, not because of the play of familiarity and unfamiliarity, knowledge and ignorance, darkness and light, truth and deceit that was at the basis of the narrative structure and characterization of the Barnabas Collins storylines in the original version.

B. THE VAMPIRE HIMSELF

The rubric of "vampire" immediately brings with it recognizable connotations that are both cultural and contextual. Although the vampire's ontology is left conveniently undiscussed in each version of the series — what is, really, a vampire? — both the original and the revival approach the vampire in aesthetic terms that inevitably have a bearing on the conceptual. There are similarities between the two interpretations of "vampire," but the ways in which the concept is presented are profoundly different, and so is the characterization that follows. Both vampires bear a physical resemblance, not only to each other, but also to their vampiric predecessors, so that "the syntax of the vampire," as Tim Kane phrases it, continues to "portray some of the characteristics of previous incarnations."[19] The iconic cape is still present, but it is distinctly modernized; the dark grey overcoats worn by Frid in the 1960s had a touch of the Victorian, and while Cross still wears the garment in 1991, its appearance resembles late twentieth-century fashion to a greater extent.

As far as aesthetic presentation is concerned, it is virtually impossible to adequately discuss any incarnation of the vampire without mentioning, even briefly, the presence of blood and fangs. The latter is, in particular, an extremely iconic presence for the vampire, and, as such, the telltale sign of the creature. Both original *Dark Shadows* and *The Revival* use fangs to communicate the presence of the vampire. The appearance of fangs here does not conform to folkloristic interpretations of the vampire, as fangs are not known to be an implement of the vampires originating from European folklore.[20] "Fangs" — defined iconographically as sharp and elongated canine teeth — are, historically, the product of twentieth-century literary and cinematic imaginations, fueled by examples such as Lee's interpretation of Dracula and, later, Anne Rice's *Interview with the Vampire* (1976), marking the beginning of her *Vampire Chronicles*. As fangs as such are an unavoidable presence in *Dark Shadows*, the impact of late twentieth-century literary and cinematic imagination is virtually impossible to ignore.

Nonetheless, while the 1960s version draws out the fangs' appearance for a number of episodes — in order to create the soap-opera-style aura of uncertainty and mystery — the 1990s remake shows them in episode one.

The discovery of the vampire is not what drives the narrative in *The Revival*, as his presence is made clear from the start. This decision to show the vampire "for what it is" from the beginning is in keeping with cinematic interpretations that closely precede *The Revival*, such as Tony Scott's *The Hunger* (1983) and Kathryn Bigelow's *Near Dark* (1987), where fangs signal the iconographical presence of the vampire from the beginning of the narrative. One can see here how the treatment of fangs in the original *Dark Shadows* and *The Revival* differs not so much aesthetically, but conceptually. In the former, the fangs are placed in the narrative tradition of classic Dracula-centered cinema, where discovering the presence of the vampire is one of the most affected moments in the narrative. Fangs, Kane reminds us, break the vampire's ability to act as a "social being," as they act as the demarcation of the killer, with "blood trickling down the chin."[21] In the latter, on the other hand, the fangs are evocative from the early moment of the vampire's introduction, as they represent the vampire's lust for blood—and the inevitable sexual lust that follows—as culturally inspired, generational presence. After all, the function of the fangs as a symbolic presence for sexual penetration has long been associated with the vampire motif, since the biting of one's neck (or even other body parts) is, as Barb Karg, Arjean Spaite, and Rick Sutherland remind us, "a highly erotic act," which is in keeping with the vampire's portrayal as a creature of extreme sexual prowess.[22]

The attention to fangs reveals how the two series propose diverging understandings of the vampire persona. Jonathan Frid's vampire is steeped not only in folklore, but also in literary and early cinematic traditions. He can transform into a bat; this power of transmutation makes him akin to Stoker's Dracula, who could transform into not only a bat, but also into an appropriately Gothic mist. Two definitive characteristics of Frid's Barnabas are his long, penetrating pauses and powerful monologues; both abound in the series, and are a reflection of the vampire's reluctant nature and conflicted self, ranging in chronology from his return to Collinwood in season two, to his encounters with his victims in later episodes. The intensity of these melodramatic moments uncovers the conceptual debt that the original *Dark Shadows* owed to classic cinematic vampire films such as Tod Browning's *Dracula* (1931), where Bela Lugosi offered an intense performance of the vampiric character, aided greatly by his theatrical manner, magnetic speech delivery, and striking Hungarian accent—so striking, in fact, that later generations often came to think of this accent as the way vampires sounded, regardless of provenance and time period.

Unlike Frid's interpretation, Cross's vampire is dramatic rather than melodramatic. The aesthetics of the vampire in *The Revival* follow cinematic depictions of the creature inspired by examples such as Terence Fisher's *Horror of Dracula* (1958). A significant scene in episode one of *The Revival* shows Barnabas biting his victims in a rather garish way; the most significant part of this is the presence of red eyes, a bloody mouth, and of course long fangs. The presentation of the act resembles a similar scene in *Horror of Dracula*, where Christopher Lee displays—for the very first time—the red eyes and long fangs that have now become an iconic part of the vampire's aesthetic mystique. This is not to say, of course, that Frid's Barnabas did not feel the influence of Lee's Dracula. There are instances (such as the one found in episode 226) where Frid's Barnabas is known to enter his victims' bedrooms through open French doors, surrounded by a menacing aura; this method of approaching victims was of course a favorite of Lee's Dracula as well. Overall, however, the bloody nature of Cross's Barnabas constructed a stronger connection to horror interpretations of the vampire such as the ones found in Fisher's movie, while Frid's incarnation was a more Gothicized version of the creature, where the dichotomy of light and darkness, alive and dead, and "good" and "evil" played a bigger part.

C. FROM "I'M FREE NOW AND ALIVE" TO "AN EXQUISITE ROMANCE"

The most significant difference between the two series is, undoubtedly, the approach that the narrative takes to the relationship between Barnabas Collins and Victoria Winters. In the 1966–71 version, the initial relationship between Victoria and Barnabas is simply based on historical curiosity. Barnabas's return to Collinwood, and the "old house" that was the principal ground for his life in the eighteenth century, is filled with both regret and wistful desires, as the ancestral home becomes the symbolic rendition of his experiences of both horror and passion before and after he was transformed into a vampire. The theme of "freedom" here emerges as particularly important in the series. Considering the socio-historical moment in which the series was developed, this focus does not come as a surprise. Jenny Diski contends that the post-war environment that gave way to the 1960s transformed this iconic decade into a time to "reinvent" identities and experience freedom—socially, politically, and even sexually—in "a climate made ready" for it.[23] The dreams of "liberation, permission, and a great enlarging of possibilities," Diski goes on to say, became a social reality that strongly opposed old social conventions and restrictions.[24] And while the focus on "new identities" emerged as an important preoccupation in the wider cultural scope, it also pervaded the narratives of numerous television series—from *Mission: Impossible* (1966–73) to *The Saint* (1962–69)—where the topic of reinvention found a prolific site for representation. This cultural experience and pursuit of new possibilities is clearly visible in the interpretation of the vampire in *Dark Shadows*, where Barnabas Collins emerges from his entombed existence—both metaphorical and literal—to openly challenge the authority of his long-dead father who, in the narrative structure of the series, had feared and subsequently trapped his young and socially unacceptable son. In charge of his own destiny, and living in a new millennium, the 1960s vampire acts as a potent allegorical representation of social reinvention.

Victoria, for her part, is inquisitive and interested in Barnabas's own history and knowledge of the Collins home. Their connection is, if anything, one of friendship—albeit an uncertain and unreliable one. As far as romance and passion go, Barnabas's interest finds an object in local waitress Maggie Evans, who is said to resemble his long-lost love Josette, and whom he later kidnaps and hypnotizes in order to make his vampire bride. It is only when his plan backfires, and the experience leaves Maggie in a regressed, child-like state, that he then turns his attention to Victoria. He then pursues her affection with a mixture of deceit, cunning, and even a touch of sorcery. Although he eventually manages to elope with the governess, a time-traveling twist transports her back to the eighteenth century, where she remains, unable to return to the present. Victoria's fate uncovers her as just another gravitational figure in the main storyline that is completely colonized by the masculine presence of Barnabas, the center of the Collins family history, whose magnetic power drives the narrative events for six whole seasons, from 1967 to 1971.

The remake, on the other hand, offers the relationship between Barnabas and Victoria a different treatment. Barnabas becomes enamored with Victoria upon their very first meeting, and the attraction, it is made clear, is mutual. Unlike in the 1960s version, where waitress Maggie bore a resemblance to Josette, in the remake it is Victoria who bears the similarity, therefore revealing the reason for Barnabas's quick infatuation. The very first episode of the series focuses centrally on Barnabas's efforts to seduce young Victoria, a feat at which he succeeds. The narrative, however, gestures towards proposing Victoria as the reincarnation of Josette, an idea that is reiterated by Barnabas himself, as he gazes at the portrait of his long-lost bride and confirms Victoria to be her reincarnation: "Josette, you have come back to me." And as the two lovers are reunited, romance is revealed as the real start of the show; Barnabas goes as far as terming their reunion as "an exquisite romance." The personalities of the two versions of Barnabas are in keeping with the different re-elaborations of the vampire motif, and its relationship to the narrative structures of both series. While Frid's original Barnabas was witty and cunning, Cross's interpretation is openly vengeful. While Frid's incarnation was love-sick and reluctant in his endeavors, Cross's version is lustful and cruel. And as the original *Dark Shadows* pivoted on Barnabas's scheming and conniving plans to regain control of his ancestral seat, the remake turns its attention to his sole purpose of positioning himself in the family circle, so that he can regain happiness with his long-lost love. The visualization of the vampire is inseparable here from the uses the series makes of central preoccupations, and while domestic disputes and invasions are pivotal in the original version, sexual desires and aims of "possession" are the definitive features of the remake.

The treatment of the vampire as a romantic creature whose endeavors are centered on regaining romantic happiness and the philosophy, as Botting puts it, that "love never dies," are distinctive features of early 1990s re-interpretations of popular vampire narratives.[25] *The Revival* is not alone in providing a distinctly romance-centered vision of the vampire in this period, and fits into a culturally sympathetic trend—in cinema, television, and even literature—of rendering the Gothic creature as a love figure. Several instances abound in this category, but one example springs to mind here. 1992 marked the release of Francis Ford Coppola's extravagant rendition of Bram Stoker's *Dracula*, in which the politicized preoccupations of the novel—in terms of invasion, identity, geography, and Empire—are replaced by the "overlaying of a distinctly romantic theme" that twisted the original text's "nastiness in confused, if not contradictory, directions."[26] The film was criticized at the time as having added layers of useless sentimentalism to the original text, and to having produced a dubious narrative where romance, as Thomas Elsaesser contends, "emasculates the potency of the very notion of the undead."[27]

In similar vein, *The Revival* converts all senseless violence on the vampire's part into necessary evils in a seemingly noble quest to reclaim love. Even when confronted with death and destruction at the vampire's hands—or, to be more specific, at the vampire's fangs—the audience is openly asked to see the horror as a subjective reality that can easily be ignored in favor of the beauty of the romantic relationship developing between Barnabas and Victoria. The Gothicized cultural anxieties of the original 1960s series, which focused on the meaning of "identity" in an increasingly globalized society, are obscured, forgotten, and replaced with a romantic transformation where monstrous villains, as Botting argues, become increasingly more "alluring."[28] In the 1991 remake of *Dark Shadows*, repulsion for the vampire's bloody actions cedes to attraction, and the only real horror remaining is that of lost love.

The decision to make romance the focus of *The Revival* can also be interpreted as the result of a conceptual process where cultural influences placed an emphasis on a "love, beauty, and conspiracy" type of storyline. Like its predecessor, the series was an American production, and it therefore fit in the wider scope of television series where popular series followed a particular pattern to elicit positive audience responses through popular characters and storylines. The early 1990s were a time of rediscovery for love series, regardless of genre and programming slot. This was the time where soap opera series such as *The Bold and the Beautiful* (1987–present) and *The Young and the Restless* (1973–present) were at the peak of popularity, both in the United States and internationally. By 1993, the show was ranked second in the American soap opera viewing ratings.[29] During this time, the female characters of these daytime shows were known to be particularly beautified with coiffured hair and permanently impeccable make up—an eroticizing feature of several television shows that, on occasions, still rings true today. One can see this feature recurring in *The Revival*, particularly in the figure of Victoria, whose appealingly dark, curly hair and permanently red lips transform her into the ideal, coveted, and sexualized prize for Barnabas. The distinction from the 1960s Victoria here—whose looks were demure and unassuming—cannot be denied. The split in aesthetics should not be interpreted as a simple sign of the times, but must be seen as a cultural re-evaluation not only of the feminine character, but also of its role in television series where seduction and conquest represent the most unavoidable part of selling to the audience. Although *The Revival* was not presented as a soap opera as such, its appearance and narrative conceptualization are clearly still indebted to the cultural framework of the early 1990s, where television created a popular spot for romanticized and sentimental relationships in a context of intrigue.

The re-evaluation of the character of Victoria in both aesthetic and narrative terms also draws attention to the presentation of the female character in relation to Barnabas himself. Historically, the vampire has been known as a predator; this notion is linked to the need to feed on living creatures—by drinking their blood—and to other conceptual resonances with overt sexuality that have been constructed by literary and cinematic interpretations over the years. In *The Revival*, the female characters are often presented not only as sexual objects of desire—with this point being particularly salient in relation to Victoria—but also as the vampire's victims. Although Barnabas does not only feed on women in the series, the relationship he holds to his female food source is revelatory. His being a predator, it would seem, extends beyond blood. Victoria, in particular, is "victimized" by Barnabas in a number of ways: firstly, she is duped into believing his identity as a distant cousin of the Collinses; she is then seduced by his outlandish stories of star-crossed lovers and reincarnation; she is finally drawn into a cross-century plot, at which center lies Barnabas's transformation into a vampire, that leaves her marooned in the eighteenth century. One could argue here that, although the plot supports romantic endeavors and the discovery of carnal desires which are intrinsic to the figure of the vampire in its 1990s context, it also strives to punish female characters such as Victoria for indulging in their sexual pleasures. While the loss of Victoria to another century was of course inherited from the original *Dark Shadows*, the cultural politics at work are significantly different. In the original, the demure Victoria's fate seemed aimed at the punishment of Barnabas himself, as the tangible consequences of his nature as an "evil being" and his plotting and scheming as a creature of cunning and deceit.

In *The Revival*, however, the sexualization of Victoria, in both aesthetic and conceptual terms, points the meaning of her fate in another direction, one that is more in keeping with soap opera narratives found in examples such as *The Bold and the Beautiful*. Louise Spence argues that, although soap operas from the 1980s onwards transformed into consumer products based on "pleasure," women—paradoxically the main source of audience for the shows—are treated as "victims" within the narratives.[30] Victoria's sexual potential is mirrored in her coiffured appearance: she is presented as the erotic prey, ready to be hunted down by the vampire. As the sexual predator, Barnabas awakens Victoria's carnal desires, for which she is chastised. This important narrative and generic element uncovers the re-evaluation of *The Revival* as not only a cultural presence, but also—one could venture to argue—as a metaphysical metaphor for the female interest in romantic storylines. Laura Stempel Mumford has pointed out how romance-centered television narratives uncover the female struggle to reconcile the pleasure that comes from watching them with the repressive sexual politics that the genre seems to reinforce.[31]

In its re-working of the female-male relationship, *The Revival* unearths the complexities of the supernatural television series—where the vampire functions as the perfect metaphorical vector for cultural discussion—as the site of contradictory and multiple experiences. This approach to the supernatural as a sexualized framework uncovers *Dark Shadows* as a highly contextual artifact, where the changes mirror the age in which it is created. The idea of pleasure extends from the narrative to the audience, as the influential flux between the two shows the ambivalence of both desire and shame. As narrative structures and genre rules converge with issues of popularity in the television framework, Barnabas Collins emerges as the catalyst for the cultural intricacies of the series, both within the diegesis and the character-audience relationship, proving how, as Gothic incarnations, vampires continue to exercise interest "personifications of their age . . . always changing so that their appeal is dramatically generational."[32]

FILMS AND TV SHOWS

The Addams Family. ABC, 1964–66.
The Bold and the Beautiful. CBS, 1987–.
Dark Shadows. ABC, 1966–71.
Dark Shadows: The Revival Series. ABC, 1991.
Dracula. Directed by Francis Ford Coppola. 1992. Columbia Pictures.
Dracula. Directed by Tod Browning. 1931. Universal Pictures.
Horror of Dracula. Directed by Terence Fisher. 1958. Universal Pictures.
The Hunger. Directed by Tony Scott. 1983. MGM.
Mission: Impossible. CBS, 1966–73.

The Munsters. CBS, 1964–66.

Near Dark. Directed by Kathryn Bigelow. 1987. De Laurentiis Entertainment Group.

The Saint. ITV, 1962–69.

True Blood. HBO, 2008–.

The Vampire Diaries. The CW, 2009–.

The Young and the Restless. CBS, 1973–.

NOTES

1. Helen Wheatley, *Gothic Television* (Manchester: Manchester University Press, 2006).

2. John Frow, *Genre* (Abingdon: Routledge, 2005), 2.

3. Wheatley, *Gothic Television*, 147. The conception of "female Gothic" here is inspired by traditional novels from inceptional Gothic, such as Anne Radcliffe's *The Mysteries of Udolpho* (1794), where the narrative follows a young heroine and her quasi-supernatural encounters in an old and mysterious mansion.

4. Ibid.

5. Milly Williamson, *The Lure of the Vampire: Gender, Fiction and Fandom from Bram Stoker to Buffy* (London: Wallflower Press), 1.

6. Fred Botting, *Gothic* (London: Routledge, 1995), 3.

7. Vivian Sobchank, "Bringing It All Back Home: Family Economy and Generic Exchange," in *The Dread of Difference: Gender and Horror Film*, ed. B.K. Grant (Austin: University of Texas Press, 1996), 146.

8. Ibid.

9. Botting, *Gothic*, 1.

10. Richard Davenport-Hines, *Gothic: 400 Years of Excess, Horror, Evil and Ruin* (London: Fourth Estate, 1998), 144.

11. Wheatley, *Gothic Television*, 149.

12. Ibid., 148.

13. Mark Dawidziak and Jay Stevenson, "Dark Shadows," *Cinefantastique* 28, no. 6 (1996): 32.

14. Enid Nemy, "*Dark Shadows* Returns to Haunt Prime Time," *The New York Times*, January 13, 1991, accessed June 8, 2013, http://www.nytimes.com/1991/01/13/arts/television-dark-shadows-returns-to-haunt-prime-time.html.

15. Wheatley, *Gothic Television*, 148.

16. Lara Parker, "Out of Angelique's Shadow," in *The Dark Shadows Companion: 25th Anniversary Collection*, ed. Kathryn Leigh-Scott (Portland, CA: Pomegranate Press, 1990), 17.

17. Wheatley, *Gothic Television*, 149.

18. Tzvetan Todorov, *The Fantastic: A Structural Approach to a Literary Genre* (Ithaca, NY: Cornell University Press, 1975), 52.

19. Tim Kane, *The Changing Vampire of Film and Television: A Critical Study of the Growth of a Genre* (Jefferson, NC: McFarland, 2006), 51.

20. Barb Karg, Arjean Spaite, and Rick Sutherland, *The Everything Vampire Book* (Avon, MA: Adams Media, 2009), 89.

21. Kane, *The Changing Vampire of Film and Television*, 46.

22. Karg, Spaite, and Sutherland, *The Everything Vampire Book*, 89.

23. Jenny Diski, *The Sixties* (London: Profile Books, 2009), 65.

24. Ibid.

25. Fred Botting, *Gothic Romanced: Consumption, Gender and Technology in Contemporary Fictions* (Abingdon: Routledge, 2008), 1.

26. Ibid.

27. Thomas Elsaesser, "Specularity and Engulfment: Francis Ford Coppola and Bram Stoker's Dracula," in *Contemporary Hollywood Cinema*, ed. Steve Neale and Murray White (New York: Routledge, 1998), 205.

28. Botting, *Gothic Romanced*, 2.

29. Gerard Waggett, "Soap Opera Nielsen Ratings," in *The Soap Opera Encyclopaedia* (New York: Harper Collins, 1997), 630.

30. Louise Spence, *Watching Daytime Soap Operas: The Power of Pleasure* (Middleton, CT: Wesleyan University Press, 2005), 224.

31. Laura Stempel Mumford, "Feminist Theory and Television Studies," in *The Television Studies Book*, ed. Christine Geraghty and David Lusted (London: Bloomsbury, 1998), 122.

32. Nina Auerbach, *Our Vampires, Ourselves* (Chicago: University of Chicago Press, 1995), 3.

TWELVE

Smart, Sexy, and Technologically Savvy

(Re)Making Sherlock Holmes as a 21st-Century Superstar

Lynnette Porter

Sherlock Holmes recently has become a hot property again, with two television adaptations supplementing the Warner Bros. film franchise starring Robert Downey, Jr. (*Sherlock Holmes*, 2009; *Sherlock Holmes: A Game of Shadows*, 2011). On television, the Great Detective rushes around modern London brandishing a smartphone (BBC's *Sherlock*, 2010–present) or has been self-exiled to New York City and drug rehab but later conveniently allowed to work with the NYPD (CBS's *Elementary*, 2012–present). In both television reboots, Sherlock Holmes is a young man at the beginning of his long friendship with Watson. The new adaptations intrigue fans as much because of Holmes's sexuality as his genius and because of his friendship with John or Joan Watson more than the episode's puzzle.

The 1991 edition of *The Television Sherlock Holmes* begins with a foreword by television favorite Jeremy Brett, who played the Great Detective in the Granada series made in the UK (*The Adventures of Sherlock Holmes*, 1984–85; *The Return of Sherlock Holmes*, 1986–88; *The Casebook of Sherlock Holmes*, 1991; *The Memoirs of Sherlock Holmes*, 1994), which was interspersed between 1987 and 1993 with television movies (e.g., *The Sign of Four*, 1987; *The Eligible Bachelor*, 1993). "I am enjoying playing Sherlock Holmes immensely," Brett wrote. "The first eighteen months were not easy due to my insecurity and determination to do my best. Now I am just enjoying every moment."[1] In a later chapter, the author added that "Having selected such a perfectionist as Jeremy Brett for his Holmes, Michael [Cox, producer of the Granada series] knew he must prepare him for the role not only with outstanding scripts—which he had—but the most thorough background information on the familiar yet enigmatic figure of the sleuth from Baker Street."[2]

That well-researched interpretation, presenting Holmes and Watson in Arthur Conan Doyle (ACD)'s original Victorian setting, provided some surprises for British (later, global) audiences. For example, "David Burke's completely fresh interpretation of Watson was to profoundly change the entrenched public image of Watson as a rather bumbling, comical figure."[3] As Nancy Beiman wrote in her tribute to Brett on The Sherlock Holmes Society of London's web site, another reason this television adaptation was and remains so popular is that Brett

> brought a sense of humor to the part. And he and David Burke and Edward Hardwicke [the second actor to play Watson] let us know that this Holmes was very good friends with John Watson. I think that Sherlock Holmes badly needed this sort of treatment. Conan Doyle never intended Holmes to be taken as seriously as some Sherlockians take him. I see many comic elements in the stories, and these were beautifully dramatized in shows like *The Redheaded League* and *The Copper Beeches*, to say nothing of the little routines that were occasionally interpolated in other shows, showing the quirks and problems that roommates can have—particularly these, the most famous roommates in literature.[4]

The Granada series placed Holmes and Watson on more equal footing, with each character having unique strengths to bring to their friendship and professional endeavors. Brett has been lauded for making Holmes more dashing and sexually desirable while keeping his portrayal in line with ACD canon. When Brett starred in the Wyndham Theatre's Sherlock Holmes play in 1988, a fan/interviewer talked with him about his portrayal of Holmes and later summarized the actor's significance within the many Holmes adaptations:

> The magnetism of his bravura performance attracts a new generation of admirers to the stories. In the years to come it will be his face they see when they read the books, and it will be his voice they hear when the great detective speaks. A part of the monument that is the legend of Sherlock Holmes now has Brett's name indelibly carved on it.[5]

By the time the 2011 edition of *Sherlock Holmes On Screen* was published, yet another actor had become the face of Sherlock Holmes for a new television audience. By then, the character had been modernized into a contemporary setting, and a new showrunner, Steven Moffat, who helms the BBC's *Sherlock*, wrote the book's introduction. Moffat deems Sherlock

Holmes on twenty-first-century television as "utterly recognizable, and utterly different, the way he has to be" if he is going to be successfully adapted for modern audiences. Holmes can survive such a contemporary reboot because he is a "most unchanging, yet most adaptable hero"[6] who has been re-imagined dozens of times previously.

Gaining network approval to revive Sherlock Holmes on television required scriptwriters to take a new approach, a challenge that production companies and casts on two continents accepted. First came the BBC's *Sherlock,* a series with high production values, innovative plots infused with ACD canon elements, and a charismatic cast. It won not only fan devotion far beyond the UK but dozens of awards as best television drama or for excellence in acting, writing, directing, editing, design, et cetera. Its popularity inspired CBS to commission a separate modernization, *Elementary,* which debuted in the United States in autumn 2013 and easily won renewal for a second season.

Sherlock, starring Benedict Cumberbatch as Sherlock Holmes and Martin Freeman as John Watson, provides high-quality entertainment on a very irregular broadcast schedule. Long hiatuses between the filming of each new batch of three 90-minute episodes may have actually helped build an audience craving more. After receiving a BAFTA Special Award for writing in 2012, Moffat commented that "*Sherlock* almost exists on starving its audience. By the time it came back this year, *Sherlock* was like a rock star re-entering the building!"[7] Certainly this "rock star" has ardent followers, so much so that producer Sue Vertue pleaded with fans to let the cast and crew complete their work when filming on location.[8] Hordes of fans descended wherever Cumberbatch, in particular, appeared, and although plenty of pleasant fan-actor encounters were reported,[9] the crew frequently had to remind onlookers to be quiet during a take or not to share video or photographs through social media. Interest in upcoming episodes has been so great that online spoilers (such as those linked through Twitter's #setlock tag) alerted fans to the production's daily activities.

Part of the appeal of the BBC's modern adaptation is that it plays up elements found in the popular Brett series: Holmes's sex appeal and the "fun side" of the Holmes–Watson friendship. As Sherlock notes in "A Scandal in Belgravia" (2.01), he appears to gain stature, both literally and publicly, from "the benefit of a good coat and a short friend." His dramatically swirling Belstaff coat, a replica now a must-have for any Sherlock cosplayer, helps create this Sherlock's aloof sexiness. John, however, knows exactly how his friend orchestrates his striking appearance and, during "The Hounds of Baskerville" (2.02), tells Sherlock to stop acting "all mysterious with your [pause] cheekbones and turning your coat collar up so you look cool." Like their predecessors, these idiosyncratic flatmates banter and often find humor in the surreal lives they lead, sometimes even giggling at crime scenes. John may seem to outsiders to be one of Sherlock's accessories, like the coat, but fans and Sherlock know his true value.

The similarities between the Brett series and *Sherlock* stop there, however, as co-creators and writers Moffat and Mark Gatiss—always with an eye toward canon—rework the familiar stories and introduce technology appropriate for a twenty-first-century scientist/detective to use. Sherlock works with a smartphone and computer, and, when his thoughts need to be visualized by the television audience, maps, equations, words, or images are overlaid on filmed scenes to represent the workings of his mind. These computer-generated graphics, as much as Sherlock's often cold, logical demeanor, emphasize the link between the detective and a computer and underscore ACD's depiction of Holmes as "a calculating machine . . . [with] something positively inhuman . . . at times."[10] The BBC's *Sherlock* is, in many ways, socially aberrant and in need of John's socializing influence, although in this adaptation both characters have their share of issues (John's PTSD and use of his illegal firearm, for starters) that make them "other" from "normal" people.

In the United States, producers who liked the award-winning *Sherlock* and hoped to develop their own series talked with Hartswood Films about bringing an American version to CBS. Vertue, head of Hartswood, declined the offer and, when CBS announced its own modern Holmes living in New York, suggested that litigation might be undertaken if the two Sherlocks seemed too much alike.[11] CBS's *Elementary*, starring Jonny Lee Miller as Holmes, distanced itself from *Sherlock* not only by changing the setting (although its second-season debut would be filmed in London) but by developing a series premise that Holmes lives in one of his father's many NYC properties after completing a stint in drug rehab. He is compelled to leave London after the death of Irene Adler—the woman with whom he built his only connection with the rest of humanity.

Elementary's casting seemed designed for maximum publicity, although the lead actor's credentials certainly proved his talent. Miller had played opposite Cumberbatch in the National Theatre's 2011 *Frankenstein*, the actors alternating the roles of Victor Frankenstein and the Creature; they shared Olivier and Evening Standard Theatre best actor awards. That Cumberbatch and Miller also would star in their respective Sherlock Holmes television series seemed to smack of stunt casting.

Similarly, in casting Lucy Liu (*Charlie's Angels, Kill Bill*) as Joan Watson, *Elementary* received a great deal of media attention, although this decision further separated the series from *Sherlock* or previous adaptations. In concept, both series seemed to be diverging wildly from ACD canon; however, each incorporates dialogue, characters, and plot points from the original stories. *Sherlock* remains far closer to Conan Doyle's concept of the characters' personalities and histories, whereas *Elementary* provides very different back stories for its lead characters and introduces far more original characters.

Comparison between these two adaptations may be unfair, as television critic Alex Strachan noted in a review of *Elementary:* "The nature of network TV is that stories have to be told in seven-minute beats, interrupted by commercial breaks. [This structure is vastly different from the uninterrupted flow of a *Sherlock* episode, which seems closer to a feature-length movie.] What's marvelous about *Elementary* is the way it has jumped hurdles and overcome the limitations of network TV, without becoming too formulaic or dumbed-down in the process."[12] Although each series faces different time constraints (with *Sherlock* having far fewer, but longer episodes spread over a longer time period, and *Elementary* having far more regularly scheduled—if shorter, commercially interrupted—episodes), they have successfully introduced new interpretations of Sherlock Holmes that have attracted a great deal of attention among fans and critics and, especially during 2012–13, invigorated the detective's presence in popular culture.

As might be expected, each series has a devoted fan base that considers its Sherlock Holmes the better. In particular, once *Elementary* was announced, some *Sherlock* fans vehemently opposed the series' premise or casting. During the series' first season, the criticism continued on Tumblr sites or other fan forums. *Elementary* fans retaliated with criticisms of the BBC series, sometimes labeling *Sherlock* fandom as "haters" who think in black-and-white "either/or" terms when it comes to a modern television adaptation of Sherlock Holmes.[13]

Commenting on the *Sherlock/Elementary* rivalry among fans, one that only seems to have become more virulent online over time, author Caitlin Moran reviewed *Elementary*'s pilot episode and concluded that

> *Elementary* has nothing to do with either *Sherlock*, or Conan Doyle. Whilst *Sherlock* is by way of a vivid love-letter to Conan Doyle—every episode competes to be the one with the most in-jokes and canonical references; it is an act of deep adoration, reverence and joy—*Elementary* has taken nothing but the names, and a whole lot of publicity off the back of an imagined rivalry.[14]

Of course, Moran may be a wee bit biased, having previously and since written glowingly about *Sherlock*, interviewed Cumberbatch several times, and moderated a British Film Institute screening of "A Scandal in Belgravia." At the introduction of her article, she took national umbrage against the US series, claiming it seems "rude" in the face of the BBC's modern adaptation. She further asked

> Why was our *Sherlock* not good enough for them? It's got a dementedly passionate fan base, Baftas up to its nuts, and international sex-cases Martin Freeman and Benedict Cumberbatch in the lead roles. I'm sorry, Uncle Sam—did all those fabulous riches in some way offend you? . . . Do you want to Super-Size Holmes?[15]

Unfortunately, the CBS adaptation failed to "Super-Size" the detective. Instead, it often has diminished him to the level of just another quirky *CSI*-type investigator who becomes the NYPD's sidekick to solve the murder of the week.

Nevertheless, *Elementary* is a highly rated television series, one that, with a larger average weekly audience and more hours of on-screen time each year than *Sherlock*, offers Miller the opportunity to play a Sherlock Holmes seen by more people, more often. During the 2012–13 US television season, for example, *Elementary* was the 15th highest-rated network series; it averaged 13 million viewers each week.[16] In comparison, *Sherlock* reached a series high of 8.8 million viewers in the UK (fans were eager to see "A Scandal in Belgravia" after an 18-month hiatus), but the series' ratings per episode have always been less than *Elementary*'s. (The audience for the first *Sherlock* episode was 7.5 million UK viewers[17]; for the first *Elementary* episode, 13.3 million US viewers.[18]) In their own ways, both *Elementary* and the critically acclaimed but schedule-challenged *Sherlock* are reboot success stories that should be considered among the most influential of Sherlock Holmes adaptations.

A. CHALLENGES IN MODERNIZING SHERLOCK HOLMES FOR TELEVISION AUDIENCES

Television audiences on either side of the Atlantic are a difficult-to-please mixture of long-time Sherlock Holmes fans (who know ACD canon extremely well) and newbies. To further complicate the audience, fans of a particular actor, such as Cumberbatch or Miller, may know little to nothing about Sherlock Holmes other than the way their favorite actor portrays him on screen. Yet other viewers may have read a few stories, watched the Brett-era television series or another of the many adaptations available on DVD, or become fans of the Great Detective after reading the ACD-inspired "thousands of pastiches, parodies and sequels in print" since the main characters and story elements published before 1923 have come into public domain.[19] Scriptwriters, like other authors who continue the Holmes saga, have begun taking more license with the characters, but any television modernization should be at least tangentially linked to canon. Dialogue should contain enough lines from the original works to satisfy Sherlockians that the writers know the subject or have at least done some research, but characters must also be updated so that all viewers are surprised and entertained by each episode. Most scripts try to provide layers of meaning so that Sherlockians can enjoy canon references but viewers new to Sherlock Holmes can easily understand the story. Trying to provide references accessible and appropriate for everyone, however, sometimes can backfire.

Perhaps that is why even *Elementary* as a title came under fire in 2012, a problem that the BBC did not encounter. *Sherlock* seems an appropriate modernization of the lead character's name, and Holmes and Watson are consistently referred to as Sherlock and John (as I refer to the BBC series' characters throughout this chapter). The informality puts viewers on a first-name basis with the characters, as well as indicates a fresh approach to the story. *Elementary,* on the other hand, seemed less of a play on "Elementary, my dear Watson" than an indication of executive producer and writer Rob Doherty's lack of knowledge about the canon. As one blogger wrote, "Regarding 'Elementary': you keep using that word. I do not think it means what you think it means."[20] The appropriately entitled Screenrant site noted that "Elementary, my dear Watson" is a line from another adaptation and (original emphasis) *"was never written by Arthur Conan Doyle."*[21] The title annoyed many Sherlock Holmes fans, as well as *Elementary* supporters who feared that this series would not be taken as seriously as *Sherlock.*

Nevertheless, as *Elementary's* first season progressed, Sherlockians noted several direct quotations from Conan Doyle within Holmes's dialogue, plus the addition of canon characters (e.g., Sebastian Moran) and plot elements (e.g., "The Adventure of Charles Augustus Milverton" worked into episode 1.20, "Dead Man's Switch"). More controversial was the addition of new characters playing major roles in weekly episodes (e.g., Detective Marcus Bell) and the unseen but manipulative presence of Holmes's emotionally distant father, plus important changes to other canon characters. Near the end of the first season, Miss Hudson is introduced as an acquaintance who worked as "the Greek interpreter" (another ACD title) on a case with the detective. After she overcomes a bad breakup with her married lover, Hudson agrees to become Holmes's one-day-a-week housekeeper; her OCD tendencies when she is stressed make her invaluable in organizing Holmes's research (1.19, "Snow Angels"). By the way, Miss Hudson is transgendered, as is the actor (gender-neutral term) portraying her; casting for *Elementary* continues to be a key part of the series' modernization of canon.

The most important casting decision to fans, who often published their complaints online, is the re-imagining of John Watson as Joan, a surgeon who loses a patient and gives up her medical practice in favor of becoming a sober companion. This Watson is no war veteran, a fact that disturbed many Sherlockians.[22] Initially hired by Holmes's father to monitor his wayward son during his first weeks out of rehab, Watson later accepts the detective's offer to become his apprentice and eventually his partner in crime detection. The famous friendship is based, in this adaptation, on a monetary relationship—employment and apprenticeship—and only gradually evolves into a personal relationship.

Sherlock co-creator Moffat believes that he and Gatiss got the blend of old and new just right, in contrast to the "American competition" posed by *Elementary*: "What we did with our Sherlock was just take [him] from Victorian times into modern day," whereas *Elementary* made "three big changes: it's Sherlock Holmes in America, it's Sherlock Holmes updated and it's Sherlock Holmes with a female Watson. I wonder if he's Sherlock Holmes in any sense other than he's called Sherlock Holmes."[23] Indeed, the characters called "Sherlock Holmes" in these series are very different men, both from each other and from Brett's character or ACD's original.

B. ASOCIAL AND ADDICTED: POINTS TO ADDRESS IN ADAPTATION

Every Sherlock Holmes, past or present (and likely future), is far from the most social of men; his work receives the majority of his focus. In canon, even close friend Watson describes Holmes as an "automaton"[24] and, ironically, appreciates being wounded if that allows him to learn of the detective's concern for him.[25] *Sherlock* and *Elementary* continue this tradition of making Sherlock Holmes "other" from the rest of society because of his obsessive concentration on his work and, especially in *Sherlock,* his lack of patience with those who cannot keep up with his deductive reasoning.

Sherlock may not become any more sentimental about the general populace but over time reveals in small ways how much John means to him. He refers to John as his only friend, who serves as a "conductor of light" to illuminate Sherlock's genius (2.02, "The Hounds of Baskerville"). In "The Reichenbach Fall" (2.03), John is first on Sherlock's mind when Moriarty threatens those closest to the detective. Sherlock then orchestrates his "death" to keep John (as well as Lestrade and Mrs. Hudson) safe. Across two seasons' episodes, Sherlock begins to show greater emotion around John and to rely on the doctor's opinion of what about his friend's behavior is "not good" socially (1.01, "A Study in Pink").

Elementary takes Holmes's less-than-conventionally-social nature to a different extreme; the series' premise revolves around Holmes's drug addiction specifically and his addictive personality more generally. Holmes prefers to be on his own or to interact with others as he sees fit, perhaps a "normal" reaction to losing the one person he loved, Irene Adler, and almost losing control of his mind through drug addiction in his grief. Almost every episode includes Holmes's attendance at Narcotics Anonymous, a meeting with a sponsor (or dealer from his past), other addicts who force Holmes to admit details about his own addiction, or Watson's comments about sobriety. For example, Watson confronts Holmes about inviting his former dealer and friend to stay in their home while the detective tries to find the man's missing daughter. The detective assures Watson her concern is appreciated but "your mistaken support-group ethos for a complete system for living . . . is not, at least for a man like me. My sobriety is on one plane; my bonds with those I consider friends is on quite another" (1.15, "A Giant Gun, Filled With Drugs"). Holmes also draws attention to himself as an addict, referring to one of Watson's former clients as "my brother-in-track-marked-arms" (1.09, "You Do It To Yourself") or, more casually, asking a crossword puzzle obsessive "You're a fellow addict, aren't you?" (1.08, "The Long Fuse"). He frequently reminds the audience that, although now sober, he will always be an addict.

Although Holmes has maintained his sobriety on his own terms during the first season's episodes, he clearly struggles with fallout from his London meltdown and drug rehab. Even when drugs are not specifically mentioned, Watson often notes Holmes's addictive behaviors. In "The Leviathan" (1.10), she calls him a "dry drunk" because of his obsession with the puzzle of opening a vault; Holmes spends hours without sleep trying to figure out a way inside, only to snap and vandalize the lock when he becomes frustrated with his inability to open it. Throughout the first season, Holmes's anger explodes, sometimes with physical violence—but only against objects, ranging from a suspect's car (1.01, "Pilot") to a bulletin board full of clues (1.21, "A Landmark Story").

Elementary's emphasis is timely, given the number of reality shows like *Celebrity Rehab* (2008–12) or self-help boot camps like *The Biggest Loser* (2004–present), in which people work on overcoming their various addictions in front of a television audience. However, portraying Holmes primarily as an addict, even if a brilliant one, limits the character's development and takes aspects of Conan Doyle's canon beyond the original context.

Elementary contrasts with *Sherlock*, which seldom refers to canon drug use, despite the first episode's drug raid on 221B. Second-season episodes show the detective desperate for a cigarette and becoming manic in nicotine withdrawal (2.02, "The Hounds of Baskerville") or causing John to worry about a potential "danger night" (2.01, "A Scandal in Belgravia"). These infrequent examples place Sherlock's substance abuse within canon but without emphasizing it.

C. THE SEXUAL SHERLOCK HOLMES

Both series also exceed ACD canon in emphasizing sexuality as a way to intrigue modern audiences to consider Sherlock Holmes from a new perspective. *Sherlock*, most obviously, teases viewers with questions about the detective's orientation. As John sits down to dinner at a restaurant with his new flatmate, he casually asks if Sherlock has a girlfriend. Sounding affronted (although he also is busy scanning the streets for a possible murderer), the detective says no. John next inquires about a boyfriend, "which is perfectly fine." Sherlock explains that relationships are not his area and emphasizes that, although flattered by John's attention, he is not interested. John, ever the heterosexual, informs Sherlock that he is not expressing sexual interest but only confirming that they are both single (1.01, "A Study in Pink"). From the pilot episode, John is frequently assumed to be Sherlock's sexual partner, and John just as often tries to correct that impression to reinforce his heterosexuality, to the point that John's mistaken orientation becomes a running joke during the first two seasons.

Although John's sexuality has been firmly established (albeit through a series of failed relationships with women during the first two seasons), Sherlock's orientation is far more ambiguous. Irene Adler reveals that Moriarty labels Sherlock "the Virgin," and, in the same episode (2.01, "A Scandal in Belgravia"), brother Mycroft condescendingly explains the case concerning dominatrix Adler, who is blackmailing the royal family. "Don't be alarmed," Mycroft says, "It's to do with sex." "Sex doesn't alarm me," Sherlock replies, but his older brother must have the last word: "How do you know?" Later in this episode, John and Adler discuss their mutual (platonic) love of Sherlock, but neither knows anything about Sherlock's sexual nature. The detective seems interested in them both: Irene as The Woman, an intellectual puzzle; John as his only friend. The BBC's Sherlock considers the body only as transport, and The Work always comes first. However, unlike John, Sherlock seems unconcerned what others say or think about him and never explains his sexual orientation.

Asking explicit questions about sexuality is a new development in Sherlock Holmes television adaptations, although fan fiction sites regularly link Sherlock and John in all sorts of sexual or romantic combinations. When photographs of outdoor location filming of the season three episode "The Sign of Three" revealed John and "Mary" (new cast member Amanda Abbingdon) in wedding attire,[26] the Internet exploded with complaints (and threats) because "Johnlock" was being challenged by the series' canon, no matter that Watson's marriage(s) also can be found in ACD canon. Slash (or same-gender sexual relationship) fiction has become a staple of most fandoms, but, to many *Sherlock* fan fiction writers, the series' tone and number of sexual teases turn what Moffat and Gatiss consider to be the greatest male-male friendship of all time into far more than bromance. Speaking on the red carpet of the 2013 BAFTA television awards, Moffat reiterated that John and Sherlock are simply best friends, but it is all right for fans to read into the relationship whatever they want.[27]

Taking a similar stance on the legendary friendship, *Elementary*'s Doherty proclaimed that Holmes and Watson would not become romantically involved,[28] which many Sherlock Holmes fans initially feared when they learned Watson's first name would be Joan. From the start, however, *Elementary* shows that Holmes has no trouble feeding his sexual appetite.

When Watson first approaches the New York brownstone where Holmes lives, she runs into a young woman Holmes has paid for a sexual work-out. Inside his home, the detective is stripped to the waist, showing off his fit physique and many of his (in real life, Miller's) tattoos. The metal frame from which he has recently been suspended is just another piece of equipment in the living room (1.01, "Pilot"). Certainly this visual intro-duction to Sherlock Holmes is atypical of other television adaptations. To *Elementary*'s Holmes, sex can be a fun experiment, and in "The Levia-than" (1.10), blonde identical twins assist him (off camera) with his re-search one night. Watson meets both young women the next morning as they prepare to leave, one blowing air kisses to and the other saluting a cordial Holmes busy making breakfast in the kitchen. The detective can-didly explains more than once to Watson that he has no qualms about meeting his sexual needs with women paid or volunteering to have sex with him.

Nevertheless, only The Woman has been able to meet Holmes's ro-mantic needs and emotionally connect him with the rest of humanity. Irene Adler becomes so important to Holmes's well-being that, when he thinks she is dead, his life spirals out of control. Even when he has been sober for months, news of Adler can possibly destroy him. In the episode "M." (1.12), he looks forward to torturing and killing Sebastian Moran, who the detective initially believes killed Irene. Only when, near the end of the first season, Holmes is reunited with Adler, who says she has been held captive by Moriarty for 18 months, do audiences see Holmes in love, and the Moriarty–Adler connection becomes the focus of a two-episode finale. "The Woman" (1.23) and "Heroine" (1.24) refer, respectively, to Adler and Watson, the women who end up in a tug-of-war for Holmes's future. Flashbacks reveal a flirtatious Holmes seduced by the enigmatic Adler; the two share pillow talk and seem besotted with each other's mind as well as body. Viewers understand just how far Holmes would go to protect Adler and how devastating must be her revelation that she is Moriarty. The Woman, whether as Adler or Moriarty, has controlled Holmes's life for years. However, she is no match for Watson, who guides Holmes into capturing Moriarty. By the end of the first season, Holmes only survives—emotionally, perhaps physically—because of Watson's intervention. Sex or sexuality is portrayed very differently on *Sherlock* and *Elementary*, but they are significant—and highly popular— aspects of these adaptations.

D. THE TECHNOLOGICALLY SAVVY HOLMES

Conan Doyle's Holmes is a man of science who uses the latest methods of his day to gather data and decipher clues. Therefore, any modern Sher-lock Holmes must be familiar with available technology. Because *Sherlock* and *Elementary* portray the detective as a young man brought up with wealth (even if both series suggest that he now has irregular access to money), he likely would have been able to own or use whatever scientific equipment and other technology he wanted. Modernized Sherlock Holmes likely is a digital native (someone who grew up with computers and the Internet). In *Sherlock,* John is a digital immigrant, being (in this adaptation) a few years older than Sherlock and not having the money for the latest gadgets. His phone, for example, is secondhand when Sherlock meets him. John is the one who has a "row with a chip-and-pin machine" at the shops (1.02, "The Blind Banker"), but he nonetheless has a far better understanding of what will attract Londoners to his blog and, consequently, Sherlock's consulting detective business. Sherlock haughtily says that he wrote a detailed account of 243 types of ash for his Science of Deduction website (a real site fans can visit), but John explains that the humorous titles on The Personal Blog of Dr. John H. Watson (many, like "The Geek Interpreter," a play on Conan Doyle's titles) attract clients (2.01, "A Scandal in Belgravia"). Sherlock understands the technical details of working with technology, such as hacking John's password or quickly texting or searching online, but he fails to grasp the human elements of web design.

He also turns 221B into a mini-lab, with body parts in the refrigerator or microwave, and sometimes is shown peering intently into a microscope. When he needs more elaborate equipment (or a full corpse), he visits the morgue or labs at St. Bart's Hospital. Not coincidentally, Sherlock is first introduced to medical man John at St. Bart's, and the hospital becomes an important setting for many of the friends' pivotal interactions (e.g., the place where Sherlock "dies" in 2.03, "The Reichenbach Fall"). Although both modern adaptations illustrate Sherlock Holmes's brilliance in seeing connections that no one else has been able to find (and doing so with great speed), Sherlock seems far more the scientist than Holmes.

Unlike *Sherlock, Elementary* minimizes the laboratory or scientific elements behind Holmes's deductions. Scenes take place at a police station instead of a lab. At home, the detective often is shown compiling models or boards linking clues; he excels in creating visual (but not computerized) representations of evidence and using them to see patterns. Holmes does not seem to own very much technology (beyond a computer and several televisions) and certainly has less scientific equipment around the house. Instead, as befitting a police procedural, he spends far more time directly assisting the NYPD, sometimes interrogating witnesses and frequently tracking down clues or suspects. In this respect, *Elementary*'s Holmes acts more like a police detective than a consulting scientist.

E. A SHERLOCK HOLMES FOR ALL (TELEVISION) SEASONS

The success of these recent Sherlock Holmes adaptations also has increased their lead actors' popularity; in the case of Cumberbatch, *Sherlock* assured his television stardom worldwide. Whereas *Sherlock* favors brooding sex appeal and computer-comparable intelligence for its "rock star," *Elementary* portrays a former "bad boy" (sex and drugs, if not the rock 'n' roll) on the road to redemption. Both interpretations gained millions of viewers and at least thousands of fans.

In focusing almost exclusively on Holmes as addict, *Elementary* makes the Great Detective seem more humanly fallible than ACD's or Brett's detective, despite the fact that Holmes's drug use is discussed in canon. In those stories, however, experimentation with illicit substances is considered "bohemian" or even part of Holmes's natural curiosity into how things work. *Elementary* presents Holmes as a man who succumbed to self-destructive behavior to deal with great loss and, in the process, nearly lost his mind. He is a man of many appetites, including sex, but has difficulty establishing close relationships. His most significant love relationship, with Irene Adler, turns out to be a sham; he has been outsmarted and manipulated by Moriarty posing as Adler. Thus, Holmes often seems like another "character" from reality television who bares his shortcomings and challenges in front of an audience and is "saved" through intervention. *Elementary* may make Holmes more relevant to modern audiences, but such emphasis on addiction minimizes what makes the detective special or unique. Nevertheless, *Elementary* has gained its own faithful fan following and proves that US viewers in particular (and international viewers watching via global syndication) will accept a Sherlock Holmes adaptation that pushes the boundaries of how far a reboot can successfully go.

Sherlock succeeds in retaining the detective's "otherness," despite John's socializing influence. As Irene Adler notes, "brainy is the new sexy" (2.01, "A Scandal in Belgravia"), and Sherlock is both. However, his lack of interest in sex or sexuality and his computer-like thought processes make him an atypical television protagonist (similar to *Star Trek*'s Spock or *The Big Bang Theory*'s Sheldon Cooper). Although the series' high-quality production values, talented ensemble cast, and creators' knowledge of and love for canon undoubtedly are reasons why so many people internationally are enamored with *Sherlock*, at least some fans may identify with Sherlock's "otherness" and interpret audiences' love of a different kind of lead character as a sign toward greater social acceptance of "otherness" in real life. In this respect, *Sherlock* may personally appeal to viewers worldwide who feel they or their peers are also "other" and find in Sherlock a character who is beloved despite being different. As well, the chemistry between Sherlock and John in this series has prompted a plethora of slash fanfiction that reflects many viewers' reading of an abiding male friendship as more sexual than that illustrated on screen. Perhaps the popularity of an asocial, seemingly asexual (or fan-reading as homosexual) Sherlock, as much as the series' high quality and entertainment value, will make this Sherlock Holmes adaptation stand out among the many past or yet to come.

FILMS AND TV SHOWS

The Adventures of Sherlock Holmes. ITV, 1984–85.
The Big Bang Theory. CBS, 2007–.
The Biggest Loser. NBC, 2004–.
The Casebook of Sherlock Holmes. ITV, 1991.
Celebrity Rehab With Dr. Drew. VH1, 2008–12.
Charlie's Angels. Directed by McG. 2000. Columbia Pictures.
CSI: Crime Scene Investigation. CBS, 2000–.
Elementary. CBS, 2012–.
The Eligible Bachelor. Directed by Peter Hammond. ITV, 1993.
Kill Bill Vol. 1. Directed by Quentin Tarantino. 2003. Miramax Films.
Kill Bill Vol. 2. Directed by Quentin Tarantino. 2004. Miramax Films.
The Memoirs of Sherlock Holmes. ITV, 1994.
The Return of Sherlock Holmes. ITV, 1986–88.
Sherlock. BBC, 2010–.
Sherlock Holmes. Directed by Guy Ritchie. 2009. Warner Bros.
Sherlock Holmes: A Game of Shadows. Directed by Guy Ritchie. 2011. Warner Bros.
The Sign of Four. Directed by Peter Hammond. 1987. ITV.
Star Trek. NBC, 1966–69.

NOTES

1. Jeremy Brett, Foreword to *The Television Sherlock Holmes* (London: Virgin Books, 1991), 13.
2. Peter Haining, *The Television Sherlock Holmes* (London: Virgin Books, 1991), 108.
3. Ibid., 111.
4. Nancy Beiman, "Jeremy Brett (1933-1995)," The Sherlock Holmes Society of London, accessed May 1, 2013, http://www.sherlock-holmes.org.uk/world/jbrett.php.
5. Gunner 54, "Jeremy Brett: Interview" (blog), 2007, accessed May 9, 2013, http://gunner54.wordpress.com/jeremy-brett-interview/.
6. Steven Moffat, Introduction to *Sherlock Holmes on Screen* (updated ed.; London: Titan Books, 2011), 7.
7. Morgan Jeffery, "Steven Moffat on 'Doctor Who', 'Sherlock', and His BAFTA Special Award," *DigitalSpy*, last modified May 19, 2012, http://www.digitalspy.com/british-tv/s7/doctor-who/news/a382427/steven-moffat-on-doctor-who-sherlock-and-his-bafta-special-award.html.
8. *Sherlockology*, "Sherlock in London: A Message From Sue Vertue," last modified April 9, 2013, http://www.sherlockology.com/news/2013/4/9/message-from-sue-vertue-090413.

9. Michael Purton, "Benedict Cumberbatch Wows Dedicated Fan After Filming Sherlock in Cheltenham," *This Is Gloucestershire,* last modified April 4, 2013, http://www.thisisgloucestershire.co.uk/Benedict-Cumberbatch-wows-dedicated-fan-filming/story-18605884-detail/story.html#axzz2TfH3J0fC. Similar articles, not to mention fan videos and blogs, flooded the Internet during April-May 2013.

10. Arthur Conan Doyle, *The Sign of Four* (London: BBC Books, 2012), 19.

11. Adam Sherwin, "Legal Thriller Looms as Sherlock Takes His Case to New York," *The Independent,* last modified January 21, 2012, http://www.independent.co.uk/arts-entertainment/tv/news/legal-thriller-looms-as-sherlock-takes-his-caseload-to-new-york-6292682.html.

12. Alex Strachan, "TV Thursday: Elementary Ends Season with Holmes vs. Moriarty," *Canada.com,* last modified May 16, 2013, http://http://o.canada.com/2013/05/16/tv-thursday-elementary-ends-season-with-holmes-vs-moriarty/.

13. Among the many posts and descriptions of the "hate wars" within Sherlock Holmes fandom throughout 2012–13, those on Tumblr sites like *WTF Sherlock* (http://wtfsherlock.tumblr.com/), *Elementary Hate* (http://www.tumblr.com/tagged/elementary%20hate), and *Things I Hate About the Sherlock Fandom* (http://www.tumblr.com/tagged/things%20i%20hate%20about%20the%20sherlock%20fandom), as well as open letters to fandom, such as "Elementary (or, Dear Sherlock Fans: an intervention)" (http://www.withanaccent.com/2012/05/22/elementary-or-dear-sherlock-fans-an-intervention/), provide representative comments and history of backlash against both *Elementary* and *Sherlock.* The *Sherlock* fans' arguments often revolve around the series' quality and number of canon references; the *Elementary* fans' arguments often emphasize that diversity (such as in the casting of Lucy Liu as Joan Watson) is a worthwhile adaptation and that Sherlock Holmes fandom is big enough to include fans of both series.

14. Caitlin Moran, "Caitlin Moran on TV: A US Holmes Feels Rude. Was Ours Not Good Enough?," *The Times,* last modified October 27, 2012, http://www.thetimes.co.uk/tto/arts/tv-radio/reviews/article3578108.ece.

15. Ibid.

16. Michael Schneider, "America's Most Watched: The Top 25 Shows of the 2012-2013 TV Season," *TV Guide,* last modified June 10, 2013, http://www.tvguide.com/News/Most-Watched-TV-Shows-Top-25-2012-2013-1066503.aspx.

17. Tara Conlan, "BBC1's Sherlock Gets Back on the Case with Nearly 9 Million Viewers," *The Guardian,* last modified January 3, 2012, http://www.guardian.co.uk/media/2012/jan/03/bbc1-sherlock-case-9m-viewers.

18. James Hibberd, "'Elementary' Premiere Gets Jolly Good Ratings," *Entertainment Weekly,* last modified September 28, 2012, http://insidetv.ew.com/2012/09/28/last-resort-ratings-elementary/.

19. Jennifer Schuessler, "Public Domain, My Dear Watson? Lawsuit Challenges Conan Doyle Copyrights," *The New York Times,* last modified February 15, 2013, http://artsbeat.blogs.nytimes.com/2013/02/15/public-domain-my-dear-watson-lawsuit-challenges-conan-doyle-copyrights/.

20. Lyndsay Faye, "A Holmes Fan's Mistrust of Elementary: An Open Apology to CBS" (blog), *Criminalelement.com,* last modified May 17, 2012, http://www.criminalelement.com/blogs/2012/05/sherlock-holmes-fans-mistrust-elementaryan-open-apology-to-cbs-lyndsay-faye.

21. Ben Moore, "CBS' Elementary Casts Eli Stone as Sherlock; Lucy Liu as Dr. Watson," *Screenrant.com,* last updated February 27, 2012, http://screenrant.com/elementary-cbs-johnny-lee-miller-lucy-liu-benm-156745/.

22. Faye, "A Holmes Fan's Mistrust of Elementary." Of the many forum posts and blogs written around this time, shortly after *Elementary*'s premise was made public, this blog clearly and politely explains Sherlockians' problems with Joan Watson.

23. Paul Jones, "Steven Moffat—Elementary Has Changed Sherlock Holmes Too Much," *Radio Times,* last modified May 17, 2012, http://www.radiotimes.com/news/2012-05-17/steven-moffat---elementary-has-changed-sherlock-holmes-too-much.

24. Conan Doyle, *The Sign of Four*, 19.

25. Arthur Conan Doyle, "The Three Garridebs," *The Casebook of Sherlock Holmes* (New York: Oxford University Press, 2009), 104.

26. *Den of Geek*, "What Do We Know About Sherlock Series 3?," last modified May 3, 2013, http://www.denofgeek.com/tv/sherlock/25483/what-do-we-know-about-sherlock-series-3.

27. *RedCarpetNewsTV*, "Steven Moffat Interview Sherlock Series 3 & 4," YouTube, last modified May 12, 2013, http://www.youtube.com/watch?feature=player_embedded&v=np_JZN_eo0E.

28. Danielle Turchiano, "CBS TCA Talk: Rob Doherty and Lucy Liu Discuss Elementary's Evolution," *Examiner.com*, last updated January 12, 2013, http://www.examiner.com/article/cbs-tca-talk-rob-doherty-and-lucy-liu-discuss-elementary-s-evolution, and Matt Webb Mitovich, "Elementary Boss: Playing Up Sherlock/Watson Sexual Tension 'Is Completely Off the Table,'" *TVLine.com*, last updated July 29, 2012, http://tvline.com/2012/07/29/cbs-elementary-sherlock-watson-sexual-tension/, among several similar articles, explain that Holmes and Watson will never become romantic with each other.

THIRTEEN

Remaking Public Service for Commercial Consumption

Jamie's School Dinners *Comes to America*

Helen Thornham and Elke Weissmann

Jamie's School Dinners (2005) has been credited[1] with starting a campaign that influenced school food policy. As an output of Channel 4, a celebrity vehicle, and an example of the Lifestyle genre, *Jamie's School Dinners* offers a pertinent case study to address the meaning of public service television in a global context. In addition to elucidating a number of contemporary issues around the status and meaning of public service principles in an increasingly international market, it also speaks to notions of genre, address, policy, and celebrity that have emerged as underpinning facets of popular culture. In what follows, we trace a number of these tensions, uncovering the program's address through textual analysis and locating it within the broader histories of public service broadcasting and the Lifestyle genre.

Jamie's School Dinners could be claimed by Channel 4 to be part of its public service remit, informing, educating, and entertaining its audience. Like most of Channel 4's output, the series was produced by an independent production company (in this case, Fresh One Productions, owned by Oliver) and created as a product for international exploitation. The series was remade in the United States as *Jamie Oliver's Food Revolution* (2010–11), where its emphasis on public service sat less comfortably, largely as a result of the specific US context. Here, it was classed as reality TV rather than as documentary and was clearly commercial in nature, being re-commissioned for a second season (even if it was dropped before all episodes were shown). The commercial nature of the program was doubly apparent when it was re-imported to the UK. Here, the US transformation undermined many of the public service values of the original series. This process highlights a significant problem for public service broadcasters across the globe: as receipts from license fees and advertising are dwindling due to channel proliferation, audience fragmentation, and the widespread acceptance of neoliberalism as commonsense ideology,[2] broadcasters and producers alike are increasingly dependent on the international exploitation of their content. The UK independent market has been particularly successful in this respect in relation to the format trade.[3] However, this sits uneasily with the broadcaster's public service commitments, particularly when the programs are more political in nature. More importantly for us, it indicates that "the public" is still defined along national lines despite the increased internationalization of both the television market and public policy.

A. PUBLIC SERVICE BROADCASTING IN THE UK

British broadcasting has operated within the system of public service practically since its inception in the early 1920s. The BBC, for example, initially set up as a private company, soon moved into the public sector. This process, which included reports from two committees, also defined the parameters of public service broadcasting.[4] Indeed, the earliest definition, offered by the Sykes Committee in advance of the Crawford Committee (1925), proclaimed that broadcasting should be a public utility and serve the public interest.[5] John Reith, invited to contribute to the Crawford Committee, extended this notion, arguing that broadcasting should not only "educate, inform and entertain," but that it could—and should—make "the nation as one man."[6] Such an image emerged from the recognition of class divisions in British society, which a mixed program could be scheduled to breach.[7] Consequently, schedules were designed with two aims in mind: to share culture and interests of different sections of society through an inclusive approach designed to showcase the best of human knowledge; and to bring important elements of British social and political life to the airwaves so that people who had traditionally been excluded (due to class, gender, or location, for example) were included. As Scannell convincingly argues, this defined a general (national) public for the first time in British history.[8]

When we compare this history with the United States, which opted for a commercial system, a further issue becomes apparent. Michele Hilmes[9] highlights that notions of the "public good" were also featured in discourses about broadcasting in the United States, where it meant something decidedly different. There, "public good" was initially understood as an opportunity for organizations to directly partake in the broadcast.[10]

The emphasis was on the ability to speak via the creation and dissemination of content rather than (as with the UK) the ability to access broadcasted content. This crucial difference, which emphasized a plurality of voices in terms of control over spectrum (US) rather than in terms of varied content (UK)[11] goes some way to explaining not only the differences in contemporary broadcasting, but also mode of address within programs. Indeed, the embedded assumption that a variety of producers (rather than varied content) automatically caters for a diverse population works to construct the audience and the public in particular ways: not only is the audience/public constructed as more enterprising in spirit, but this enterprise is written along liberal, business driven models that, arguably, define American public life more generally. In contrast, the British version of "the public good" assumes the need for a paternalistic role of the (upper middle-class led) state,[12] which knows what is best for the nation as a whole. The comparison with the United States thus reveals that the BBC constructed the audience in ways that suggested their inherent passivity and separation from the broadcaster. In turn, the British broadcaster is the active benefactor that designs its schedule to offer a deliberate variety of high and low cultural elements enjoyed by different sections of the audience. The public, then, is perceived as receiving—as consumers—even if that is of material for public consumption.[13]

Such a definition of the British public as receiving rather than participating in broadcasting remained central for the best part of seventy years, even as "the public" and "public service broadcasting" were continuously redefined. While we don't have the scope to enter into a detailed history, one crucial redefinition is worth noting. This relates to changes brought into the system as a result of the 1986 Peacock Report.[14] As Scannell details, the Report took an alternative approach to broadcasting and in the process altered the language used to speak about broadcasting for the foreseeable future. Where previous reports had thought of broadcasting as a utility and public service, Peacock saw in it a commercial entity. In this process, he also redefined the audience from a national public to *private consumers* which meant that broadcasting in the UK should become more focused on the individual and that broadcasting itself should move away from providing a service to becoming a commodity. As several writers[15] have argued, this resulted in the wholesale commercialization of British television, where public service broadcasting was an optional add-on, reduced in definition to specific programs. As Holland[16] argues, this undermined the construction of public service broadcasting *as a system*, which recognized viewers and listeners as citizens coming together as national, regional, or other specific publics. In other words, Peacock's recommendations were largely in line with the neoliberal ideology Margaret Thatcher's and later governments embraced, where the emphasis was on the positive impact of the market and the "active" consumers-as-individuals.

A further change worth noting was the increased introduction of digital technologies to broadcasting, which also facilitated a redefinition of the public. These technologies were understood to provide audiences with greater access to two-way communication, and hence would enable them to shape broadcast content themselves. This is particularly evident in the policy decisions taken by the Blair government, which aimed to use these technologies to "ameliorate the 'digital divide' as a means of combating social exclusion and political apathy."[17] While the audience's ability to shape broadcast content had been part of public service broadcasting long before the Blair government, the 1990s saw concerted efforts, particularly by the BBC and Channel 4, to involve audiences in making programs, as the BBC's ambitious *Video Nation* project (in different formats, since 1993) indicated. This participatory approach, also evident in Channel 4's *4Thought* series (2010), redefines the public in much more traditional ways as participating in a Habermasian public sphere and in so doing re-evokes a masculine-defined sphere of politics while undermining other aspects of the public that broadcasting in the UK, particularly in its early forms on the BBC and later on Channel 4, had explicitly included.

Public service broadcasting in Britain, then, had been transformed significantly by the early 2000s. By then, it was clear that it was no longer a public utility, meant to be accessible by all, bringing the nation together as a general public. Rather, the national public, if it still existed, was now understood to consist of consuming individuals who might participate—if that was their choice, to use another neoliberal watchword—in a masculine-defined public sphere of politics and social policy. The need to engage with each other's culture, to be educated and informed, to be represented in diverse ways, and most importantly to be brought together as one was increasingly perceived as archaic.

B. CHANNEL 4 AND LIFESTYLE PROGRAMMING

Choice, the individual, and consumerism are some of the key underlying ideologies of contemporary broadcasting, written not only into scheduling and the availability of different channels, but also into the modes of address, and the discourses and representations of key characters of the programs themselves. Indeed, it is clear when we consider the wider socioeconomic and political contexts that these ideologies have been central not just to broadcasting, but also to popular culture, politics, civic life, and the economy more generally. As Angela McRobbie has argued, drawing on Giddens[18] and Beck,[19] neoliberal consumerist identities are part of a longer and wider shift working to construct the individual as discerning, self-monitoring *agent*.[20]

In relation to broadcast content, our suggestion is that the Lifestyle genre and the 8 p.m. slot for Channel 4's schedule can be read as exemplary of these ideologies, and it is in their wider context that *Jamie's School Dinners* is located. In what follows, we discuss the generic traits of the Lifestyle genre, particularly in relation to the ideologies of individualism, neoliberalism, and choice, before specifically focusing on *Jamie's School Dinners*—which claimed, at least overtly, to be *more* than the others.

Lifestyle has become a central feature for the evening line-up of Channel 4. It attracts a young middle-class audience which, as a result of its particular make-up (of reasonably affluent, cultured/educated, independent consumers), returns significant advertising revenue for the channel.[21] Following early successes in the 1990s, Lifestyle is now a hallmark of the 8–9 p.m. slot on weekdays for Channel 4, where it is a lucrative genre also for the production companies that produce and subsequently franchise their formats for sales across the world.

Despite its contemporary status in a primetime slot, the Lifestyle genre has a longer history—one that saw it originally as a predominantly daytime, female-oriented genre, aimed at housewives and mothers.[22] Since 1990, however, the genre has undergone some changes, the most obvious being the shift from daytime to evening scheduling, which has necessitated further alterations in relation to content, mode of address, and style. Charlotte Brunsdon[23] and Rachel Moseley[24] have both discussed these changes in relation to gender, and it is worth noting these briefly here. For Brunsdon, the change in scheduling is seen as an overall feminization of British television in that period because on a broad level, genres perceived as feminine were now being seen in the evening slot, which was previously dominated by genres traditionally considered masculine (documentary and political chat shows)[25] or aimed at the whole family (variety programs). Moseley has suggested, on the other hand, that the alteration in scheduling resulted in a "masculinization" of the genre[26] which has worked to establish it as "gender-neutral" over the past two decades.[27] This process, of course, is built on the notion that the Lifestyle genre in its original form was problematic for the coveted demographic described above. The consequence, we suggest in keeping with Moseley, was a convoluted and complex process of "masculinization" that has actually worked to promote ideologies of neoliberalism, individualism, and capitalism as *the* shared cross-gender cultural values. What is notable from Moseley and Brunsdon's analysis is the interrelation of *content* and *time-slot* when thinking about gender and gendered address.

The masculine address was overtly achieved by including an increasing array of bloke-y characters such as "Handy" Andy Kane, the carpenter on *Changing Rooms* (1996–2004); Gordon Ramsay, who gained notoriety for his swearing; or indeed the "new lad" Jamie Oliver. Such characters also work as celebrities—unique individuals who are constructed as such (rather than, for example, as characters), which, in turn, underpins notions of individualization, celebrity, and neoliberalism, not least because in many cases, the centering of such characters also enhanced their careers. In addition, there was an increased emphasis on elements traditionally considered masculine, particularly the notion of competition,[28] evident in *Masterchef* (1990–present) or *Changing Rooms* and utilized in *Hell's Kitchen* (2004–09), and *Sarah Beeny's Selling Houses* (2012–present). Moreover, these programs included the notion of self-improvement as a central driving force behind participation. This notion, as theorists[29] have argued, is connected to a discourse that emphasizes a middle-class sensibility and is directed at the neoliberal individual in control of "his" own destiny via the avenue of consumption. In other words, these programs relied on an address to a subject that looked increasingly like a (metrosexual) spin on the traditional Cartesian (masculine) subject.[30]

Channel 4's Lifestyle programs further underwent a shift in the late 2000s. In the light of a review of public service broadcasting under the late Blair government, Channel 4 sought to redress its role as public service provider. It had become overly commercial as a result of gaining control of its own advertising time in 1993, and because it used programs such as *Big Brother* (2000–present) to refocus on a young, affluent, and urban audience.[31] By 2009, it also became clear that it needed to find alternative revenue streams as audiences splintered in the multi-channel era.[32] Channel 4 saw the review as an opportunity to increase public service programs, which included quality drama, but also documentary. Within this climate, Channel 4 also remodeled many of its Lifestyle programs to fit the more caring, and clearly educational mold it aimed to achieve as a whole. These included programs such as *How to Look Good Naked* (2006–08), which emphasized body consciousness as a socio-cultural issue, rather than constructing it as a matter of "bad taste" as with *What Not to Wear* (2001–07). *Supersize versus Superskinny* (2008–present) investigates the medical and socio-psychological issues that accompany dietary choices. *Superscrimpers* (2011–present) is constructed in response to the financial crisis of 2007–08, by offering domestic and local money-saving advice. These contemporary Lifestyle programs can also be read as masculinized, not least because of the use of male experts who have replaced the female presenters of earlier versions of the genre (Gok Wan instead of Trinny and Susannah, Dr. Christian Jenssen instead of Gillian McKeith). They also offer a particular appeal to the audience as both discerning *and* culturally or socially aware—offering a sort of public service Lifestyle genre, and in so doing re-imagining the public along lines of public policy and economics. It is within this context that *Jamie's School Dinners* set a remarkable example.

C. *JAMIE'S SCHOOL DINNERS*

Jamie's School Dinners is at the forefront of this most recent shift in Channel 4's broadcasting. Indeed, it clearly influenced and shaped the public service agenda that has been reimagined and reproduced in the particular ways noted above. These changes are also evident in the social and civic premise that the program pertains to have. Labeled "documentary" rather than Lifestyle, it re-imagines cooking as an issue of national importance related to health, well being, education, and family values. It also re-positions cooking as an activity about which we need to be educated, rather than simply entertained. Of course, such claims also draw on the many discourses of youth as needing protection, as problematic, and as inherently different from previous generations.[33] By focusing on children and school dinners, *Jamie's School Dinners* works with the potent device of power imbalance which positions the viewer in a powerful role, which mirrors some of the earlier hierarchies discussed above even if they are here less clearly structured around class (though this features too, as we will see later). Within this context, Oliver's public persona is also deliberately re-written, from "new lad" and chef to caring father and citizen who acts as (literally) paternalistic individual.

In addition to the paternalistic stance of early public service broadcasting, the program also rehashes a deliberately national address. These are "our children"—the children of the nation—whom we are all called upon to care for, along with the campaign leader, Oliver. Moreover, it develops the educational content of the documentary into a political campaign, which the nation is called upon to join (for example, by "taking action" via an online petition which resulted in over 270,000 signatures).[34] As viewers, we are also offered characters with whom to identify, be that the school dinner cook and reluctant campaigner, Nora Sands, or (more likely) the parents who are shown again and again being addressed by Oliver in his crusade to find potential political allies. Eventually, this campaign, which we see unfold over four weeks, leads Oliver to the prime minister, where Oliver delivers the votes of the online petition. Of course, this understanding of "our children" and the viewer as citizen is based on an extremely porous premise. The assumption is that this is an issue in which everyone has some investment—even if we need to be educated about what *exactly* is happening in "our" schools to be able to create change in terms of policy and perception.

Despite these overt political and civic elements, the program nevertheless operates within the Lifestyle genre and its neoliberal agenda. This is perhaps most apparent in the way Nora is presented. Like any other subject of Lifestyle television, she is a woman in need of a makeover. In this case, this makeover relates to her attitudes towards freshly cooked dinners. Accustomed to re-heating pre-cooked and packaged food, Nora is at first reluctant to embrace Oliver's fresh food campaign. Instead, she complains about the amount of time and work the preparations take, and again when she doesn't receive the recipes in writing but is instead expected to write them down herself. She whines when she doesn't know what she will cook the next day. It is only later, when she convinces other dinner ladies, that her "progress" is revealed. Her attitudes to fresh food, as well as her white cooking uniform which includes an unflattering hat (a uniform she is allowed to take off when she joins the campaign trail) and her noticeable regional accent, clearly mark her as different from the middle-class celebrity cook, Oliver. Instead she is strongly coded as working class in need of improvement. In that respect, she is aligned with the parents who pass banned junk food to their children through the school fences. This representation invites the audience to position themselves as middle class, discerning, and knowledgeable, a position which, commentators[35] have shown, is squarely in line with one key convention of Lifestyle television. Indeed, Biressi and Nunn argue that makeover programs allow viewers "to explore the hierarchies of social difference and to review their own relative position within them."[36] In this context, then, the viewers are again framed as neoliberal subjects, in charge of their own destinies. The main difference relates to the overt political and civic messages the program also claims.

Jamie's School Dinners, then, precisely articulates a public which is both defined by traditional *and* contemporary understandings of public service broadcasting. It marries the paternalistic and classist approach which imagines the viewing public as one nation with the "post-1980s ascendancy of the political values of consumerism, choice and individual self-reliance."[37] The public sphere becomes defined by the citizens' ability to take control and participate—as long as they can first transform themselves to adhere to the middle-class values that are presented as commonsensical.

D. THE AMERICAN REMAKE

The problematic definition of the public in *Jamie's School Dinners* is further undermined when it is compared with the American remake. Before we can investigate the re-import's impact on the meanings of the original, it is important to gain a better understanding of the American version. *Jamie Oliver's Food Revolution*, in contrast to the British version, is not addressed to a nation as a whole. Instead, it is focused on specific individuals and a particular locale. The latter is evident in the opening lines spoken by Ryan Seacrest: "beautiful Huntington, West Virginia, population fifty thousand, home of Marshall University, and recently named the unhealthiest city in America." This address is accompanied by images of the city's sights, including a "welcome to Huntington" sign, the university, and the city center, before cutting to images of unhealthy food, obese people on the streets and in doctors' surgeries—images which we will encounter again later in the program, when they will be contextualized in small-scale narratives about specific individuals. To compare this briefly with *Jamie's School Dinners*, in the original series, Oliver appears in an educational environment, pictured showing children different vegetables before sitting amongst them while they eat their lunches. He addresses the camera directly, with the sound of the school environment nearly drowning him out, suggesting a direct cinema documentary style. When the sound is faded out and Timothy Spall begins his narration, the emphasis is on "school dinners" and again "our children," indicating that this is a general problem that the nation as a whole has to deal with, rather than a specific town.

Jamie Oliver's Food Revolution is also about specific people—not least Oliver himself. He is introduced as the "one man [who] will be trying to save 50,000 lives." In contrast, in the British version, he appears as someone who tries to take on the role of government, since "they don't seem to have the answers." This sets up two very different personas for Oliver. In the American version, he appears as single-handed savior who is on a near-impossible mission; in the British, he is a concerned citizen and father doing his civic duty. The opening of the American version also introduces what Seacrest calls "resistance," embodied in the two very specific figures of the radio DJ and one outspoken dinner lady, Alice (a more extreme version of Nora, clearly set up to mirror her). More importantly, in the British version, Nora is representative of a general, and noticeably plural, "dinner ladies," although she does visually dominate the introductory scenes. In the American version, Alice is constructed as an individual problem—as part of the "resistance." As a result of this individualization, the public and civic framework falters and the overt political aim becomes negated, and—considering the apparent scale of the mission—also less possible.

How individualized this mission actually is becomes apparent in the very first scene after the introductory section. Here, the local radio DJ, Rod Willis, states in the language of liberal America: "I really take issue with someone coming in and telling us how we should live our lives." The argument of individual responsibility versus Oliver's (and Britain's more general) paternalistic stance is staged in the radio debate and post-interviews, when Willis accuses Oliver of grandee-ism.[38] Of course this mirrors an age-old discourse of cultural difference between the two countries that is problematic at best.[39] By staging this opposition as a fight (heated up in the post-debate interviews with Willis and Oliver), the program aims not only to create the suitable tension to keep viewers entertained (and note the absence of this extreme staging in the British version), but places the viewers in a position where they have to choose clearly defined sides, with the aim, of course, that they will be swayed—as Willis will be—towards Oliver's.

In sum, such a staging of oppositions, locales, and individuals means that Oliver's paternalistic campaign can be cloaked in the guise of neoliberal choice. The US program presents choices and perspectives constructed as dichotomous for the individual viewer. In turn, this means that the program is completely divorced from a collective address that defines groups of people (such as dinner ladies, parents, policy makers, and finally the audience *as a whole*), from which policy and thereby a definition of the public as the nation can be extrapolated. Instead, even the viewers are defined as individuals, free to choose (and invited to choose). In order to make the argument compelling, the program also needs to develop Oliver and the other characters *as characters*. Their behavior becomes stereotyped and—with the help of carefully crafted editing and decisions on the part of the participants, particularly Oliver, Alice, and Willis—their behavior also becomes performative. Oliver renders this visible by frequently emphasizing that he *is* performing a role— be that of the apprentice on his first day in the school, of the "polite Brit" who comes to America, or the concerned father who dresses up in a pea costume to make his teachings to the kids more fun.[40] The program, then, is not a civic call to action, as the British one claimed, but a showcasing of Oliver's variable (star) persona as well as the creation of new stars (in particular Alice) in the name of neoliberal debate, conducted for the entertainment of (perhaps) politically aware individual viewers.

E. CONCLUSION

What is particularly notable for us is that the differences between the British and American version only become visible through the re-import of the program to Channel 4 (as *Jamie's American Food Revolution*). Sitting between similar Lifestyle programs, the re-import draws attention to the problematic framing of the original "documentary" and in the process, undermines its public service function more generally. In particular, it makes visible the contradictions, discussed below, that are heightened in the American remake, but contained in the British version too.

Oliver's performance is self-consciously and self-reflexively foregrounded in the American remake, which in turn throws into question the authenticity of Oliver's "passion" in the British original. By comparison, Oliver comes across as relatively understated, but the narrative in both versions is so similar that his emotional reactions are betrayed as narratively motivated and hence inevitably performed. As a result, a level of fakery creeps into the experience of the original version which undermines its value as public service. Public service, then, must be authentic, non-replicable or, at least, non-performing.

The re-import to Britain, on a much more fundamental level, also makes the series' commercial value visible. Rather than being a campaign designed to change the national public, the series becomes a commodity to be traded for financial gain. That British programs are internationally successful as formats is not news to a British viewing public.[41] However, the commercial exploitation emphasizes the monetary value of the program, there to enhance Oliver's business empire, which by 2005 included a restaurant, TV series, books, and advertising contracts. This is also related to the notion of authenticity, raising issues around notions of "unique" television versus the "mass produced"[42]—which the commercial exploitation via the format trade explicitly introduces.

The program's international value also undermines its specific national public service value. If we are addressed as a nation, how can the exact same issue be of relevance to just one locale elsewhere? What this question suggests is that for public service television to work, it must indeed speak to a particular public and not—at the same time—to others. In the case of *Jamie's School Dinners* this public was, as we have seen, very clearly defined as national.

As a result of the above, the series also becomes less issue based. Within the British context, the porosity of the school dinner narrative in which supposedly everyone is invested (be that for nostalgic or parental or public policy reasons) becomes increasingly obvious. Because everyone can engage with the narrative, it seems self-sufficient when seen only in the British context. But as soon as the American version is played back to us, this sentiment is lost as we gape at the bizarre American eating habits and political opinions, and because we are constantly aligned with individuals rather than publics. As a result, the narrative in both versions becomes less about the *issues* and more about the *hero* Jamie Oliver.

Overall, then, the re-import of the program highlights the fact that our own versions are actually far less issue based, less public service focused, less authentic, more hero-centered, and more commercially interested than we would like to admit. In part this stems from the normative viewing conditions that structure our reception and make these issues less visible for us. However, they are also better disguised in a British context that wants to operate as a public service. Seeing the American remake, then, creates the critical distance that uncloaks both the representational disguises *and* our normative perceptual habits.

This, of course, also has implications for our understanding of public service and the public more generally. Indeed, it unmasks the hidden and complex *notion* that we have of public service broadcasting. Thus, unlike Scannell, who was able to return to broadcasting reports that clearly defined what the term should imply, we are struck by just how intangible the concept has become. The contradictions that the remake of the program makes visible suggest that public service broadcasting should be addressed to a specific public (and only to that), should be authentic (but what in an era of postmodern performativity might that be?), should not be commercial (but perhaps it can be in Britain), and should be issue based (but who defines what counts as an issue?). Perhaps even less tangible is the fact that it should be connected to a particular address (that draws us in as citizens who might be able to take "action") and to a particular, but badly defined, *experience* of viewing. What all of this indicates is that the notion of "the public" is emotive, and a lived and embodied experience which, for British viewers, decreasingly operates as a clear agenda.

Jamie's School Dinners and its American remake, then, make visible the problem that public service broadcasting in the post-Peacock era faces. If it is defined by particular programs, such as this one which we have dubbed an example of public service Lifestyle, then it suffers from a lack of clear understanding of its component parts, and most of all "the public" itself. As long as it remains an emotive notion that needs to operate within a commercial system (in which programs need to be exploited via the format trade, for example), it can all too easily be unmasked as performed, inauthentic, not issue based and, most of all, not really addressed to us—the viewing nation as public. With this specific (and last) bastion of public service broadcasting pulled from under us like the proverbial rug, the ideal of public service television turns into a falling house of cards.

FILMS AND TV SHOWS

4thought TV. Channel 4, 2010–.
Changing Rooms. BBC, 1996–2004.
Hell's Kitchen. ITV, 2004–09.
How to Look Good Naked. Channel 4, 2006–08.
Jamie Oliver's Food Revolution. ABC, 2010–11.
Jamie's School Dinners. Channel 4, 2005.
Masterchef. BBC, 1990–.
Sarah Beeny's Selling Houses. More4, 2012–.
Superscrimpers. Channel 4, 2011–.
Supersize versus Superskinny. Channel 4, 2008–.
What Not To Wear. BBC, 2001–07.

NOTES

1. Rachel Williams, "Jamie's School Dinners Shown to Have Improved Academic Results," *The Guardian,* last updated March 29, 2010, http://www.guardian.co.uk/education/2010/mar/29/jamie-oliver-school-dinners-meals.
2. David Hesmondhalgh, *The Cultural Industries* (London: Sage, 2007).
3. Andrea Esser, "Audiovisual Content in Europe: Transnationalization and Approximation," *Journal of Contemporary European Studies* 15, no. 2 (2007): 163–184; Andrea Esser, "Television Formats: Primetime Staple, Global Market," *Popular Communication: The International Journal of Media and Culture* 8, no. 4 (2010): 273–292; Jean K.

Chalaby, "The Rise of the Super-Indies: Policy-Making in the Age of the Global Media Market," *International Communication Gazette* 72, no.8 (2010): 675–693; Jeanette Steemers, *Selling Television: British Television in the Global Marketplace* (London: BFI, 2004).

4. Paddy Scannell, "Public Service Broadcasting: The History of a Concept," in *Understanding Television*, ed. Andrew Goodwin and Garry Whannel (London, New York: Routledge, 1990), 11–12.

5. Largely, this emphasis on broadcasting as a public utility stemmed from the recognition that wavelengths were scarce and hence needed to be tightly regulated in order to guarantee the quality of the service in the public interest.

6. Reith cited in Scannell, "Public Service Broadcasting," 14. Of course, such a definition indicates a significant bias towards masculine-defined aspects of public, social, and private life. However, as Scannell shows, the early definition of public service broadcasting explicitly addressed women as an important public that needed to be taken into consideration if the nation was to be brought together as one.

7. David Cardiff and Paddy Scannell, "Broadcasting and National Unity," in *Impacts and Influences: Essays on Media Power in the Twentieth Century*, ed. John Curran, A. Smith and P. Wingate (London: Methuen, 1987), 157–173; Kate Lacey, "Radio in the Great Depression: Promotional Culture, Public Service, and Propaganda," in *Radio Reader. Essays in the Cultural History of Radio*, ed. Michele Hilmes and Jason Loviglio (New York, London: Routledge, 2002), 21–40.

8. Scannell, "Public Service Broadcasting," 16.

9. Michele Hilmes, *Network Nations: A Transnational History of American and British Broadcasting* (London, New York: Routledge, 2011).

10. By the mid-1930s, however, the regulation of the American system concentrated ownership in elite hands—interestingly, in the supposed interest of public service. As Hilmes highlights, this meant that public service became defined as the offerings of a station that was run as a business, whilst non-profit organizations were seen as propagandistic. Michele Hilmes, "British Quality, American Chaos," *Radio Journal: International Studies in Broadcast and Audio Media* 1, no. 1 (2003): 18.

11. Hilmes, "British Quality, American Chaos," 13–27.

12. Patricia Holland, "Conceptual Glue: Public Service Broadcasting as Practice, System and Ideology," (paper presented at MIT2 Television in Transition, Cambridge, Massachusetts, 2003), http://web.mit.edu/cms/mit3/papers/holland.pdf.

13. For a discussion of public consumption versus private consumption see Logemann, Jan E., *Trams or Tailfins: Public and Private Prosperity in Post War West Germany and the United States* (London: University of Chicago Press, 2012).

14. Alan Peacock, *Report of the Committee on Financing the BBC* (London: Her Majesty's Stationary Office, 1986). Whilst earlier committees redefined public service broadcasting in relation to its aims and scope (for example, the recognition that ethnic or gender minorities needed to be more expressly served in the Annan Committee 1974), the Peacock Report asked the much more fundamental question if public service broadcasting was a desired option.

15. Holland, "Conceptual Glue"; Georgina Born, "Strategy, Positioning and Projection in Digital Television: Channel Four and the Commercialization of Public Service Broadcasting in the UK," *Media, Culture and Society* 25, no. 6 (2003): 773–799.

16. Holland, "Conceptual Glue."

17. Born, "Strategy, Positioning and Projection in Digital Television," 774.

18. Anthony Giddens, *Modernity and Self-identity* (Cambridge: Polity, 1991).

19. Ulrich Beck, *Risk Society: Towards a New Modernity* (London: Sage, 1992).

20. Angela McRobbie, *The Aftermath of Feminism: Gender, Culture and Social Change* (London: Sage, 2009), 19.

21. See "BARB Weekly Top Ten, week 19 March," last updated 2013, http://www.barb.co.uk/viewing/weekly-top-10?_s=5&period[]=201305060119.

22. See Dorothy Hobson, *Soap Opera* (Cambridge: Polity Press, 2003); Catherine Johnson and Helen Wheatley, "The 8–9 Slot: 1990–92 and 1997–98," paper presented to

the Midlands Television Research Group, Warwick University, November 4, 1999; Andy Medhurst, "Day for Night," *Sight and Sound* 9, no. 6 (1999): 26–27.

23. Charlotte Brunsdon, "Lifestyling Britain. The 8–9 Slot on British Television," *International Journal of Cultural Studies* 6, no. 1 (2003): 5–23.

24. Rachel Moseley, "Makeover Takeover on British Television," *Screen* 41, no. 3 (2000): 299–314.

25. Johnson and Wheatley, "The 8–9 Slot."

26. We can see similar changes, for example, as documentary genres have moved to docudrama and docusoap. See John Corner, ed., *New Challenges for Documentary 2nd Ed.* (Manchester: Manchester University Press, 2005); Stella Bruzzi, *New Documentary: A Critical Introduction* (London: Routledge, 2006); Thomas Austin and Wilma De Jong, eds., *Rethinking Documentary: New Perspectives, New Practices* (Maidenhead: Open University Press, 2008).

27. Rachel Moseley, "'Real Lads Do Cook… But Some Things Are Still Hard to Talk About'. The Gendering of 8–9," *European Journal of Cultural Studies* 4, no. 1 (2001): 33.

28. See Walkerdine for a discussion on the gendered elements of competition. Valerie Walkerdine, *Children, Gender, Videogames: Towards a Relational Approach to Multimedia* (Basingstoke: Palgrave MacMillian, 2007).

29. Gareth Palmer, "'The New You'. Class and Transformation in Lifestyle Television," in *Understanding Reality Television*, ed. Sue Holmes and Deborah Jermyn (London, New York: Routledge, 2004), 173–190; Anita Biressi and Heather Nunn, "Bad Citizens: The Class Politics of Lifestyle Television," in *Exposing Lifestyle TV. The Big Reveal*, ed. Gareth Palmer (Aldershot, Burlington: Ashgate, 2008), 15–24; Julie Doyle, and Irmi Karl, "Shame on You: Cosmetic Surgery and Class Transformation in *Ten Years Younger*," in *Exposing Lifestyle TV. The Big Reveal*, ed. Gareth Palmer (Aldershot, Burlington: Ashgate, 2008), 83–100.

30. For a feminist critique of the Cartesian subject as masculine see Adrianna M. Paliyenko, "Postmodern Turns against the Cartesian Subject: Descartes 'I', Lacan"s 'Other'," in *Feminist Interpretations of René Descartes*, ed. Susan Bordo (Pennsylvania Press 1999), 141–166.

31. Maggie Brown, *A Licence to Be Different. The Story of Channel 4* (London: BFI, 2007).

32. Mark Sweeney and Leigh Holmwood, "Big Brother Axed by Channel 4," *The Guardian*, last updated August 26, 2009, http://www.guardian.co.uk/media/2009/aug/26/big-brother-dropped-channel-4.

33. See for example Paul Hodkinson, "Youth Cultures: A Critical Outline of Key Debates," in *Youth Cultures: Scenes, Subcultures and Tribes*, ed. Paul Hodkinson and Wolfgang Dieke (London: Routledge, 2007), 1–23.

34. Jamie Oliver, "How the Feed Me Better Campaign Happened," last updated September 2006, http://www.jamieoliver.com/media/jo_sd_history.pdf.

35. Palmer, "'The New You'"; Biressi and Nunn, "Bad Citizens."

36. Biressi and Nunn, "Bad Citizens," 15.

37. Ibid., 16.

38. And we encounter the same argument again in an interview with Alice Gue.

39. Valerie Camporesi, *Mass Culture and the Defence of National Traditions: the BBC and American Broadcasting, 1922 – 1954* (Florence: European University Institute, 2000); Hilmes, *Network Nations*.

40. However, he also keeps emphasizing that this is "real," particularly when one disenchanted participant points out that "this is TV." The effect of this continuous need to stress the reality of the series, the people, and his motives, is of course that we are reminded that it might actually not be.

41. One of the most successful British films of the mid-2000s was *Slumdog Millionaire* (Danny Boyle, 2008), which is based on the premise of the Indian remake of *Who Wants to Be a Millionaire* (ITV, 1998–present).

42. For a discussion of the emphasis on the unique over the mass produced, see scholarship on the Arts and Crafts Movement, e.g., Ruth Ellen Levine, "The Influence of the Arts-and-Crafts Movement on the Professional Status of Occupational Therapy," in *American Journal of Occupational Therapy* 41, no.4 (1987): 248–254; Mary Ann Stankiewicz, "From the Aesthetic Movement to the Arts and Crafts Movement," *Studies in Arts Eduction* 33, no. 3 (1992): 165–173. The dichotomy between mass produced versus unique also underlies Adorno and Horkheimer's critique of the mass media. Theodor Adorno and Max Horkheimer, *Dialectic of Enlightenment* (London, New York: Verso, 1979).

FOURTEEN

Who Are We? Re-Envisioning the Doctor in the 21st Century

Paul Booth and Jef Burnham

Since *Doctor Who* premiered in 1963, twelve distinct personalities and visages have defined the character of the Doctor.[1] Given his Time Lord ability to regenerate, the Doctor's identity is never stable. The original twenty-six-year run of the series saw seven actors inhabiting the role, each with his unique version of the character. The 1996 TV movie introduced an eighth personality, and the 2005 New *Who* reboot has added four more (so far). Each Doctor is different enough that one can commonly find fans of the show identifying themselves through the persona of one particular iteration: "My Doctor is the Second," "My Doctor is the Fourth," etc. After 50 years, one would be hard pressed to find a more iconic role than the Doctor. Yet, the Doctor actually problematizes the notion of "iconicity"; he does not exemplify it. Although there are a few traits that one could ascribe to the character of the Doctor, "Doctorish"[2] characteristics more frequently appear to apply to specific iterations rather than to the character as a whole.

The role of the Doctor offers opportunities for an actor to categorically break with his predecessors yet remain tethered to one particular persona. Within the *Doctor Who* universe, each of the Doctor's regenerations problematizes the process of identifying the character according to a singular, textually "real" identity. This has created a complex character onto whom the fan audience can place their own interpretations. In the classic series, establishing the Doctor's character was a slow, often inconsistent progression, as *Doctor Who* fans could choose from the various regenerations' multitude of characteristics across its twenty-six seasons (plus TV movie). In terms of narrative, this progression creates what cult scholar Matt Hills calls a "hyperdiegesis," the sense that a storyworld is larger than any text could hope to depict.[3] We posit a similar term in the depiction of character in classic *Who*: a *hypercharacterization*, which we define as gaps in character back story, identity, or persona that create the impression of an "unknowable" characterization. This hypercharacterization leads to more fannish work on the part of the audience and highlights a Barthesian "writerly" conception of the character.[4] This hypercharacterization was augmented by the ephemeral nature of the television program: until the 1980s, video recorders were rare, and reruns on BBC even more so.

New technology and changes in television textuality heralded a shift in fans' conceptions of the Doctor's character in the New *Who* reboot. Fans of the series have positioned the New *Who* Doctors (Nine, Ten, and Eleven[5]) as amalgams of the first eight, convincingly poaching characteristics from the original series. This amalgamation occurs because multiple iterations of the Doctor can be "known" at once: through DVDs, streaming, and downloading, *Doctor Who* is literally never unavailable.[6] The immediacy and availability of the show offers a concise build-up of the character with immediate technological reinforcement. Instead of hypercharacterization, New *Who* generates *hypocharacterization*, which in turn highlights a Barthesian "readerly" conception of the character.[7] Whereas fans of classic *Who* made use of textual *absence* to create an "open" space of character identification, the always available technology of the rebooted New *Who* creates an indelible textual *presence* that closes narrative gaps and facilitates greater cult character structure. This hypocharacterization illustrates a textual excess of characteristics, prescribing (rather than facilitating) fannish construction of the character.

New *Who* is both diegetically *connected to* and also extra-diegetically *separate from* the classic series.[8] As a reboot, New *Who* articulates a nuanced reading of the evolution of the Doctor's character. Just as the show seems to intimate textual connections between classic and New, so too does it introduce variations in the series: updates to mythology (the Time War), to characters and costumes (e.g., the Cybermen), and to set design (the TARDIS control room). Yet the Doctor maintains his own personal connections to the past as well, which manifest in his characterization. Looking at the show through the lens of the Doctor's changing character contributes to our understanding of the changing cultural values of televisual characterizations, deepens research on changing technologies of viewership, and articulates an intervention in the production of fan knowledge.

A. THE CHARACTER AND IDENTITY OF THE DOCTOR

In one of the few structural analyses of characters in television narratives, Roberta Pearson identifies six elements by which audiences make meaning from characters: psychological traits, physical appearance, speech patterns, interactions, environment, and biography.[9] From combinations of these six elements, any number of permutations arises. We know some characters more fully through, for instance, their psychological traits rather than their environment (that *Hamlet* takes place in Denmark is an interesting element to the story, but not as readily identifiable to the character of Hamlet as his psychological profile, which is why Shakespeare's story can be set in different locales). But it is this very mutability that makes character an inherently unstable entity, for characters are not just the result of a hypothetical, "all-knowing" author (itself a mutable concept in a post-Barthesian world[10]), but also emerge from active audiences as well.

For the first seven incarnations of the Doctor, fans had three main sources of information about their favorite protagonist. The primary source was the television show itself: the characterizations of the actors who played the role each helped solidify a particularly salient portrayal. However, until the mid-1980s, video recording technology was relatively scarce, and so fans did not always have access to the primary text (especially as organized fandom for the show didn't spring up until the mid-1970s).[11] Thus, a secondary source became relatively canonical during this period: the Target imprint series of novelizations of individual episodes.[12] The third source for information about the Doctor's character was fan magazines and newsletters, official paratextual publications (like *Doctor Who Magazine*), and other professionally published nonfiction books like Terrance Dicks and Malcolm Hulke's 1972 *The Making of Doctor Who*.

In order to determine what characteristics most defined the first seven Doctors, we culled material from fanzine archives and fan writings that specifically described either the Doctor's appearance or the Doctor's personality. We summarize these findings in Table 14.1. Even a cursory examination of Table 14.1 reveals fluidity to the Doctor's character, from what scholar Piers Britton calls the "titanic egocentricity and deviousness" of the First Doctor, to the "avuncular" Third, the anti-heroic and "frightening" Fourth and Sixth Doctors, and the "impish cunning" of the Seventh.[13] This mutability could result from fans artificially separating one Doctor from another (i.e., fans may be choosing to emphasize particular differences instead of similarities). During the classic run of the series, fans rarely had opportunities to enact full comparisons between portrayals of the Doctor—the lack of repeat viewings and dearth of recordings means that many fans based their comparisons on memory (which, famously, "cheats") or on already-extant descriptions.

Table 14.1. The First Eight Doctors

Doctor	Characteristics	Appearance
First Doctor: William Hartnell	• Most human, arrogant, gleeful, irascible, lovable[1] • Magical[2] • Cruel[3] • Seniority and experience[4] • Youngest Doctor, oldest actor[5] • Spoiled, obstinate, and impulsive[6] • Hubris[7]	An Edwardian ensemble—suit coat, tie, checked trousers
Second Doctor: Patrick Troughton	• Manipulative[8] • Detective[9] • Humor, compassion, intelligence, and mystery; whimsy and uncertainty[10] • Anti-authoritarian authority figure[11]	Scruffy, baggy trousers, too-large coat, tie, hats
Third Doctor: Jon Pertwee	• Full of warmth, compassion, and emotions[12] • Science (not magic)[13] • Upper-middle-class English intellectual, arrogant, rude, impeccably dressed, and constantly moralizing[14] • Charismatic, pompous, opinionated, right-wing, and patronizing[15] • Paternalist[16] • Gentlemanly and civilized[17] • Sherlock Holmes, middleman between human and alien,[18] demon and fallen angel[19]	Fancy dress, "dandy," ruffled shirts, velvet coats, silk ascots, boots
Fourth Doctor: Tom Baker	• Wittier, sillier, bolder, madder[20] • Angry, cynical, dissatisfied, mercurial, alone[21] • Depth, anger, a bit of a dark side[22] • Daft, playful, thoughtful, heroic[23] • Eccentric[24] • Iconic[25] • Adventurous, playful, whimsical[26] • Quirky, arbitrary, comforting[27] • Quizzical and childlike[28] • Irascible, curmudgeonly, manic, and sharp—but he was also profoundly benevolent and generous of spirit[29]	Wide-brimmed hat, long scarf, long overcoat, (first tan, then light brown, then purple), white shirt (sometimes with question marks on lapels), sweater vest
Fifth Doctor: Peter	• Playing it straight, a real character: a believable, bewildered hero[30]	Cricketing outfit, blond

Davison	• Fast-paced, not quite as eccentric as what went before, and looks pretty, but is still surprisingly thoughtful[31] • Cricket jacket and scarf[32]	straight hair, young, cute
Sixth Doctor: Colin Baker	• Narcissistic and cutthroat to some, loyal and caring to others[33] • Loud, jarring portrayal, mood swings and his patchwork coat, a jerk[34] • Unlikeable[35] • Alieness [sic][36] • Pompous, demanding[37] • Darker, more complex Doctor[38] • Complex, manipulative[39] • Good, heroic, pompous, judgmental, funny[40]	Multi-colored cloak, blond curly hair, portly, cat badge
Seventh Doctor: Sylvester McCoy	• Cute, but underlying menace[41] • Played games[42] • Depth[43] • Manipulative[44] • God or God-like[45] • Humorous[46] • Darker, aggressive, demigod, darker and manipulative, Thor, nasty, mythical[47]	Umbrella, Panama hat, sweater with question marks on it, cream colored jacket
Eighth Doctor: Paul McGann	• Sneaky[48] • Passionate[49] • Beautiful[50] • Magician and fool[51]	Dark green velvet frock coat, a silver waistcoat and a cravat, which he finds in the hospital; long, flowing hair

For the most part, classic *Who* fans rarely used specific comparisons between Doctors—although, at the same time, there are some specific comparisons within the classic series that indicate that fans are actively constructing characters from those that came before. James Bow, for example, compares the portrayal of the Seventh Doctor to the Second in his discussion.[14] And in 1982, with the regeneration of the Fourth to the Fifth Doctor, Rose Collier notes, "'I quite like Peter Davison as Doctor Who. He's much better than I thought he'd be, a mixture of Tom Baker and Patrick Troughton.'"[15] And Jason Miller echoes Collier's assessment of the Fifth Doctor, but adds the First Doctor to the mix, noting, "here's a thirty year old who plays old and crotchety, and young and sweet, all at once."[16] Here, the comparisons between classic Doctors don't so much indicate a fluidity of *character*, but rather a comparison of *actor*. And, more to the point, these fans are making these comparisons based on their own observations—not so much based on characteristics emerging within the *Doctor Who* corpus itself.

Although these comparisons of classic *Who* Doctors are rare, the larger point is not whether or not these fans are identifying similarities, but rather that *the fans themselves are co-creating that personality*. The Doctor of classic *Who* represents what we're calling a "hypercharacterization," or the sense that fans can fill in the personality gaps to determine the most salient features of a fictional character. There are, for fans, unnoted similarities between *all* the Doctors: they are male, they are white, they are British, they are all over the age of 18, etc. But when fans construct the Doctor's personality *as a whole*, each fan must pick characteristics that are deemed the most appropriate and the most relevant for him/herself. And, perhaps surprisingly, there does seem to be some consistency in the way these seven are identified. For example, John Tulloch and Henry Jenkins note that "there is a 'different,' 'eccentric' and 'idiotic' side to the Doctor which is inflected differently in different eras of the show."[17]

This type of hypercharacterization relies on what cultural theorist Roland Barthes described as a "writerly" sense to textuality. In a writerly text, the reader is put in a position of control, and takes an active role in constructing meaning out of the multifarious number of meanings there could be. For Barthes, a writerly text is open and rewritable, and offers multiple discourses for the creation of meaning, all of which are accessible to the reader.[18]

The first seven Doctors are writerly because with each additional interpretation, a *greater discourse for viewer understanding arises*. The addition of new interpretations opens up, rather than closes, the generative properties of fan hypercharacterizations. For example, very few fan characteristics of the First Doctor survive—perhaps because there wasn't a huge fan base for the show pre-1970s, or perhaps because there was a relative dearth of material from which to construct that character.[19] Many of the characteristics attributed to the First Doctor, then, arrive via hindsight or retrospect, and are tinged with nostalgia (and possibly influenced by other mechanisms, like the Target novelizations). With the Fourth, Fifth, and Sixth Doctors in particular, however, interpretations become more varied and more impassioned, perhaps because of the emerging home video market (VHS tapes of *Doctor Who* became available in 1983, the last year of Fifth Doctor Peter Davison's tenure in the role).

In classic *Who*, the inherent "unknowable" qualities of the Doctor led to a viewer-initiated construction of the characteristics most applicable to the character. Characters sit in an uneasy space, as viewers have to navigate between a character's semiotic fictionality and the emotional connection the viewer may feel for the character in order to make sense of that character's affective role.[20] Roberta Pearson phrases the difficulty as a "paradox at the heart of the fictional character."[21] In other words, to create affective viewership, audience members must negotiate between understanding that a character is *diegetic* but intuiting that character as *mimetic*. Understanding any form of character in the televisual realm is difficult at best; as Jason Mittell points out, our understanding of any television character is always already constrained by our knowledge of the person who portrays that character.[22] For Pearson, the physical appearance of the actor determines our understanding of the character: "like all television characters . . . [understanding] is conflated with the actor who embodies him."[23] Any understanding of the Doctor's character first emerges from the physical characteristics of each actor and the costume choices envisioned by the production staff. Physically, the twelve men who have played the Doctor are all considerably different from one another, although notably they all conform to standard patriarchal, racial, and heteronormative representational modes.

Characters are the nexus through which audiences understand the narrative and also by which authors make connections to the viewers. They are the focal point by which meaning is cohered and condensed. When classic *Doctor Who* presented such an open character in the guise of the Doctor, it developed a similarly open relationship with its audience. If audiences cohere to a text through character, then, the Doctor offered a chance for viewers to engage in a non-structured but highly motivated (and personal) way.

B. THE EIGHTH DOCTOR

With fan reaction to the Eighth Doctor, we start to see major comparisons to the previous incarnations as constitutive of character itself. In Lance Parkin's "Eighth Wonder," he explores the characterization of the Eighth Doctor based solely on the movie, and even details the various ways in which some fans point to Eight as an amalgamation of the early Doctors.[24] The Eighth Doctor fuses the others' personalities as well, as Parkin points to the various ways in which the early Doctors were distinctive from one another and how fans easily identified them.[25] Fan website classicdoctorwho.co.uk criticizes the Eighth Doctor's look for being too similar to previous incarnations: "he was styled a little too similar to Tom Baker in terms of his hair and his outfit."[26] However, Parkin also distinguishes Eight from the rest, possibly suggesting that the aforementioned fan-held notion that he is an amalgamation of earlier Doctors is inherently flawed.[27]

Ultimately, Parkin's argument situates the Eighth Doctor as a massive rupture at the heart of *Doctor Who* continuity. After 15 years, fans were able to not only see a new Doctor, but also expand on a working chronology of his character. At the same time, massive technological shifts in the mid-1990s, including the popularity of the Internet and home video market, heralded a shift in the way fans *could* construct the character. For fifteen years fans were able to revisit classic *Who* as a historical text, leading to a (re)articulation of the Doctor's character. The Eighth Doctor represents a bridge between classic and New, between hyper- and hypo-characterization. He is both writerly and readerly at the same time.

C. THE NEW *WHO* REBOOT

Whereas classic *Who*'s cultural positioning as episodic television before contemporary video recording and digital technology created open spaces upon which viewers could inscribe their own version of the character, New *Who*'s location within a network of digital files and home videos prescribes those characteristics in order to maintain character consistency. We summarize the characteristics of the New *Who* Doctor in Table 14.2.

The point here is not just that fans are describing the Doctor in terms that might be used to describe the classic series hero, but that these characteristics have been asserted for the New *Who* reboot *as already present within the* Doctor Who *corpus itself.* The key difference between hyper-characterization in the classic series and this hypocharacterization in the New is that the characteristics have been reified in the series. This isn't the interpretation of a character as it evolves through fannish discourse and nostalgic remembrance, but the direct articulation of what those characteristics *are*, textually, diegetically, and canonically. This has the effect of establishing the character of the Doctor in the New *Who* reboot as what Barthes might call a "readerly" text. In a readerly text, meaning is fixed and pre-determined, making the "work" of reading easier to complete. Although multiple meanings are possible, there are clear efforts by the author to create a singular standard interpretation.

One method that fans use to construct this consistency is by drawing on specific elements from the past. When the New *Who* reboot premiered in 2005, fan discourse focused on iconography about the Doctor from his past characterizations. The New *Who* Doctor is rebooted via the deliberate layering of familiar tropes. This creates a hypocharacterization of the Doctor, for the fan is no longer "filling in the gaps" of the character. Instead, the gaps are always already filled in by the diegesis. For example, in her assessment of Doctor Nine, Barbara Hambly identifies moments when the Ninth Doctor purloins elements from the past: "I absolutely had the sense that this person actually used to be Jon Pertwee and Tom Baker and the others—other than the superficial mannerisms, I could hear their voices delivering the lines just as well as his."[28] Elizabeth Bear concurs: "Because Four was irascible, curmudgeonly, manic and sharp—but he was also profoundly benevolent and generous of spirit, and it seemed to be that Nine captured those elements as well." [29]

Table 14.2.   The New *Who* Doctors

Doctor	Characteristics	Appearance
Ninth Doctor: Chrisopher Eccleston	• Brooding, introverted, alien, youthful, serious, authority[1] • Everyman aspect[2] • Callous and condescending[3] • Emotional and affectionate[4] • Darker[5] • Upbeat personality and patent optimism[6] • Charming, goofy, fast-moving, guilty, flirtatious, jealous[7]	Black leather jacket; muted, dark-colored shirt; black trousers; boots; cropped hair
Tenth Doctor: David Tennant	• Alien and alone, playful and mysterious[8] • Likeable and odd, strange and familiar, alien and inviting, scruffy, disrespectful of authority, projecting great authority[9] • Menacing[10] • Pained and lonely, comic and tragic, quiet and overblown, passionate, emotional, flirtatious[11] • Charming, funny[12]	Tight suit; brown overcoat; occasional glasses; sneakers; slightly messed-up hair
Eleventh Doctor: Matt Smith	• Ruthless[13] • Childish and adult, energetic, hilarious, confident[14] • Profound and wide, angry, practical, humorous, witty, impatient, sentimental, contradictory[15] • Fluid and awkward, camp and authoritative, unusual-looking and appealing[16]	Bow tie; occasional fez; suit jacket; pants slightly too short; vest; boots; lanky; long, floppy hair

Perhaps because of his part in reviving the role, Christopher Eccleston's Ninth Doctor was often compared to previous incarnations, including the Eighth Doctor ("his Byronic brooding quality and unconventional good looks").[30] Not all comparisons are flattering, as Bob Furnell argues that Eccleston's "interpretation of the Doctor [is] odd and I just can't believe it's the same character I grew to love in the original series."[31] In "We ♥ Chris," a love letter to Christopher Eccleston, Robert Smith?[32] writes about the way in which the Doctor (as portrayed by Eccleston) is a fully formed, complex, emotional character.[33] To understand the character, all viewers have to do is pay attention in a readerly way to the nuances throughout the Ninth Doctor's single season in order to construct a hypo-characterization. His identity precepts are always already formed by the previous series. The classic series *foregrounds* and therefore *foreshadows* the reboot. The Ninth Doctor becomes a fixed character, contrasted with previous Doctors whom viewers came to understand only through their writerly intervention.

In this analysis, we're drawing on the works of fans who know both the classic and New series well. While it might appear coincidental (that is, the fans might not specifically mention which Doctor), the similarities between these knowledgeable fans' descriptions of the classic vs. New Doctors is significant precisely because *these fans know their Doctors*. Our examples of classic Doctor interpretation mainly draw from classic-era fanzines, while our examples of New Doctor interpretation come from newer fanzines. The comparisons between characteristics, even if implicit, draw on a body of knowledge that fans share. The hypercharacteristics defined in the past help to shape the hypocharacteristics in the present.

For example, in her many descriptions of David Tennant's characterization of the titular hero, Laura Mead uses the same terms for Ten that were used in the past to describe Four:

> he is brave and inquisitive even in the face of terror . . . thinks, talks and runs his way out of sticky situations. But this isn't down to cowardice: equally, he will run towards danger without batting an eyelid.[34]

Furthermore, her litany of examples compares Ten to Five as well:

> He's eloquent to a fault . . . he prefers to neutralize or deconstruct a threat rather than destroy it, recognizing beauty even in the most frightening, disgusting or unexpected of situations. . . . He is steadfast, loyal and honest. . . . He is passionate, sweet, and uncompromisingly moral, unarmed but never powerless.[35]

And she also compares Ten to characteristics also interpreted as belonging to Eight: "He is comfortable, relaxed and huggy around everyone . . . an emotionally intelligent, expressive . . . figure."[36] Helen Kang uses terms to describe the Tenth Doctor that would seem more applicable to the Sixth—"He is imperfect . . . he has flaws"[37] —and Barbara Hambly offers a comparison between Six and Nine as well—"the Doctor himself [is a] villain . . . by a well-meaning but ill-judged mistake."[38] Neil Lambess argues that Tennant's Doctor is "alien and alone, playful and mysterious"—characteristics that have been used multiple times in the past to describe the Seventh Doctor.[39] Andrew Cartmel, former script editor of the Seventh Doctor era, writes that Tennant "was scruffy and disrespectful of authority, while himself projecting great authority."[40] Compare this with LM Myles, writing about the Second Doctor: "The irony is that despite his anti-authoritarianism, the Doctor himself is an authority figure."[41] The comparison to the Second Doctor is made explicit by Matthew Kilburn, who argues persuasively that "Tennant's [Doctor] owes a lot to the [S]econd Doctor too, particularly in . . . his apparent childishness in the face of authority."[42]

Matt Smith's Eleventh Doctor doesn't escape comparisons to the classic Doctors. In his description of "The Wedding of River Song" (6.13), Will Barber argues that Smith "plays all sides of The Doctor in this story. One minute he is angry and very similar to Hartnell; the next he is winking at the camera just like Troughton with a great mix of [Tom] Baker as well."[43] Again, other comparisons become implicit. Sean Twist uses the "old man in a young man's body" descriptor again while going on to describe him explicitly as exhibiting "shades of Troughton, shades of Davison."[44]

Andrew Cartmel argues that Tennant was "likable and odd, strange and familiar, alien and inviting."[45] These descriptors mirror things other fans have said about the First, Fourth, Fifth, and Seventh Doctors, but they are also the very characteristics by which Cartmel defines a "Doctorish" Doctor. For Cartmel, "Doctorishness" describes the distillation of the most significant characteristics of the first six Doctors, which he used as a template for shaping McCoy's Doctor during his time as script editor.[46] Yet, Cartmel's "Doctorishness" comparison mirrors the hypercharacterization of classic *Who*—during his script editor days, he seemed less concerned about poaching characteristics of previous Doctors than he is about augmenting and developing those previous characteristics in new directions.[47] In fact, authorship is especially difficult to determine in terms of *Doctor Who*.[48] Hills shows how, for example, the Russell T. Davies era both relies on and eschews notions of authorship.[49] It's not necessarily possible to assert with impunity that New *Who* showrunners Russell T. Davies or Steven Moffat *did* or *did not* create a character by poaching characteristics from the past, but fans often assert just that.[50] For fans, the showrunner often inherently solidifies the creation of the Doctor's personality. In his own description of creating characters, Davies notes that "characters are really blurs, but that doesn't mean they're vague; it means they're alive."[51] Although in his *The Writer's Tale* he never lays out his "blueprint" for creating the Doctor, he does intimate that he often used elements from classic *Who* to help define the New series, including a few "Doctorish" qualities like the character's honesty and his eschewing of weaponry.[52]

Yet, Barbara Hambly attributes the Ninth Doctor's character to Davies, arguing he had a major role in shaping the character: he "pegged that combination of wisdom, quiet courage and daffiness."[53] Such characterizations, fans note, can be inconsistent. For example, as Lloyd Rose points out, "Ten had four years in which he was alternately adorably flirtatious and blankly indifferent—pretty much, as far as I can tell, depending on the scriptwriter."[54] She goes on to show how *Doctor Who*'s characterizations are necessarily filtered through an authorial lens:

> These are the sort of vagaries of television. Audiences . . . expect char-
> acter and story consistency, and it's nice if the show gives the impres-
> sion that someone involved knows where it's going. And producers try
> to provide this. But these are really the qualities of a novel—a story
> created by one person, worked on at leisure, and presented to the read-
> er in finished shape. Television [is] made on the run, and the scores of
> people and the amount of material involved mean that nothing can be
> entirely controlled.[55]

Doctor Who has always been free-flowing and enigmatic, and the Doctor's
character even more so. He didn't have two hearts until the start of the
Third Doctor's tenure; his regenerations were limited to twelve in the
Fourth. Classic *Who* facts become dispersed by different personnel over
twenty-six years, and thus can be contradictory. The New *Who* reboot has
replicated this dispersal of information, but done so quickly and has
therefore been forced to develop new languages of characterization. Dave
Owen argues that the new series "deliberately followed the path of the
original series, by beginning with an enigma and gradually fleshing it out
with a tangible framework."[56] In doing so, the producers (re)constructed
the mythos of *Doctor Who* in a far shorter period of time than the classic
series did, all the while drawing connections between the two. The mythos of the Doctor in classic *Who* developed organically over an extended
period of time. Therefore, the rapid pace at which New *Who* constructed
the same mythos, which necessarily draws on events and assertions from
Classic *Who*, may also account for the perception of the Doctor as an
amalgamated figure made up of elements of previous Doctors.

D. THE DOCTOR'S CHARACTER

So "Who" is the Doctor? Cordone and Cordone contend that it is his Time
Lord nature that best determines his characteristics, arguing that the
show

> can be organized under the meta-narrative that the Doctor is . . . a Time
> Lord, which makes him a member of the aristocracy. . . . His primary
> traits stem from this fact and are immutable, while other traits stem
> from the social context or the desire of the producers at the time of
> production and can evolve.[57]

But of course, as Wood and Miles demonstrate, up until 1969 the Doctor
wasn't a Time Lord at all: his home planet remained a mystery and yet the
audience could still attribute characteristics to the character.[58] Matt Hills
shows that it's the Doctor's "alien-ness . . . relying on different actors'
performance codings of 'the alien'" that determine the character.[59] In
contrast, Alan McKee's analysis of an audience's understanding of the
politics of *Doctor Who* reveals that, for many audience members, the Doctor is "too thin a character" to reveal anything about himself at all.[60]

Doctor Who fans must use semiotic productivity to connect the key characteristics that define the Doctor's *hypercharacterization*. The first eight Doctors' characteristics elide typification, creating "gaps" in fans' complete understanding of the character. To create the character, then, fans assert the primacy of key attributes. Perhaps because of the lack of visual recording technology—at least for the first five or so Doctors—fans only had at their disposal photographs, audio recordings, and novels with which to understand the character. More important for these different media, then, were psychological characteristics.

In contrast, the New *Who* Doctors' personalities are always already prescribed for the fans by the textual presence of the show. There are fewer "gaps" to fill in, a hypocharacterization, as the character is always present. In direct contrast to the "unfolding" text of the classic *Who*, the New *Who* reboot is always unfolded, always accessible.[61] It is always possible to revisit old episodes (even classic) which makes recognition of the Doctor's personality quirks that much easier. It is no surprise that Tennant's Doctor is so often compared to Tom Baker's—with a quick flip of the DVD, a comparison is immediate.

The part of the Doctor is at once iconic and mutable. It is owned by twelve different actors, but presented as a singular whole. It is deliberately opaque, but dramatic and variable as well. In fifty years, one character emerged from the combination of twelve personas, but twelve separate interpretations of this particular entity provided historiographical periodization to equip readings of production. But even with its inconstant coherence, the formation of the Doctor's character has shifted in the era of the New *Who* reboot. Whereas the production of classic *Who* allowed mystery and enigmatic "gaps" in character to result in a hypercharacterization of the Doctor, the production of current *Doctor Who* foregrounds a hypocharacterization of his diegetic elements instead.

Twelve incarnations in and we know even more—and even less— about the Doctor than we did when the series started in 1963. But we know the ultimate lesson of *Doctor Who's* changing lead character: as David Butler muses: "people change, was the lesson, but that didn't necessarily mean they stopped caring about us underneath."[62] The Doctor is now, as he was then, a madman with a box: both old and young, both human and alien; the Doctor is forever unknowable and yet meaningfully familiar, always looking out for humankind.

FILMS AND TV SHOWS

Doctor Who. BBC, 1963–89.
Doctor Who. BBC, 2005–.
Doctor Who. Directed by Geoffrey Sax. 1996. Fox Network.
The Five Doctors. Directed by Peter Moffatt. 1983. BBC.

NOTES FOR TABLE 14.1

1. Robert Smith?, "Backwards, Forwards, Sideways, Hmm?," in *Time, Unincorporated: The Doctor Who Fanzine Archives Vol 2*, ed. Graeme Burk and Robert Smith? (Des Moines, IA: Mad Norwegian Press, 2010), 41.
2. Hugh Sturgess, "'Science, Not Sorcery, Miss Hawthorne,'" in *Time, Unincorporated: The Doctor Who Fanzine Archives Vol 2*, ed. Graeme Burk and Robert Smith? (Des Moines, IA: Mad Norwegian Press, 2010), 69.
3. Lou Anders, "The Doctor's Darker Nature," in *Time, Unincorporated: The Doctor Who Fanzine Archives Vol 2*, ed. Graeme Burk and Robert Smith? (Des Moines, IA: Mad Norwegian Press, 2010), 321.
4. Laura Mead, "David Tennant's Bum," in *Chicks Unravel Time: Women Journey Through Every Season of Doctor Who*, ed. Deborah Stanish and LM Myles (Des Moines, IA: Mad Norwegian Press, 2012), 138.
5. Ibid., Teresa Jusino, "All of Gallifrey's a Stage: The Doctor in Adolescence," in *Chicks Unravel Time: Women Journey Through Every Season of Doctor Who*, ed. Deborah Stanish and LM Myles (Des Moines, IA: Mad Norwegian Press, 2012), 165.
6. Jusino, "All of Gallifrey's a Stage," 159.
7. Ibid., 163.
8. Bow, "The Two Clowns with Skeletons in the Closet," 327.
9. Lance Parkin, "Something Took Off from Mars," in *Time, Unincorporated: The Doctor Who Fanzine Archives Vol 1* (Des Moines, IA: Mad Norwegian Press, 2009), 96.
10. Myles, "Identity Crisis," 39.
11. Ibid., 42–43.
12. Jan Vincent-Rudski, "What Has Happened to the Magic of *Doctor Who*?," in *Time, Unincorporated: The Doctor Who Fanzine Archives Vol 2*, ed. Graeme Burk and Robert Smith? (Des Moines, IA: Mad Norwegian Press, 2010), 54.
13. Sturgess, "Science," 70.
14. Scott Clarke, "Wine, Cheese and Moralising," in *Time, Unincorporated: The Doctor Who Fanzine Archives Vol 2*, ed. Graeme Burk and Robert Smith? (Des Moines, IA: Mad Norwegian Press, 2010), 106–107.
15. Mike Morris, "10 Official Writer's Guidelines for the Pertwee Era," in *Time, Unincorporated: The Doctor Who Fanzine Archives Vol 2*, ed. by Graeme Burk and Robert Smith? (Des Moines, IA: Mad Norwegian Press, 2010), 114.
16. Matthew Kilburn, "Was There a Hinchcliffe Era?," in *Time, Unincorporated: The Doctor Who Fanzine Archives Vol 2*, ed. Graeme Burk and Robert Smith? (Des Moines, IA: Mad Norwegian Press, 2010), 172.
17. Mike Morris, "10 Things I Want to Say about the Graham Williams Era (Taking in 'Why Various Other Shows are Rubbish' on the Way)," in *Time, Unincorporated: The Doctor Who Fanzine Archives Vol 2*, ed. Graeme Burk and Robert Smith? (Des Moines, IA: Mad Norwegian Press, 2010), 182.
18. Parkin, "Something Took Off from Mars," 96.
19. M. Khan, "Calling a Spade, a Spade," in *Tides of Time* 27 (2001): 19.
20. Graeme Burk, "A Year in the Life," in *Time, Unincorporated: The Doctor Who Fanzine Archives Vol 2*, ed. Graeme Burk and Robert Smith? (Des Moines: Mad Norwegian Press, 2010), 165–166.
21. Rob Matthews, "Heart of Darkness," in *Time, Unincorporated: The Doctor Who Fanzine Archives Vol 2*, ed. Graeme Burk and Robert Smith? (Des Moines, IA: Mad Norwegian Press, 2010), 175–176.
22. Ibid., 177.
23. Morris, "10 Things I Want to Say About the Graham Williams Era," 182–183.
24. Sean Twist, "Five by Five," in *Time, Unincorporated: The Doctor Who Fanzine Archives Vol 3*, ed. Graeme Burk and Robert Smith?, (Des Moines, IA: Mad Norwegian Press, 2011), 265.
25. Lance Parkin, "Seriously Silly," in *Time, Unincorporated: The Doctor Who Fanzine Archives Vol 1* (Des Moines, IA: Mad Norwegian Press, 2009), 111.

26. Elizabeth Bear, "We'll Make Great Pets," in *Chicks Dig Time Lords: A Celebration of Doctor Who by the Women Who Love It*, ed. Lynne M. Thomas and Tara O'Shea (Des Moines, IA: Mad Norwegian Press, 2010), 12.

27. Ibid., 12--13.

28. Ibid., 13.

29. Ibid., 14.

30. Paul Magrs, "My Adventures," in *Time, Unincorporated: The Doctor Who Fanzine Archives Vol 2*, ed. Graeme Burk and Robert Smith? (Des Moines, IA: Mad Norwegian Press, 2010), 21.

31. Morris, "10 Things I Want to Say About the Graham Williams Era," 182.

32. Twist, "Five by Five," 265.

33. Graeme Burk, "The Rise, Fall and Decline of John Nathan-Turner," in *Time, Unincorporated: The Doctor Who Fanzine Archives Vol 2*, ed. Graeme Burk and Robert Smith? (Des Moines: Mad Norwegian Press, 2010), 256.

34. Sean Twist, "Don't You (Forget About Me)," in *Time, Unincorporated: The Doctor Who Fanzine Archives Vol 2*, ed. Graeme Burk and Robert Smith? (Des Moines, IA: Mad Norwegian Press, 2010), 266.

35. Mike Morris, "Untrue Grit," in *Time, Unincorporated: The Doctor Who Fanzine Archives Vol 2*, ed. Graeme Burk and Robert Smith? (Des Moines, IA: Mad Norwegian Press, 2010), 293.

36. Kilburn, "Assured Tennancy," 5.

37. Tansy Rayner Roberts, "The Ultimate Sixth," in *Chicks Unravel Time: Women Journey Through Every Season of Doctor Who*, ed. Deborah Stanish and LM Myles (Des Moines, IA: Mad Norwegian Press, 2012), 111.

38. Ibid.

39. Ibid., 114.

40. Ibid., 120.

41. Morris, "10 Things I Want to Say About the Graham Williams Era," 182.

42. Twist, "Don't You (Forget About Me)," 267.

43. Dave Rolinson, "Authorship in the John Nathan-Turner Era," in *Time, Unincorporated: The Doctor Who Fanzine Archives Vol 2*, ed. Graeme Burk and Robert Smith? (Des Moines, IA: Mad Norwegian Press, 2010), 275.

44. Bow, "The Two Clowns with Skeletons in the Closet," 327.

45. Sarah Groenewegen, "Don't Tell the Sisterhood," in *Time, Unincorporated: The Doctor Who Fanzine Archives Vol 2*, ed. Graeme Burk and Robert Smith? (Des Moines, IA: Mad Norwegian Press, 2010), 337.

46. Mark Hanlon, "Era Review: 'The McCoy Years,'" in *The Tides of Time* 8 (1992): 10.

47. David Carroll, "Seasons 25 and 26: An Overview," *Burnt Toast* 6 (1990): http://www.tabula-rasa.info/BurntToast/Issue06/S25-26.html.

48. Jonathan Blum, "Eight Wonderful Things about the TV Movie," in *Time, Unincorporated: The Doctor Who Fanzine Archives Vol 2*, ed. Graeme Burk and Robert Smith? (Des Moines, IA: Mad Norwegian Press, 2010), 353.

49. Eric Briggs, "Blowing Kisses to the Past, Making Love to the Future," in *Time, Unincorporated: The Doctor Who Fanzine Archives Vol 2*, ed. Graeme Burk and Robert Smith? (Des Moines, IA: Mad Norwegian Press, 2010), 357.

50. Lloyd Rose, "What's a Girl to Do?," in *Chicks Dig Time Lords: A Celebration of Doctor Who by the Women Who Love It*, ed. Lynne M. Thomas and Tara O'Shea (Des Moines, IA: Mad Norwegian Press, 2010), 46.

51. Kelly Hale, "Timing Malfunction: Television Movie + The BBC Eighth Doctor Novels = a Respectable Series," in *Chicks Unravel Time: Women Journey Through Every Season of Doctor Who*, ed. Deborah Stanish and LM Myles (Des Moines, IA: Mad Norwegian Press, 2012), 249.

NOTES FOR TABLE 14.2

1. Cartmel, "What Does It Mean To Be Doctorish?," 31.
2. Russ Flinn, "The Ninth Doctor: Resurrection or Regeneration?," in *Whotopia* 6 (Dec. 2005): 11.
3. Furnell, "Aliens of London," 18.
4. Bonnie Gale, "Fanreaction," in *Whotopia* 6 (Dec. 2005): 37.
5. Graeme Burk, "Counting to Ten," in *Time, Unincorporated: The Doctor Who Fanzine Archives Vol 3*, ed. Graeme Burk and Robert Smith? (Des Moines, IA: Mad Norwegian Press, 2011), 164.
6. Jez Strickley, "The Oncoming Storm," in *Whotopia* 11 (June 2007): 6.
7. Lloyd Rose, "Resurrection," in *Time, Unincorporated: The Doctor Who Fanzine Archives Vol 3*, ed. Graeme Burk and Robert Smith? (Des Moines, IA: Mad Norwegian Press, 2011), 38–39.
8. Lambess, "The Tenth Doctor Debut," 8.
9. Cartmel, "What Does It Mean To Be Doctorish?," 27.
10. Ken Holtzhouser, "Voyage of the Damned," in *Whotopia* 13 (May 2008): 39.
11. Burk, "Counting to Ten," 164–165.
12. Nina Kolunovsky, "How Do You Kill a Wasp?," in *Time, Unincorporated: The Doctor Who Fanzine Archives Vol 3*, ed. Graeme Burk and Robert Smith? (Des Moines, IA: Mad Norwegian Press, 2011), 179.
13. Gary Phillips, "Day of the Moon: Episode Two," in *Whotopia* 23 (May 2012): 42.
14. Katie Steely-Brown, "That Odd British TV Show," in *Fish Fingers and Custard* 11 (Aug. 2012): 13.
15. Keith Topping, "First Eleven," in *Time, Unincorporated: The Doctor Who Fanzine Archives Vol 3*, ed. Graeme Burk and Robert Smith? (Des Moines, IA: Mad Norwegian Press, 2011), 262–264.
16. Robert Smith? "Squee-mendous," *Time, Unincorporated: The Doctor Who Fanzine Archives Vol 3*, ed. Graeme Burk and Robert Smith? (Des Moines: Mad Norwegian Press, 2011), 279.

NOTES

1. For the sake of this chapter, we will be confining our analysis to the television series and TV movie, not the ancillary (non-canonical) films of the 1960s, the Big Finish audio adventures, or the (sort of) non-canonical *Scream of the Shalka*.
2. Andrew Cartmel, "What Does It Mean To Be Doctorish?," in *Time, Unincorporated: The Doctor Who Fanzine Archives Vol 3*, ed. Graeme Burk and Robert Smith? (Des Moines, IA: Mad Norwegian Press, 2011), 26.
3. Matt Hills, *Fan Cultures* (New York, NY: Routledge, 2002), 137.
4. Roland Barthes, *S/Z: An Essay*, trans., Richard Miller (New York, NY: Hill and Wang, 1974).
5. At the time of writing, the BBC has not aired any episodes with the Twelfth Doctor (Peter Capaldi), and thus we have no fan research to describe the character.
6. With the notable exception of classic series episodes that were wiped from the BBC's archive. However, audio recordings do exist of these missing episodes.
7. Barthes, *S/Z*.
8. Matt Hills, *Triumph of a Time Lord: Regenerating Doctor Who in the Twenty-First Century* (London, UK: IB Tauris, 2010), 4.
9. Roberta Pearson, "Anatomising Gilbert Grissom: The Structure and Function of the Televisual Character," in *Reading CSI: Television under the Microscope*, ed. Michael Allen (London: I.B. Tauris, 2007).
10. Roland Barthes, "The Death of the Author," in *Image-Music-Text*, trans. Stephen Heath (New York, NY: Hill and Wang, 1977).

11. Miles Booy, *Love and Monsters: The Doctor Who Experience, 1979 to the Present* (London, UK: IB Tauris, 2012); Andrew O'Day, "Event TV: Fan Consumption of Televised *Doctor Who* in Britain (1963-Present)," in *Doctor Who in Time and Space*, ed. Gillian Leitch (Jefferson, NC: McFarland Press, 2013).

12. Lance Parkin, "Canonicity Matters: Defining the *Doctor Who* Canon," in *Time and Relative Dissertations in Space*, ed. David Butler (Manchester, UK: Manchester University Press, 2007).

13. Piers Britton, *TARDISBound: Navigating the Universes of Doctor Who* (London, UK: IB Tauris, 2011), 19–20.

14. James Bow, "The Two Clowns with Skeletons in the Closet," in *Time, Unincorporated: The Doctor Who Fanzine Archives Vol 2*, ed. Graeme Burk and Robert Smith? (Des Moines, IA: Mad Norwegian Press, 2010), 327.

15. "TV Mailbag," from *Morbius* 12 (March/April 1982), 3.

16. Jason Miller, "Dwellings of Simplicity," in *Time, Unincorporated: The Doctor Who Fanzine Archives Vol 2*, ed. Graeme Burk and Robert Smith? (Des Moines, IA: Mad Norwegian Press, 2010), 288.

17. John Tulloch and Henry Jenkins, *Science Fiction Audiences: Watching Star Trek and Doctor Who* (New York: Routledge, 1995), 126.

18. Barthes, "Death."

19. Booy, *Love and Monsters*.

20. James Phelan, *Reading People, Reading Plots: Character, Progression, and the Interpretation of Narrative* (Chicago, IL: University of Chicago Press, 1989).

21. Pearson, "Anatomising Gilbert Grissom," 40–41.

22. Jason Mittell, *Complex TV: The Poetics of Contemporary Television Storytelling*, prepublication edition, MediaCommons Press, 2012: http://mediacommons.futureofthebook.org/mcpress/complextelevision/character/, 6.

23. Pearson, "Anatomising Gilbert Grissom," 44.

24. Lance Parkin, "Eighth Wonder," in *Time, Unincorporated: The Doctor Who Fanzine Archives Vol 1* (Des Moines, IA: Mad Norwegian Press, 2009), 118.

25. Ibid., 120.

26. "Paul McGann—The 'Canon' Doctor," http://classicdoctorwho.co.uk/78-doctors/80-paul-mcgann-the-canon-doctor-who.

27. Parkin, "Eighth," 121–124.

28. Barbara Hambly, "Regeneration—Shaping the Road Ahead," in *Chicks Unravel Time: Women Journey Through Every Season of Doctor Who*, ed. Deborah Stanish and LM Myles (Des Moines, IA: Mad Norwegian Press, 2012), 12.

29. Bear, "We'll Make Great Pets," 14.

30. Cartmel, "What Does It Mean To Be Doctorish?," 31.

31. Bob Furnell, "Aliens of London," *Whotopia* 6 (Dec. 2005): 18.

32. Smith? spells his name with the question mark.

33. Robert Smith?, "We ♥ Chris," in *Time, Unincorporated: The Doctor Who Fanzine Archives Vol 3*, ed. Graeme Burk and Robert Smith? (Des Moines: Mad Norwegian Press, 2011).

34. Mead, "David Tennant's Bum," 139.

35. Ibid., 140.

36. Ibid., 141–142.

37. Helen Kang, "Adventures in Ocean-Crossing, Margin-Skating and Feminist-Engagement with *Doctor Who*," in *Chicks Dig Time Lords: A Celebration of Doctor Who by the Women Who Love It*, ed. Lynne M. Thomas and Tara O'Shea (Des Moines, IA: Mad Norwegian Press, 2010), 44.

38. Hambly, "Regeneration—Shaping the Road Ahead," 18.

39. Neil Lambess, "The Tenth Doctor Debut," *Time Space Visualizer: The Journal of the New Zealand Doctor Who Fan Club* 72 (Feb. 2006): 8.

40. Cartmel, "What Does It Mean to be Doctorish?," 27.

41. LM Myles, "Identity Crisis," in *Chicks Unravel Time: Women Journey Through Every Season of Doctor Who*, ed. Deborah Stanish and LM Myles (Des Moines, IA: Mad Norwegian Press, 2012), 42.

42. Matthew Kilburn, "Assured Tennancy: A Few Answers for 2005 from 2010," *The Tides of Time* 31 (2005 [revised Aug. 2010]): 8.

43. Will Barber, "The Wedding of River Song Review," *Fish Fingers and Custard* 9 (March 2012): 25.

44. Twist, "Five by Five," 290–291.

45. Cartmel, "What Does It Mean to be Doctorish?," 27.

46. Ibid.

47. Andrew Cartmel, *Script Doctor: The Inside Story of Doctor Who 1986–89* (London, UK: Reynolds & Hearn, 2005).

48. Hills, *Triumph*, 25–53.

49. Ibid., 48.

50. James Chapman, *Inside the TARDIS* (London, UK: IB Tauris, 2006).

51. Russell T. Davies and Benjamin Cook, *The Writer's Tale: The Final Chapter* (London: BBC Books, 2010), 64.

52. For example, Ibid., 65, 168, 200.

53. Hambly, "Regeneration—Shaping the Road Ahead," 12.

54. Rose, "What's A Girl to Do?," 47.

55. Ibid., 49.

56. Dave Owen, "The Death of *Doctor Who*: Verdict Overturned," in *Time, Unincorporated: The* Doctor Who *Fanzine Archives Vol 3*, ed. Graeme Burk and Robert Smith? (Des Moines, IA: Mad Norwegian Press, 2011), 20.

57. Michelle Cordone and John Cordone, "Who Is The Doctor? The Meta-Narrative of *Doctor Who*," in *Ruminations, Peregrination, and Regenerations: A Critical Approach to Doctor Who*, ed. Chris Hansen (Newcastle, UK: Cambridge Scholars Press, 2010), 8.

58. Tat Wood and Lawrence Miles, *About Time 2: The Unauthorized Guide to Doctor Who 1966–1969, Seasons 4 to 6* (Des Moines, IA: Mad Norwegian Press, 2006), 275.

59. Matt Hills, "'Gothic' Body Parts in a 'Postmodern' Body of Work? The Hinchcliffe/Holmes Era of Doctor Who (1975–77)," *Intensities: The Journal of Cult Media* 4 (2007):   http://intensitiescultmedia.files.wordpress.com/2012/12/hills-gothic-body-parts-in-postmodern-body-of-work.pdf, 15.

60. Alan McKee, "Is Doctor Who Political?" *European Journal of Cultural Studies* 7, no. 2 (2004): 209, quoting an anonymous fan.

61. John Tulloch and Manual Álvarado, *Doctor Who: The Unfolding Text* (New York, NY: St. Martin's Press, 1984).

62. David Butler, "Introduction," in *Time and Relative Dissertations in Space*, ed. David Butler (Manchester, UK: Manchester University Press, 2007), 8.

FIFTEEN

"More Village"

Redeveloping The Prisoner

Peter Clandfield

The seventeen episodes of *The Prisoner*, the 1967–68 ITC Television production about an ex-secret agent imprisoned in a mysterious Village, develop a pioneering example of the series-spanning narrative arc. Patrick McGoohan's central character tries persistently to escape, while the never-identified powers behind the Village, represented by a succession of figures occupying the role of No. 2, deploy increasingly elaborate ways of coercing the prisoner, "No. 6," into explaining his resignation. In the opening episode, "Arrival," the first No. 2 (Guy Doleman) tells the protagonist, "I don't think you realize what a valuable property you've become": this reference to the secret agent as Cold War commodity also anticipates the way McGoohan's No. 6 has become an icon of principled individualism, and the series a reference point for critiques of intrusive surveillance, synthetic sociability, and manufactured consensus. The ambiguity of the series finale, which can be read as depicting the protagonist's ultimate escape from the Village, or his final co-option by the forces behind it, or something else again, made the work something of a popular and critical failure in 1968; these same provocative qualities, however, have helped the series to sustain, and be sustained by, pioneering, persistent, and notably eccentric fan cultures.[1]

Given this distinctive history, *The Prisoner* represents both provocation and obstacle for remakes, and the 2009 American Movie Classics "reinvention" or "reimagining" of the property as a six-episode miniseries has had a lukewarm reception. Tim Goodman concludes, "The origi-

nal 'Prisoner' opened the door to decades of innovative television. Remaking it now seems pointless."[2] Sue Short assesses the reinvention as "a
contemporary production with an eye on global (particularly American)
appeal." Noting that the protagonist is now played by American Jim
Caviezel as a New Yorker working in surveillance, Short points out that
in the new Village, "the repeated 'mirage' of the twin towers (a symbol of
6's lost world) places the production on a par with other post-9/11 telefantasy, yet has little coherent meaning." For Short, "the miniseries clearly aims to sell itself as a quality production, and looks ravishing, yet fails
in its aspirations to emulate the original, with little to compare the two."[3]
In simpler terms, the header for a brief review in the *Independent* dismisses the AMC series as "a lacklustre US remake of a British classic."[4]
Yet, while oriented toward the US market as Short notes, and backed by
AMC, the series was made (in Namibia and South Africa) by Britain's
Granada Productions (since rebranded as ITV Studios), with British writer and executive producer Bill Gallagher and British director Nick Hurran. Many British actors are involved, and while some adopt American
accents, the most prominent role—though possibly, I will argue, not the
most important—has Ian McKellen as 6's adversary, 2, whose voice, demeanor, and costuming mark him as a British imperial figure, a re-working of the original's various officer-class No. 2s.[5] The Village itself,
played by the Namibian resort of Swakopmund, includes features, such
as vehicles, evoking the 1960s, but appears overall as an extra-national,
extra-temporal space, designed according to generalized ideals of heritage and harmony. To treat the original *The Prisoner* as an unalterable
monument of British cultural heritage, or as a television landmark beyond all possible extension, would be to replicate some of the establish-
mentarian attitudes the original series questions, while to dismiss the
"reinvention" as redundant is to overlook both its significant features
and its potential to reactivate those of the original.

In the final moments of the AMC miniseries, 6, having finally been
persuaded not merely to accept the Village but even to take over as its
leader, muses, "It has to be possible to do this the right way. . . yeah . . .
make a *good* village. . . ." Indicating 6's capitulation to the values of the
Village, these remarks apparently offer neater closure than does the original series. Yet, the suggestion that a "good village" is still in the future
can be heard as an ironic, self-reflexive comment on the limitations of the
miniseries; further, 6's remarks could evoke a gap between the potential
and the achievement of the original series, and hint that its concerns have
implications beyond the capacity of any one version to explore fully. The
multi-layeredness of the final lines illustrates the depth that the miniseries does achieve in part, and these lines also highlight the value of moving past judgment of the remake to focus on intertextual relations between the two productions, and on some of what has been made of *The
Prisoner* by fans, critics, and marketers.

Intertextuality in this instance is not only a matter of allusion, quotation, and narrative weaving of common threads; it is a connection affecting interpretation of both original and remake, and drawing attention to what Mikhail M. Bakhtin and others theorize as the dialogic relations among texts. As Graham Allen summarizes, for Bakhtin, "One cannot understand an utterance or even a written work as if it were singular in meaning, unconnected to previous and future utterances or works."[6] Utterances—including novels and screen texts—call back to previous ones, but also ahead to future ones. Bakhtin outlines the process of "re-accentuation," whereby the "images and languages" of works are subject to changing interpretations and uses as their "background animating dialogue[s]"—influential social concerns and debates, plus prevailing definitions and connotations of words, tropes, or discourses—evolve, so that "The historical life of classic works is in fact the uninterrupted process of their social and ideological re-accentuation."[7] Thus, the 1967–68 *The Prisoner*, gaining "classic" status from ongoing interpretation and recycling, is not a fixed standard by which the reinvention can be assessed; nevertheless, as the newer production participates in the re-accentuation of the older one, this renewed attention to the older work raises additional ways of interpreting the newer. I will focus on reading the two series—and some of their re-accentuations—as critiques of the assumption that social harmony can be prefabricated, and as warnings against too-ready acceptance of manufactured environments and cultural experiences.

A. REMAPPING THE VILLAGE

The AMC *Prisoner* opens with Caviezel's 6 waking in a rugged desert and witnessing an elderly man fleeing pursuers. The man is dressed in the khaki-trimmed black blazer (evoking a British "public" school uniform) that McGoohan's No. 6 normally wears as a Village inmate. "Tell them all that I got out," he whispers, urging Caviezel's bewildered character to seek out other would-be escapers, and adding as his dying words the standard Village salutation, "Be seeing you" (1.01, "Arrival"). This opening literal instance of "common threads" between original and remake is ambiguous, like the final lines cited above: it makes homage to the original's resolute protagonist, yet apparently relegates the 1960s series to the status of prologue.[8] The remake's opening episode includes other pointed recreations of details and incidents from the original, notably a version of the sequence in which the disoriented protagonist, on his first morning in captivity, finds that even the most expensive map available from the Village shop shows nothing of the outside world. In the remake, 6 demands "the biggest [map] you got," and is offered a wallet-sized effort which startlingly unfolds to the dimensions of a ping-pong table, though still depicting only the Village. The visual joke implies that the

Village and the miniseries itself, despite their compactness, contain more than they seem to.

The two series differ clearly in narrative structure. While the original develops an overall narrative arc, episode-to-episode continuity in the middle can be uncertain.[9] Other than McGoohan's No. 6, the only continuing characters are in supporting roles. The remake has a tighter arc and much more assertive continuity. Whereas the original has No. 6 defeat or defy a new No. 2 in almost every episode, while No. 1 remains a mystery, the reinvention positions one figure, McKellen's overlordly "2," as the enduring force behind the Village. 2 is as prominent, and as enigmatic, in every episode as 6. Other major characters also evolve through the narrative, which parallels the experiences of 6 in the Village with flashbacks to his recent past in New York. The second episode, "Harmony," explores 6's past encounter with a woman called Lucy (Hayley Attwell), and their conversation reveals details of his work for a company called Summakor: "My job is to look for patterns, how we live," he tells her, adding that "finding out what is going on is not good news." The idea that something has gone wrong with "how we live" will prove important to later revelations about the nature of the Village. Despite his growing suspicion of Lucy's motives, 6 is evidently attracted to her; meanwhile, in the current timeline of the Village, he is similarly interested in yet wary of 313, a sympathetic doctor (Ruth Wilson). Both relationships evolve, to converge in the fourth episode, "Darling," when a version of Lucy appears in the Village as 4–15. In its recourse to triangular romantic tension involving attractive people, the newer series seems, as Short suggests, formulaic.[10] However, it does not become a dystopian remake of *The Bachelor* (2002–present), thanks partly to other substantial plotlines, particularly that of 2's relationship with his restless son, 11–12, and the mystery surrounding 2's wife, M2, who lies in their palatial home, apparently comatose except in brief drug-induced periods of normal activity.

B. 2, 6, 11–12, & 909

While the original series is family-oriented in that it treats sex and (usually) violence circumspectly even by 1960s television standards, the newer one offers an updated take on matters of familiality and sexuality, particularly in the third episode, "Anvil," which reveals a romantic liaison between 11–12 and 909, a Village man who works for 2. The relationship crosses boundaries both of class, since 909 lives in a trailer park on the outskirts of the Village, and age, since 11–12 (played by Jamie Campbell Bower, b. 1988) is barely adult in appearance, while 909 (played by Vincent Regan, b. 1965) is solidly middle-aged. The men's bond is depicted sympathetically, with romantically lit shots of their eye contact as they talk in a Village bar (which apparently caters to queer or alternative tastes, indicating that the Village offers superficial acceptance of diversity). 11–12 is apprehensive but somewhat reassured by 909's evident sincerity:

11–12: "It's good. This. I mean . . .you choosing me."

909: "I seem to recall it was you chose me."

The romantic harmony, however, will be broken. Short argues that "The theme of being trapped in a relatively idyllic 'prison' is brought home via [11–12's] outlawed homosexuality imprisoning the young man within his father's expectations."[11] Significantly, however, the "outlawing" of 11–12's and 909's relationship is depicted as a particularly harsh example of the way individual freedom will be curtailed in the Village when it conflicts with 2's agenda. The relationship is compromised partly by the intervention of 6, who witnesses the bar encounter. 6 suspects that 909 is watching him and 313, and he threatens to reveal the lovers' relationship to 2 unless they arrange for surveillance to end. But 2 is already monitoring his son, and after he indicates plans to interrogate 909, a desperate 11–12 fatally stabs his lover, who willingly submits to this fate. Thus summarized, the episode may sound like a retrograde reassertion of stereotypes of homosexuality as inherently unstable and tragic. However, 11–12's role in the remainder of the series foregrounds his strength. Immediately after 909's death, 2 enjoins 11–12 to find "someone . . . your own age," but the final episode finds the justifiably angry young man, after 2 has goaded him more crudely about his sexuality, placing flowers at 909's grave. In fact, 11–12, rather than 6, embodies the strongest challenge to 2's controlling agenda, maintaining his individual sovereignty.

Thus, while the inclusion of 11–12 seems one of the reinvention's clearest departures from the original, it also brings the most sustained reaccentuation of the original's concern with distinctions between genuine personal choice and manipulated pseudo-choice. In the original opening episode, No. 6 warily wanders the Village, chaperoned from a distance by No. 2, who points out, via loudhailer, a vigorous older couple as models of assimilation: "They didn't settle for ages. Now they wouldn't leave for the world." When No. 6 retorts, "You mean you brought them around to your way of thinking?," No. 2 replies evenly, "They had a *choice*." The combination of urbane veneer and underlying authoritarianism sets a pattern for No. 2s in the original and for 2 in the remake, in whose opening episode McKellen's 2 responds to 6's "Why are you keeping me here?" with a crisply disingenuous "I see no locked doors." In the remake's finale, 2 presents 6 with an ultimatum: "You choose. This life, or no life" (1.06, "Checkmate"). While 6 will be coerced into accepting the former option, 11–12, looking on here, actively chooses the latter option in revolt against his father, first smothering—and apparently killing—his

comatose mother, then hanging himself. Arguably, 11–12 is the true protagonist of the series, if a tragic one.

11–12's insistence on rights of choice is particularly significant in light
of the singular conditions, revealed gradually through the inquiries of
both 6 and 11–12, which govern the reinvented Village. The Village exists
as the dream of 2's wife, M2—or in the oneiric space she generates under
the influence of what are presumably very powerful drugs indeed. Writ-
er-producer Bill Gallagher explains the premise, ostensibly based on the
ideas of Carl Jung: not only consciousness but also the unconscious may
have multiple levels, including a collective storehouse of dreams and
images that all human beings are affected and connected by. The Village
is a hitherto-unknown level of the unconscious which 2—or Mr. Curtis,
as he is known in New York as the CEO of Summakor—and M2 have
figured out how to access and activate. Gallagher insists that "The Village
is not some virtual world," but the Village is perhaps most intelligible as,
indeed, a virtual reality collectively experienced.[12] 11–12 turns out, in
fact, to be a virtual being: in the fifth episode, "Schizoid," he learns from
his temporarily awakened mother that having been born in the Village,
he exists only in its dimension. He is the child 2 and M2 were unable to
have in reality; the opportunity to create him was part of their motivation
for conceiving the Village, but the demands of her dreaming (mysterious
holes open up in the Village when she is awake) mean that M2 cannot
take up her parental role except very briefly. Paradoxically, however, the
fact that 11–12 is synthetic, seemingly just a character in his parents'
story, makes him a more substantive presence in the series as an embodi-
ment of sovereign individuality. If a prefabricated being proves to be gay,
the implication is that orthodox heterosexuality is not a particularly fundamental human quality, or not something straightforward enough to be
synthesized. Choice, on the other hand, is implied through 11–12's actions to be a fundamental aspect of human identity. As an artificial being
who insists on making his own choices and questions the terms of his
existence, 11–12 is something of a remake of Frankenstein's monster—a
poster-being for creation as a process of recycling.

"It was all a dream" is a proverbial cop-out resolution for fantastic
narratives, but its use in the AMC *The Prisoner* has important intertextual
resonances. The most salient source for the dream/virtual reality conceit
is, I would argue, not Jung, but a specific episode of the original series, to
which many of the premises of the reimagined Village can be traced. The
effect reverses that of the unexpectedly large map mentioned above: the
reinvention proves smaller than it seems. Yet the episode, "Living in
Harmony" (1.14), is particularly audacious, and the remake's use of it
points to several aspects of its significance.

C. LIVING IN HARMONY

The original *Prisoner* gains distinctiveness from the location used for the Village: Portmeirion, North Wales, which according to Robert Fairclough was developed by architect Clough Williams-Ellis as "a site for implementing his belief that architecture could be developed in harmony with a naturally beautiful area." Between the 1920s and the early 1960s, "The buildings and statuary that went into the creation of the village were salvaged from all over the United Kingdom . . . and restored in a variety of Mediterranean and classical styles," creating what Catherine Johnson sums up as "a surreal location that appears to transcend time and space."[13] But "Living in Harmony," the fourteenth episode in the original British running order, achieves surreal dislocation by going somewhere seemingly unrelated to the rest of the series.

Paradoxically, "Living in Harmony" varies the established formula of *The Prisoner* by remaking it in terms of another formula, that of Westerns. Omitting the usual title sequence, the episode opens with McGoohan as a sheriff who resigns by turning in badge, gun, and horse and leaving town, only to be set upon and taken to another town, Harmony, where he is forced to make a stand against an authoritarian local order. The name of the town is significant: in a previous episode, "A Change of Mind" (1.12), No. 6 is denounced by the Village Council for his "spirit of disharmony" and subjected to orchestrated harassment, which he eventually turns back against the No. 2 responsible. "Living in Harmony" is the kind of Western, prominent in the postwar era, that questions the codes of its genre rather than remaking them with minor variations; Fairclough notes that the episode features allusions to several such works.[14] McGoohan's character confronts the corrupt Judge (David Bauer) who controls Harmony and who seeks to co-opt him by making him sheriff: he resists carrying a gun or co-operating with the town's regime, but is eventually manipulated into trying to protect a saloon girl, Kathy (Valerie French), from the attentions of a volatile, hard-drinking gunslinger, the Kid (Alexis Kanner). After the Kid kills Kathy in a fit of jealousy, McGoohan's character defeats him in a duel, but is gunned down by the Judge. No. 6 then regains consciousness and discovers that he has been immersed in a virtual reality fabricated with mind-altering drugs, electronic apparatus, and an elaborate set and props: the Judge is No. 2, and the Kid is No. 8, who has masterminded the operation, with No. 22 as Kathy. The experiment suggests that not only chemicals but also familiar plot-patterns, like those of the Western, can lend themselves to (attempts at) mind control. The strategy harmonizes with the idea that subjectivity (individual consciousness and conscience) is made partly through engagement with familiar narratives. Individuals are texts, understanding and expressing themselves through tropes and structures from other texts. The idea behind putting No. 6 into a virtual Western is presumably that his response to its conventions may reveal important information, but this experiment fails, as the reawakened No. 6 quickly reasserts his defiance, staring down his would-be manipulators in the Village control room.

Despite this non-violent demonstration of No. 6's moral authority, the episode ends with a further violent twist, as No. 8, accosting No. 22 at the saloon set, reverts to his role as the Kid and kills both her and himself. The deaths are depicted in strikingly unrealistic ways (strangled, No. 22 can still speak to No. 6 before dying), and as Chris Gregory comments, "The final scene reminds us that, although what we have been observing for most of the episode has been given a (somewhat unlikely) quasi-realistic explanation, it is the world of the Village itself which is the real 'nightmare'. 'Living in Harmony' is a dream within a dream." Gregory points out also that the ending emphasizes that it is not only No. 6 who has been immersed in the synthetic environment of Harmony, but also the other major players.[15] Hence the way in which "Living in Harmony" is a blueprint for the collective virtual reality of AMC's reimagined Village.

Recognition of the significance of "Living in Harmony" to the remake also cues attention to the original's critique of television as a prime purveyor of fabricated experience. The older series remakes itself with every episode, as each new No. 2 tries new strategies for eliciting information, while No. 6 pursues new avenues of escape. Not only in "Living in Harmony" but in other episodes leading up to the finale, Village authorities place No. 6 in scenarios recycling familiar narratives. The succeeding episode, "The Girl Who Was Death" (1.15), is both a Bond spoof and *The Prisoner*'s carnivalesque self-parody. Other instances of the critique of television are more subtle. Gregory argues that the prominence of screens, such as those on which Village authorities monitor No. 6, "represents a visual commentary on the relationship between the viewer and the TV screen itself."[16] The critique of television's effects also, arguably, figures in the provocatively ambiguous revelations of the finale. Having outlasted yet another No. 2 in a marathon interrogation in the penultimate episode, No. 6 is feted as victorious and granted one of his persistent demands: access to No. 1. But No. 1 is revealed—in fleeting, enigmatic glimpses—as No. 6 himself. One interpretation of the revelation is that No. 6 is his own jailer, and that we create our own prisons, but it seems just as plausible to suggest that No. 1 is the culture industry as represented by McGoohan, whose role in *Danger Man* (1960–61; 1964–66), the relatively orthodox and successful secret agent series that preceded *The Prisoner*, had made him the highest-paid star on British television. In this reading, No. 1's identity, along with the eccentric way in which it is suggested, leaves *The Prisoner* with a built-in warning about its own manipulative potential.

Even the technical limitations of 1960s television reinforce the warning, by calling attention to the constructedness of the series. In "Living in

Harmony," No. 6 emerges from the virtual reality clutching headphones to his ears, and the image evokes the artificial, tinny sound of the episode itself and also cues awareness of the way the series has its audience "living in harmony" through its imposing use of music, both diegetic and non-diegetic. No. 6 goes on to confront cardboard cutouts of figures from his Western experience in the now-deserted "Harmony," recognizable as a studio lot; thus, the sequence reminds us that we are watching two-dimensional television. Technical limitations of the original series are more noticeable when it is viewed alongside the remake, and these very limitations—the visible and audible built-ness—also serve to draw attention to the convergence between the technical facility and efficiency of the remake and that of Summakor *within* the remake.

Summakor apparently manipulates the unconscious lives of its Villagers so efficiently that the mechanisms concerned are virtually invisible. AMC's corporate motto is "Story Matters Here," and narrative is an important tool of manipulation for Summakor—one which, in the absence of detailed depiction of means whereby the Village's people have been conveyed to its Jungian level, seems to be a sovereign force. The second episode, the one entitled "Harmony," for example, introduces 6's purported brother 16, who tells stories of their past. 16 actually succeeds in persuading 6 of their kinship, but then reveals the deception and attempts to escape by swimming, only to be—in another quotation from the original series—smothered by "Rover," the large white balloon that polices would-be escapers. In the end, the AMC series has 6 himself, having learned the secrets of the Village, submitting to narratives of therapy and compliance and "living in harmony" for good. It appears that 2, in his capacity as Summakor's CEO, has brought Michael/6 to the Village not only to find out what he knows about the company's aims, but also to subject him to a particularly gruelling job interview. As noted, Caviezel's character ends up inheriting the role of Village overlord—while 313 is the new dreamer, and a major factor in 6's decision to stay, since in reality (according to 2) she suffers from an intractable personality disorder. Like the Judge/No. 2 in "Living in Harmony," 2 manipulates the chivalrousness of his target, but this time succeeds in making him work for the organization that has imprisoned him. Meanwhile, Curtis/2 and his wife/M2 return to their lives in New York, seemingly little affected by the loss of 11–12. Evidently, Summakor's project is to expand the Village as a therapeutic space, a kind of psychic suburb or gated community to which those unhappy in and with the real world can be relocated—a world where, in a way, *only* story matters.

D. FANDOMS

If the remake leaves ambiguity about whether 6's acceptance of Village life is to be seen as selling out, definitely somewhat sinister is AMC's bid to *pre-make* the reception of the remake by providing an online graphic novel, games, downloadable wallpapers, etc.[17] AMC is not so much telling viewers how to interpret the remake as pre-mapping spaces for engagement with it. Such attempted channeling of fan culture is now common, but is particularly ironic in this instance, since both original and remake are important precisely for their commentary on the contrivance of choice and the spread of prefabricated culture. Yet, AMC's attempt to synthesize fandom for the remake usefully prompts attention to the evolution of fan culture of and from the original. Joanne Morreale argues that "*The Prisoner* presaged [Guy] Debord's warning of the dominance of the spectacle, and [anticipated] Debord's pessimistic conclusion . . . that there is no free agency, no place to escape."[18] Mentioning various fan productions, Morreale asserts that the original *The Prisoner* "has simply become another commodity that endlessly replicates itself" through merchandising that exploits its cult status.[19] This assessment seems too ready to concede the hegemony of commodity culture, foreclosing engagement with particular recyclings of *The Prisoner*. True, there are commercialized reworkings of the original series, notably a 1989 television advertisement, using Portmeirion locations and original theme music, and appropriating the original protagonist's iconic individualism, where a figure called No. 21 uses a Renault 21 automobile to escape Rover.[20] More complex is the parodic *The Prisoner* remake in the *Simpsons* episode "The Computer Wore Menace Shoes" (12.06). Homer, stumbling on a scheme using fake flu shots to promote frantic Christmas shopping, is kidnapped and imprisoned, as No. 5, on "The Island," where he meets No. 6 (voiced by McGoohan himself), steals the raft No. 6 has laboriously built, and escapes after puncturing Rover with a fork. Possibly, the parody signals the ultimate institutionalization of *The Prisoner*, since *The Simpsons* serves to capture viewers for the Fox network and thus illustrates TV-that-subverts-TV as a commercial genre in itself. Then again, the end of the episode eerily foresees the end of the remake: after the whole family is imprisoned by the organization behind The Island, Marge tells Homer, "Once you get used to the druggings, this isn't a bad place."

There has accumulated an assortment of official *The Prisoner* merchandise and spin-offs that parallels what AMC markets—novelizations and comics, for example—but there is also much more eccentric material. Fan responses to *The Prisoner* have a distinctive history that blurs critical and commercial boundaries.[21] Fan fiction sites offer surprisingly few *The Prisoner*-related works: as of 29 May 2013, *FanFiction.net* hosts only twenty-two, most based on the original; by contrast, there are 49,548 for *Doctor Who*. *Archive of Our Own* has eighteen works for the 1967–68 series and

four for the remake, and 21,863 under " *Doctor Who* & Related Fandoms."
[22] However, *The Prisoner* has inspired distinctive creative responses, for
example in British pop music of the 1970s and 1980s. In 1977, the pub
rock band Dr. Feelgood released the LP *Be Seeing You*, with cover featuring band members in wide-lapelled versions of McGoohan's iconic blazer. In 1980 The Teenage Filmstars recorded "I Helped Patrick McGoohan
Escape," a sympathetic recap of the way McGoohan's life was affected by
the series; in 1982–83, as The Times, the band re-recorded the song and
made a video at Portmeirion. Another 1980s band, The Prisoners, evoked
the series with its name, with the iconography of album covers, and
indirectly, like The Times, with a sound harkening back to the 1960s. And
in 1987 the music program *The Tube* produced "The Laughing Prisoner,"
featuring host Jools Holland as a TV personality who resigns, plus Portmeirion performances by post-punk/New Wave bands Siouxsie and the
Banshees and XTC.[23] Beyond their interest in *The Prisoner*, what links
these various acts is independence: durable, and successful on their own
terms, they have never necessarily been interested in spectacular stardom. Their uses of *The Prisoner* are partly commercial, but not necessarily
more so than, for instance, those of an academic analysis.

While *The Prisoner* seems under-explored by fan fiction, *The Prisoner*-
fandom has an internet presence, one favoring documentary modes. The
appreciation society Six of One, founded in 1976–77 at the time the series
was rebroadcast in Britain, maintains UK and US webpages with links to
The Prisoner-related materials.[24] Six of One itself has become an object of
online debate, with some former members contending, under the site
name "sixofone-info," that the original society has become "a shameful
version of its former self."[25] Yet, disharmony among *Prisoner* fans can be
seen as aptly reflective of the challenging spirit of the original series.
"sixofone-info" has links to another large fan site, *The Unmutual*, which
includes some fan fiction and an extensive news archive, covering personnel involved with the series even in minor roles. The site counters
tendencies to treat McGoohan as a cult figure and acknowledges the
people whose labor was vital to *The Prisoner*.[26] Such *The Prisoner* fan work
offers evidence that sustained intellectual response to a television production need not be confined to academic Villages.[27]

E. CONCLUSION: *PRISONER* GEOGRAPHIES AND OTHER VILLAGES

In *Fan Cultures* (2002), Matt Hills covers "cult geographies," noting pioneering examples in *The Prisoner* fans' pilgrimages to Portmeirion.[28] In a
more allusive take on geographies of *The Prisoner*, Catherine O'Flynn's
novel *The News Where You Are* (2010), about the evolving physical and
cultural geography of Birmingham, has a scene in an area called Byron's

Common, with a resident remarking, "My sister visited and said she thought a big white ball would chase us if we tried to leave. I like it, though, it's wipe-clean."[29] Byron's Common is a fictionalized version of Dickens Heath, a suburb developed since the 1990s in a neo-traditional style and touted as "Truly a village for the 21st Century."[30] The understatement of O'Flynn's allusion registers the enduring familiarity of the original series, reflecting patterns of audience response that cannot readily be prefabricated. O'Flynn speaks not just to the possibly superficial heritage status of *The Prisoner* but also to its capacity to address material questions concerning living spaces—a capacity the newer series shares.

Early in the remake's finale, an expansive 2, accompanied unwillingly by 11–12, visits an area where new houses are being completed—under the billboard slogan "More Village"—and receiving new residents. 2 praises the scene; 11–12, unimpressed, remarks, "They're buildings. Houses." 2 replies grandiloquently: "More Village means that our way of life is becoming the very consciousness of the Universe." He then greets an admiring fan, autographing a large 2 on the bib of her overalls and praising her as one of those who "choose life." Since there is scant attention to the means whereby people are actually placed in the Village (or to whether they really have had any choice), these scenes of construction stand in metaphorically—but they can also be read metonymically and materially. 11–12's retort points to the significance of settings for both series, in another example of his resistant role. Like O'Flynn's allusion, 11–12's remark suggests that Portmeirion is important not so much as the authentic, auratic home of *The Prisoner*, or a spiritual home for fans, but for what it represents as "buildings": a designed heritage community of a kind promoted, under the rubric of "New Urbanism," by neo-traditional architects and developers in recent decades, as at Dickens Heath and as in 2's reimagined village. The original Village is a prison for McGoohan's protagonist, but is also figured as a place where many residents (like those pointed out by the first No. 2) believe themselves happy. There is debate concerning the extent to which New Urbanism is a means of solving urban problems, rather than, like earlier kinds of suburban development, often in practice an exclusionary means of evading them.[31] Examples of New Urbanist rhetoric eerily similar to that of McKellen's 2 include an electronic billboard inside Vancouver International Airport in 2008–09 that promoted Concord Pacific "communities for world-class living" in Western Canada: "Each a master-planned world unto itself with parks, schools, daycares, shops, restaurants and resort-style amenities. All primely centered in urban vibrancy, living synergy and orchestrated contentment." And Prince Charles, the current Royal No. 2, has recently published *Harmony: A New Way of Looking At Our World*, a book in which he condemns both the horizontal sprawl of twentieth-century suburbs and the vertical starkness of modernist mass housing, and promotes an alternative in developments such as the Village of Poundbury, Dorset, which his patronage has helped to promote as a realization of neo-tradi-tional urban design.[32] The New Urbanist resemblances of the Village also evoke Peter Weir's film *The Truman Show* (1998), where the manufactured landscape of the studio staging the corporate-controlled life of the title character is "played" by the real New Urbanist community of Seaside, Florida. Both the television operation in the film and the activites of Summakor in the 2009 *Prisoner* resonate with Max Horkheimer's and Theodor W. Adorno's view of mass housing and mass entertainment as parts of an overarching cultural system of control disguised as choice which is imposing standardization on human beings themselves.[33] If the newer *The Prisoner* can be seen as a reimagining of *The Truman Show*, the commonalities also indicate how Weir's film reinvents elements of the original *The Prisoner*, such as the location in a prefabricated community, along with the vision of the culture industry as No. 1.

In a less pessimistic mode than Horkheimer's and Adorno's, the two *The Prisoners*, alongside Weir's film and O'Flynn's novel, offer warnings about possible dangers of ongoing remakings of the built world and of the ways we inhabit it. As the balance and nuance of O'Flynn's allusion to Dickens Heath suggest, the problem is not necessarily with the details of a particular new Village (walkability is a virtue of Poundbury, if also of the Village), but rather with the idea that happiness can be designed or orchestrated. To treat the original *The Prisoner* as an eternal landmark would be to fall into the same assumptions underlying uncritical celebrations of neo-traditional, heritage-based architecture and design. And not to acknowledge that, despite limitations, the remake does succeed in developing key concerns of the 1960s series would be to allow the heritage of the original to rise up, Rover-like, to smother re-accentuation.

FILMS AND TV SHOWS

The Bachelor. ABC, 2002–.
Danger Man. ATV, 1960–61, 1964–66.
The Prisoner. AMC, 2009.
The Prisoner. ITV, 1967–68.
The Simpsons. Fox, 1989–.
The Truman Show. Directed by Peter Weir. 1998. Paramount.

NOTES

1. On production and reception of *The Prisoner*, see Chris Gregory, *Be Seeing You...: Decoding The Prisoner* (Luton: University of Luton Press, 1997), Chapter 2; Catherine Johnson, *Telefantasy* (London: BFI, 2005), Chapter 2.
2. Tim Goodman, "TV review: 'Prisoner' remake captive of past," *San Francisco Chronicle*, November 13, 2009, http://www.sfgate.com/news/article/TV-review-Prisoner-remake-captive-of-past-3210094.php.

3. Sue Short, *Cult Telefantasy Series* (Jefferson: McFarland, 2011), 28.

4. John Walsh, "*Welcome to Lagos,* BBC2; *The Prisoner,* ITV: An uplifting gem of a documentary from the refuse tips of Lagos contrasts with a lacklustre US remake of a British classic," *The Independent,* April 18, 2010, http://www.independent.co.uk/arts-entertainment/tv/reviews/welcome-to-lagos-bbc2brthe-prisoner-itv-1947511.html.

5. McKellen lends 2 his associations with previous roles as Gandalf and various Shakespearean leads. The remake thus addresses the US niche market for productions foregrounding British cultural heritage. See Jeannette Steemers, "British Television in the American Marketplace," in *American Remakes of British Television: Transformations and Mistranslations,* ed. Carlen Lavigne and Heather Marcovitch (Lanham: Lexington, 2011), 1–16.

6. Graham Allen, *Intertextuality* (London: Routledge, 2000), 19.

7. Mikhail M. Bakhtin, *The Dialogic Imagination: Four Essays,* ed. Michael Holquist, trans. Caryl Emerson and Michael Holquist (Austin: University of Texas Press, 1981), 420–421.

8. On "quotation" in remakes as a form of intertextuality, see e.g., Constantine Verevis, *Film Remakes* (Edinburgh: Edinburgh University Press, 2006), 18–20. Quotation—like this reference to Verevis's book—is a way of acknowledging an important source while maintaining the momentum of one's own story.

9. On debates about running order, see e.g., Gregory, *Decoding The Prisoner,* 93.

10. Short, *Cult Telefantasy Series,* 28.

11. Ibid., 28–29.

12. "Beautiful Prison: The World of *The Prisoner,*" prod. Michael Brosnan (London: Granada, 2009).

13. Fairclough, *The Prisoner,* 113; Johnson, *Telefantasy,* 56–57.

14. Fairclough, *The Prisoner,* 91–92.

15. Gregory, *Decoding The Prisoner,* 153.

16. Ibid., 48.

17. See http://www.amctv.com/shows/the-prisoner. As of May 2013, not all the site's features work.

18. Joanne Morreale, "The Spectacle of *The Prisoner,*" *Television & New Media* 7, no. 2 (2006), 224.

19. Ibid., 225.

20. On the Renault commercial, see Gregory, *Decoding The Prisoner,* 212n4; Fairclough, *The Prisoner,* 137.

21. On the way the original series blends avant-garde and commercial, see Johnson, *Telefantasy,* 59–64.

22. See http://www.fanfiction.net; http://archiveofourown.org. Thanks to Sarah Winters for pointing out this information, and for further suggestions on fan cultures.

23. On musical re-accentuations of the series, see e.g., Fairclough, *The Prisoner,* 126–127.

24. See http://www.sixofone.co/ and http://www.netreach.net/~sixofone/.

25. See http://www.sixofone-info.co.uk/about.htm.

26. See http://www.theunmutual.co.uk/. On the inherent irony in views of McGoohan as a cult figure, see Gregory, *Decoding The Prisoner,* 197–198.

27. There are definite resemblances between universities and The Village: both feature distinctive buildings in which people pursue information and interrogate one another. . .

28. Matt Hills, *Fan Cultures* (London: Routledge, 2002), 198–99; on *The Prisoner* fan conventions see e.g. http://www.portmeiricon.com/.

29. Catherine O'Flynn, *The News Where You Are* (London: Penguin, 2010), 95.

30. See http://www.visitsolihull.com/explore-solihull/about-the-area/dickens-heath.

31. See Jill Grant, *Planning The Good Community: New Urbanism in Theory and Practice* (Abingdon: Routledge, 2006), Part 3.

32. HRH The Prince of Wales, Tony Juniper, and Ian Skelly, *Harmony: A New Way of Looking At Our World* (London: Blue Door, 2010), 238–242.

33. Max Horkheimer and Theodor W. Adorno, "Enlightenment as Mass Deception," trans. Edmund Jephcott, in *Dialectic of Enlightenment* (Stanford: Stanford University Press, 2002), 94–95.

Index

Forbes, Michelle, 24
Forbrydelsen (Danmarks Radio,
2007–12), 3, 131–132, 134–135, 137,
138, 139; Sarah Lund, 132, 134–135,
137, 138, 139
The Forest of Hand and Teeth (2009), 13
Forrest, Jennifer, 23
Fox, Michael J., 142
Fox Network, 53, 230
Frankenstein, play (National Theatre,
2011), 174
Frankenstein, Victor (National Theatre,
Frankenstein), 174
Fraser, Brent David, 31
Fratkin, Stuart, 143
Freeman, Martin, 173, 175
French, Eve, 117, 118, 122, 123, 124,
129n35
French, Valerie, 227
Fresh One Productions, 187
Freud, Sigmund, 37, 38, 59
Frid, Jonathan, 156, 161, 162–163, 164
Friday Night Lights, film (2004), 3,
97–99, 100, 101, 102–106, 107, 109,
112n32; Boobie Miles, 103, 105; Don
Billingsley, 103, 104–105, 107; Gary
Gaines, 98, 103, 104–107, 112n32;
Maria, 105; Mike Winchell, 103, 105;
Permian Panthers, 98, 102, 103–104,
105–106, 112n32; Sharon Gaines,
101, 106, 112n29
Friday Night Lights, series (NBC,
2006–11), 3, 97–99, 100, 101–103, 105,
106–109, 110n13, 112n29, 112n32;
Buddy Garrity, 100, 108–109; Coach
Eric Taylor, 97, 98–99, 100, 102, 103,
105, 106–108, 109, 110n3; Dillon
Panthers, 97, 98, 102, 107–109; East
Dillon Lions, 107–108; Jason Street,
103; Julie Taylor, 105; Lyla Garrity,
105; Matt Saracen, 101, 103; Ray
'Voodoo' Tatum, 106; Slammin'
Sammy Meade, 102; Tami Taylor,
101, 106, 107, 110n3, 112n29; Tim
Riggins, 103; Tyra Collette, 105–106
*Friday Night Lights: A Town, A Team,
and a Dream* (1990), 97, 98, 100,
103–104, 110n13, 111n26
Friday the 13th, films, 25

Friedan, Betty, 114
Friedman, Brent V., 31
Fringe (Fox, 2008–13), 2, 31–33, 46,
53–64n16, 138; Astrid Farnsworth,
54, 56, 58, 64n11; David Robert
Jones, 56; Elizabeth Bishop, 55;
Faux-livia, 54, 56, 62; Henrietta
Bishop, 62; Lieutenant Broyles, 56,
59, 62; Lincoln Lee, 54; Massive
Dynamic, 54; Nina Sharp, 54, 56, 59;
Observers, 32, 36n31, 58, 62–63;
Olivia Dunham, 31–32, 54, 55–56,
58, 59, 62, 63, 138; Peter Bishop, 31,
54–56, 58, 59, 60, 62, 63; September,
58, 63; Walter Bishop, 31–32, 53,
54–55, 56, 57, 58, 59, 61, 62;
Walternate, 54, 55, 56, 57, 58, 59, 61,
62; William Bell, 54, 55, 56, 57, 59, 62
From Russia With Love (1963), 69
Frow, John, 156
Fulci, Lucio, 12
*Fundamental Principles of the
Metaphysics of Morals* (1785), 132, 133
Furnell, Bob, 211

Gabel, Seth, 54
Gaines, Gary, 98, 103, 104–107, 112n32
Gale, Cathy, 68–70, 76–77, 77–78
Gallagher, Bill, 222, 226
Game of Thrones (HBO, 2011–), 2
Gandalf, 234n5
Garrett, Kelly, 115, 117, 119, 120, 121
Garriga, Jaume, 57
Garrity, Buddy, 100, 108–109
Gatiss, Mark, 174, 177, 180
General Hospital (ABC, 1963–), 61
Geraghty, Christine, 6, 15
Get Christie Love!, film (1974), 129n39
Get Christie Love!, series (ABC,
1974–75), 129n39
Get Smart (NBC, 1965–70), 77
Gibson, Mel, 7, 129n52
Giddens, Anthony, 190
G.I. Joe (Claster, 1983–86), 43
G.I. Joe: Renegades (The Hub, 2010–), 42
Gitlin, Todd, 37
Glimmer Twins. *See* The Rolling Stones
Going, Joanna, 160
Gok Wan, 192

Goldberg, Leonard, 119
Goldfinger (1964), 71
Golightly, Gage, 145
Goodman, Tim, 221
Gore, Al, 57
Gough-Yates, Anna, 120, 121, 130n54
Gråbøl, Sofie, 132
Granada Productions, 171, 172, 222. *See also* ITV Studios
Gray, Jonathan, 39
The Greatest Event in Television History (Adult Swim, 2012–), 1
Green, Lorne, 24
Greenberg, Harvey Roy, 27
Gregory, Chris, 228
Griffin, Lorie, 142
Grimes, Rick, Sherriff, 7–8
Groundwork of the Metaphysics of Morals. See Fundamental Principles of the Metaphysics of Morals (1785)
Gue, Alice, 195, 196, 200n38

Hair, musical, 76
Hale, Mike, 53, 56
Halperin, Victor, 12
Hambly, Barbara, 210, 212, 213
Hamilton, Linda, 83, 94, 96n18
Hamlet, play, 205
Hamm, Jon, 1
Hampton, James, 142
Hanauer, Terry, 92
Happy Days (ABC, 1974–84), 42
A Hard Day's Night (1964), 71, 72
Hardwicke, Edward, 172
Hargitay, Mariska, 138
Harmony: A New Way of Looking At Our World, 232
Harris, Jared, 56
Hartnell, William, 206, 213
Hartswood Films, 174
Hart to Hart (1979–84), 1
Hasselhoff, David, 25
Hassler-Forest, Dan, 11
Hawaii Five-O (CBS, 2010–), 1, 40, 49
Haynes, Colton, 145
Haywire (2012), 116
Hebdige, Dick, 44
Hector (*The Iliad*), 59
Heidegger, Martin, 55

Hell's Kitchen (ITV, 2004–09), 192
Hendry, Ian, 65, 66, 67, 74
Herman, Barbara, 137
Hibberd, James, 64n2
Higson, Charlie, 13
Hills, Matt, 204, 213, 214, 231
Hilmes, Michele, 188, 199n10
HIMYM. See *How I Met Your Mother* (2005–)
Hitchcock, Alfred, 58, 60
Hoechlin, Tyler, 146
Hofer, Johanna, 38
Hogle, Jerrold, 12, 13
Holland, Jools, 231
Holland, Patricia, 189
Holmes, Sherlock, character: in canon, 42, 172, 174, 177, 178, 181, 183; in *Elementary* (CBS, 2012–), 41, 42, 171, 174, 175, 176, 177, 178–179, 180–181, 182, 183, 186n28; figure of, 171, 172–173, 175, 176–177, 178, 179, 181–182, 183, 206; in Granada series, 171–172, 173, 178, 183; in *Sherlock* (BBC, 2010–), 171, 173–174, 175, 177, 178, 179–180, 182, 183–184. *See also* Sherlock Holmes, canon; Sherlock Holmes, franchise
Homeland (Showtime, 2011–), 84
Honey West (1965–66), 129n39
Horkeheimer, Max, 201n42, 233
Horror of Dracula (1958), 162–163
Houghton, Harry, 67
House, M.D. (Fox, 2004–12), 41
Howard, Scott, 142–144, 146, 148
Howard, Todd, 142, 143–145, 147, 148
How I Met Your Mother (CBS, 2005–), 38, 40, 46–48, 49; Barney Stinson, 47–48; Lily Eriksen, 47–48; Marshall Eriksen, 47–48; Robin Scherbatsky, 47–48; Ted Mosby, 47–48
How to Look Good Naked (Channel 4, 2006–08), 192
The Hub, 42–43
Hughes, Alan, 73
Hulke, Malcolm, 205
The Hunger (1983), 162
Hurran, Nick, 222
The Hurt Locker (2008), 84
Hutcheon, Linda, 5, 9

Contributors

PAUL BOOTH (Ph.D.) is an assistant professor in the College of Communication at DePaul University. He is the author of *Digital Fandom: New Media Studies* (Peter Lang, 2010), which examines fans of cult television programs, and *Time on TV: Temporal Displacement and Mashup Television* (Peter Lang, 2012). He is the editor of *Fan Phenomena: Doctor Who* (Intellect, 2013). He has also published articles in *Communication Studies, Transformative Works and Cultures, Television and New Media, Critical Studies in Media Communication, New Media and Culture,* and in the books *Transgression 2.0* (Continuum, 2010), *American Remakes of British Television* (Lexington, 2011), and *Battlestar Galactica and Philosophy* (Wiley-Blackwell, 2008).

JEF BURNHAM (M.A.) is a member of the adjunct faculty in DePaul University's College of Communication and Columbia College Chicago's Film and Video Department. He has been published in *Sherlock Holmes and Philosophy* (Open Court, 2011) and *Reading Mystery Science Theater 3000* (Scarecrow Press, 2013). He also serves as the editor-in-chief of the Chicago-based website FilmMonthly.com, for which he has written since 2007.

PETER CLANDFIELD (Ph.D.) is an assistant professor in the Department of English Studies at Nipissing University in North Bay, Ontario. He specializes in twentieth-century literature and cultural studies. His publications include articles in the *Iowa Journal of Cultural Studies* and the *Canadian Journal of Film Studies,* as well as book chapters in *The Wire: Urban Decay and American Television* (Continuum, 2009), *The Pedagogy of Adaptation* (Scarecrow Press, 2010), and *Popping Culture* (Pearson, 7th ed. 2012).

STEVEN GIL (Ph.D.) recently completed his doctoral studies at the University of Queensland in Australia. His thesis examined the presence of scientific discourse in contemporary science fiction television produced in North America. His work has been published in *Networking Knowledge* and the *Australasian Journal of Popular Culture.*

KAREN HELLEKSON (Ph.D.) is a founding co-editor of the fan studies journal *Transformative Works and Cultures*(journal.transformativeworks. org). She has published extensively in fan studies, science fiction, and media studies, and she was a contributor to *American Remakes of British*

Television (Lexington, 2011). She is the co-editor of *Practicing Science Fiction* (McFarland, 2010) and *Fan Fiction and Fan Communities in the Age of the Internet* (McFarland, 2006), and the author of *The Science Fiction of Cordwainer Smith* (McFarland, 2001) and *The Alternate History: Refiguring Historical Time* (Kent State University Press, 2001).

CARLEN LAVIGNE (Ph.D.) teaches communications at Red Deer College in Alberta, Canada. She has published articles in the *Australasian Journal of Popular Culture,* the *Journal of Popular Television,* the *Canadian Review of American Studies, Femspec,* and *The Journal of Dracula Studies.* She has contributed chapters to *Sherlock Holmes for the 21st Century* (McFarland, 2012) and *Technologies of Intuition* (YYZ Books, 2006). She is the co-editor of *American Remakes of British Television* (Lexington, 2011) and the author of *Cyberpunk Women, Feminism and Science Fiction* (McFarland, 2013).

RYAN LIZARDI (Ph.D.) is an assistant professor at the SUNY Institute of Technology. He wrote his doctoral dissertation on nostalgic contemporary media, and he has published works in *Eludamos: Journal of Computer Game Culture, Democratic Communiqué,* and *Flow.* He places a research emphasis on the connection between ideology and representations of the past in media.

HEATHER MARCOVITCH (Ph.D.) is the head of English at Red Deer College in Alberta, Canada. She is the co-editor of *American Remakes of British Television* (Lexington, 2011) and *Mad Men, Women and Children: Essays on Gender and Generation* (Lexington, 2012), as well as the author of *The Art of the Pose: Oscar Wilde's Performance Theory* (Peter Lang, 2010).

JAMES W. MARTENS (Ph.D.) is a retired historian and the former head of history at Red Deer College in Alberta, Canada. He was a contributor to *American Remakes of British Television* (Lexington, 2011), and has also published articles for the Historical Society of Alberta and the *Canadian Journal of History.* He has lectured on British history and culture for more than 25 years.

KIMBERLEY MCMAHON-COLEMAN (Ph.D.) teaches in Learning Development at the University of Wollongong. Her work has been published in a number of journals, and in *Fanpires: Audience Consumption of the Modern Vampire* (New Academia Publishing, 2011), and *Open Graves, Open Minds: Representations of Vampires and the Undead from the Enlightenment to the Present Day* (Manchester University Press, 2013). She is also the co-author of *Werewolves and Other Shapeshifters in Popular Culture: A Thematic Analysis of Recent Depictions* (McFarland, 2012). The book focuses on the figure of the shapeshifter in literature and popular culture, and how it is used as a metaphor for difference.

MATTHEW PAPROTH (Ph.D.) is an assistant professor of English at Georgia Gwinnett College. He is co-editor of the journal *Notes on Teaching English,* and he has published in the *Journal of Popular Television* and contributed chapters to *Drama and the Postmodern: Essays Assessing the Limits of Metatheatre* (Cambria Press, 2008) and *Zadie Smith: Critical Essays* (Peter Lang, 2008).

LORNA PIATTI-FARNELL (Ph.D.) is a senior lecturer in communication studies at Auckland University of Technology. She is also president of the Gothic Association of New Zealand and Australia (GANZA). Her numerous publications include articles in the *Journal of Popular Culture,* the *Australasian Journal of Popular Culture, Otherness: Essays and Studies,* and *M/C: The Journal of Media and Culture,* and book chapters in *The Culture and Philosophy of Ridley Scott* (Rowman & Littlefield, 2013), *It Came from the 50s!: Popular Culture, Popular Anxieties* (Palgrave, 2011), *The 'Richard and Judy Book Club' Reader: Popular Texts and the Practices of Reading* (Ashgate, 2011), and *Boundaries* (Cambridge Scholars Publishing, 2007). She is the author of *Food and Culture in Contemporary American Fiction* (Routledge, 2011), *Beef: A Global History* (Reaktion, 2013), and *The Vampire in Contemporary Popular Literature* (Routledge, 2013).

LYNNETTE PORTER (Ph.D.) is a professor in the Humanities and Social Sciences department at Embry-Riddle Aeronautical University in Daytona Beach, Florida. She is the editor of *Sherlock Holmes for the 21st Century* (McFarland, 2012). Her many television-related publications include *Lost's Buried Treasures* (Sourcebooks, 2007), *Finding Battlestar Galactica* (Sourcebooks, 2008), *Saving the World: A Guide to Heroes* (ECW, 2007), and *The Doctor Who Franchise* (McFarland, 2012). She is a contributing editor for online popular culture magazine *PopMatters.*

WILLIAM PROCTOR is a Ph.D. candidate and lecturer at the Centre for Research in Media and Cultural Studies at the University of Sunderland, UK. His thesis explores the reboot phenomenon in popular culture and he has published a number of articles on the reboot in *Scope: An Online Journal of Film and Television Studies* and *Scan: Journal of Media Arts Culture.* More recently, William has published an article which investigates fan responses to the Disney takeover of Lucasfilm for *Participations: The International Journal of Audience Research* and has a chapter in the edited collection *Fan Phenomena: Batman* (University of Chicago Press, 2013). His most recent article, on Batman scribe Scott Snyder, has been translated into Polish and published in *Zeszyty Komiksowe.* William is creator and editor of the popular culture website *Infinite Earths* (infiniteearths.co.uk).

CRISTINA LUCIA STASIA (Ph.D.) teaches in the Women's and Gender Studies department at the University of Alberta. She has published chapters in collections including *Bisexuality and Transgenderism: Intersexions of the Others* (Routledge, 2004) and *Third Wave Feminism: Critical Explorations* (Palgrave Macmillan, 2nd ed. 2007). Her recently completed manuscript *Heroine Abuse: Feminism, Femininity and the Female Action Hero* argues that female power has become a pervasive but meaningless concept and charts the depoliticization of popular feminism through an analysis of female action cinema.

HELEN THORNHAM (Ph.D.) is a research fellow at the University of Leeds. She has published on issues relating to gender, young people, place, identity, narrative, and digital technology. Her book *Ethnographies of the Videogame: Narrative, Gender and Praxis* (Ashgate, 2011) investigates the gendered, lived, and narrated power relations embedded in gaming experiences.

ELKE WEISSMANN (Ph.D.) is reader in film and television at Edge Hill University. She is vice-chair of the Television Studies Section of the European Communication Research and Education Association (ECREA). Her previous publications include *Transnational Television Drama* (Palgrave Macmillan, 2012) and *The Forensic Sciences of CSI: How to Know about Crime* (VDM, 2010).

CPSIA information can be obtained at www.ICGtesting.com
Printed in the USA
BVOW08*0241180214

345199BV00002B/3/P